VIOLENCE IN THE HOME

To Vivien, my wife and
Hilary and Jeremy, my children

Violence in the home

M.D.A. FREEMAN
University College London

SAXON  HOUSE

Published by

Saxon House, Teakfield Limited,
Westmead, Farnborough, Hants., England

 British Library Cataloguing in Publication Data

Freeman, Michael David Alan
    Violence in the home.
    1. Conjual violence - Great Britain
    I. Title
    301.42'7   HQ614

ISBN 0 566 00129 2

Printed by David Green (Printers) Ltd, Kettering, Northamptonshire

Contents

v

Part III OTHER FAMILY VIOLENCE

Preface

Not many years ago the student of violence in the home was on a relatively uncharted ocean. There were no books, little or no legislation and the subject had barely attracted the attention of the police, the medical profession, social workers or lawyers.

All this has now changed. The 'discovery' of child abuse in the 1960s and wife abuse a decade later has led to a variety of legislative, professional and academic responses. There are now a large number of books on the subject or aspects of it.

This book is, however, different. First, it is the only book written on the subject by a lawyer and the first to discuss in depth legal responses to the problem. Secondly, it is the first book to attempt to integrate the problems of wife abuse and child abuse and to apply to each a relatively consistent theoretical framework. Thirdly, the book draws attention also to newer aspects of the problem (newer that is in surfacing to public attention): husband battering, 'granny bashing', and violence between children are thus briefly considered. The general theme of this book is that the problems it discusses cannot be solved or ameliorated until they are properly understood; that the emphasis on a psychopathological model of the behaviour in question is misconceived and misleading; and that the problems are in fact endemic in society, in the way we perceive and treat women and children.

There are other aspects of the problem of violence in the home which I should have liked to have treated in this book. Rape, particularly of wives by husbands, and sexual abuse of children are two of the more significant omissions. Both are the result of the need to keep the book down in length for publishing considerations. A chapter on the sexual abuse of children has been published separately as an article in *Family Law*.

A large number of persons and organisations have assisted me with the writing of this book. It would be invidious to single out names and take up too much space to list them all. By avoiding the mentioning of anyone I also obviate the need to put in the traditional disclaimer. I cannot, however, fail to mention expressly the patience, willingness and hard work of my secretary, Miss Su-fong Tsou ('Sophie') who coped manfully (or womanfully) with a complex and often untidy manuscript and never complained. My thanks also are due to my wife, Vivien, and children Hilary and Jeremy who put up with me, bad-temper, tiredness and all, as I prepared the manuscript. That I did not join the ranks of battered husbands says a lot for my wife's tolerance and good humour. I suppose I ought to add that all three of them are still relatively unscathed!

The book was largely written in 1977. Certain revisions took place in the early months of 1978 to take account of *Davis v Johnson*, the Domestic Proceedings and Magistrates' Courts Act 1978, and the Home Office Review of the Criminal Injuries Compensation Scheme. None of these developments could, however, be treated in the depth which I should have liked. Other updating has been fitted into the notes. The law, as stated, is, therefore, accurate as at the writing of this preface.

M.D.A. Freeman
4 August 1978

1 Violence: some preliminary remarks

We live, as we always have done, in a violent society, of which the family is a true microcosm. Indeed, more violence takes place within the privacy of the immured family than in the outside world. Further, the family is a real cradle of violence, which can be seen as a family affair as conditions of childhood and experiences of family life socialise into a culture of violence.

There is no evidence that family life is any more brutal now than it was in past generations. The last 20 years, however, have seen a gradual awakening of interest in, and understanding of, the dimensions of violence within the home. This book discusses the problems thus raised and appraises some of the legal responses to those problems. This opening chapter explores some more general questions about the meaning, causes and incidence of violence.

The meaning of violence

Walter has defined violence as 'destructive harm . . . including not only physical assaults that damage the body, but also . . . the many techniques of inflicting harm by mental or emotional means'. [1] This is a useful definition for it comprehends a large spectrum of acts and omissions which members of families perpetrate upon one another. Contemporary criminology has taught us to be wary of definitions. What constitutes 'violence' is always a social construction. [2] Acts of violence which are deemed legitimate are characterised as means of control or punishment. [3] Corporal punishment of children comes into this category. Violence, on the other hand, to quote Walter, 'is generally understood as unmeasured or exaggerated harm to individuals, either not socially proscribed at all or else beyond established limits'. It is often, he adds, 'socially defined to include the processes that *originate* as authorised, measured force, but that go beyond the prescribed conditions and limits'. [4] The line between socially acceptable force and illegitimate violence is thus a thin one.

Aetiology

Questions about the origins of violence have been asked by

sociologists, ethnologists, psychologists and others and, needless to say, there is no agreement among the different disciplines as to the answer. Controversy has long raged over the question whether or not man has an instinct of aggression, an innate aggressive drive that would account for his endemic violent behaviour, or whether, on the other hand, aggressive behaviour is environmentally grounded and essentially learned behaviour.

Instinct conceptions of aggression break down into two types of theory. For Freud [5] aggression is a constantly driving force whose energy must be released in some manner. There were, he argued, impulses toward self-destruction which motivated the individual to kill himself. This self-destruction was prevented by turning aggressive impulses outward. In other words, man attacked others as an outlet for the energy of his death instinct. Subsequent research offers little support for this hypothesis. [6] Hartmann's [7] views diverge from those of Freud. According to him the attacked objects invite the discharge of aggressive energy rather than instigating aggressive impulses. Again subsequent research does not support Hartmann's theory. [8] Instinct conceptions still have their supporters. Anthony Storr is an eloquent advocate for their cause. He writes: 'in man, as in other animals, there exists a physiological mechanism which, when stimulated, gives rise both to subjective feelings of anger and also to physical changes which prepare the body for fighting. This mechanism is easily set off and, like other emotional responses, it is stereotyped and, in this sense,"instinctive".' [9] Instinct theories may be discredited [10] but explanations of the origins of violence are still sought in biological factors.

Other studies show an association between the male sex hormone androgen and aggression, higher levels of the hormone being correlated with increases in aggressive behaviour. [11] But men with normal as well as those with low androgen levels have been known to commit violent acts, as have women without excess androgen and normal estrogen levels. Theories which seek the origins of violence in hormonal patterns are thus not adequate explanations of the phenomenon. Brain disorders may account for some violence but are too rare to explain the majority of violent incidents. [12] The recent discovery that a number of prisoners in maximum security mental hospitals had an additional 'Y' chromosome led some to seek an explanation of violence in this factor. [13] And, although further studies have shown an increased frequency of the XYY genotype in males in penal institutions, it is known that many males with this chromosomal abnormality are not known for their violent tendencies. Further, there is an increasing number of violent women. There may

2

be almost as many husbands battered by wives as vice versa and child abuse is commonly perpetrated by mothers. Women cannot have this abnormality. It has also been found that the XYY offenders discovered in the research had been convicted predominantly of property offences. [14]

Social learning theory, on the other hand, which views violence as a learned phenomenon, is supported by a number of laboratory studies [15] as well as clinical studies. [16] Furthermore, survey research on family interaction strongly supports the theory. Thus Owens and Straus [17] found that those who experienced violence as children tended to favour the use of violence to achieve personal and political ends. They write: 'observing and experiencing violence tends to provide a powerful learning situation because (among other things) such experience provides the entire script for behaviour, not just attitudes of approval or disapproval. Among the important elements of this script are the specific types of situations in which violence is used, the appropriate affective states, and the appropriate response to such situations, that is, the type and intensity of violence'. [18] They did however find less of a relationship between exposure to violence and the extent to which women approved of interpersonal violence. They postulate two possible reasons for this. First, women are subject to more societal pressure to disapprove of violence than are men, with the result that the effects of exposure to violence may be considerably mitigated by the operation of normative factors that tend to suppress approval of violence. Second, as women are biologically weaker they may feel more threatened by violence and it may be less useful to them.

Steinmetz's study of the methods used to resolve family conflict also supports the social learning thesis. [19] She found that children are likely to use similar methods to resolve disagreements between themselves and their brothers and sisters as their parents use to resolve marital conflict and that between themselves and their children. The data from her study suggest that 'specific patterns of family conflict resolution methods exist and these patterns are learned and utilized in interactions with different family members.' [20] Further support for the social learning theory is the finding of Sears, Maccoby and Levin [21] and Eron, Walder and Lefkowitz [22] that physical punishment of children tends to increase rather than decrease their aggressive behaviour. And this aggression may not cease with the attainment of adulthood for there is clear evidence that child abusers were frequently abused children themselves. [23]

An understanding of family violence is thus important if we are to understand violence in the wider society. Where we find violence

3

prevalent in society we are likely also to find that that society is characterised by high levels of violence experienced during childhood. That is not to say that ghetto riots or football hooliganism [24] are to be totally explained in terms of violence learned during family inter-action, nor that such phenomena are modelled on such experiences. But in part such attributions may be made. This is important for it suggests that attempts to reduce the level of violence in society require measures to be taken to eliminate its use in the family setting. And, as this book demonstrates, one cannot be optimistic about achieving this.

The history and incidence of violence

Violence is rooted in our earliest myths and history. Cain murdered his brother Abel because, the Bible tells us, the Lord did not respect Cain's offering and preferred Abel's. [25] Romulus killed his twin Remus when, it is said, Remus ridiculed Romulus's strength and authority. [26] The Greek myth of Oedipus tells of parricide, filicide, fratricide and multiple suicides in three generations of one family. [27]

History teaches us that violence is not atypical or anomalous. [28] The history of most nations had been characterised by it. There is certainly no evidence that it is more prevalent today than in the past. [29] Football hooliganism is often taken to be a contemporary malaise but in 1893 an observer at a match in Shrewsbury noted that 'the shouting and horseplay on the highways were a terror to peaceful residents passing homewards'. [30] Violent confrontations between rival political groups which excited the public imagination in 1977 are reminiscent of the marches and clashes in the 1880s in such quiet sea-side resorts as Weston-super-Mare and Worthing between the Salvation Army and their opponents who called themselves the 'Skeleton Army'. [31]

Violence against children and wives is similarly firmly rooted in our history and culture. The Report of the Commissioners on the Employment of Children in Factories of 1833 remarked on 'acts of severity and cruelty towards children employed in factories' and on the practice of spinners or slubbers, often the child's parents, to beat children in the factories. [32] A generation later in 1867 Florence Davenport-Hill quoted one Mary Thorpe of Bulwell who told of children pinned to the knee to keep them to their work. [33] In *The Classic Slum* Roberts recalls Salford before the First World War:

4

no-one who spent his childhood in the slums during those years will easily forget the regular and often brutal assaults on some children . . . Among fathers administering such punishments were men who had received forty-eight strokes of the birch — at the local prison for small mis-demeanours . . . In its city windows the NSPCC displayed photographs of beaten children and rows of confiscated belts and canes. Gallantly as it worked, the society hardly touched the fringe of the problem. [34]

Using children for begging purposes and pre-maiming or blinding them to make them valuable objects of pity has been common through-out history. Maria Colwell's name now conjures up in the public's mind the brutality which caretakers are capable of inflicting upon innocent children but in earlier generations names like Margaret Waters [35] or the O'Neill twins [36] brought forth similar reactions.

Violence perpetrated upon wives and other women folk is a common theme in 19th century literature. The novels of Charles Dickens and Mrs Gaskell particularly are replete with examples of working-class domestic brutality. [37] In the middle of the century a campaign began, which culminated in 1878 with the development of the concept of the separation order, to publicise the plight of battered working-class women and rescue them from their distressful situation. Descriptions of the condition of these women written by John Stuart Mill and J.W. Kaye and others read like contemporary essays on the same theme. Thus, we read of 'a bulldog set at the heels of a wife, blows with a poker, attempted murder by hanging, stabbings, murder in a fit of drunkenness' not in Erin Pizzey's *Scream Quietly or the Neighbours will Hear* but in an article by Mill in *The Sunday Times* of August 1851.

We do not know how much violence there is and there is no way of measuring its incidence accurately. Even with homicide figures cannot be ascertained with absolute certainty. Similarly, we can only estimate how much violence exists in the family setting. The accuracy of commonly quoted statistics, e.g. that in Great Britain two children a day die at the hands of their parents, may be doubted. [38] This book reports what we know from existing research and what we may speculate as to how much family violence there is. Certainly, if we take murder as a paradigm of violence, we note that it is mostly a family matter. Only a minority of murders occur between strangers. Nor is this a finding unique to Western culture. Bohannan, [39] in studying native African homicide and suicide, found that murder occurred predominantly among kinsmen, though the patterns of kinship differ from those in more complex, urbanised societies. Nor is conjugal violence short of murder a phenomenon prevalent only in Western civilisation. Schlegel [40] rated 45 societies and revealed that three-quarters of them permitted husbands to aggress against their wives. Amongst all the uncertainty one thing is clear: the home is a very dangerous place and we have more to fear from close members of our own family than from total strangers.

Notes

[1] E. Walter, *Terror and Resistance: A Study of Political Violence*, OUP, 1969, p.8.
[2] See, for example, H. Becker, *Outsiders*, Free Press, 1963.
[3] *Cf.* W.J. Goode, 'Force and Violence in the Family', *Journal of Marriage and the Family*, vol.33, 1971, p.624.
[4] Op.cit., note 1, p.12.
[5] S. Freud, *Beyond the Pleasure Principle*, Hogarth Press and Institute of Psycho-Analysis, 1948.
[6] See L. Berkowitz, *Aggression — A Social-Psychological Analysis*, McGraw-Hill, 1962, ch.1.
[7] H. Hartmann, 'Notes on the Theory of Aggression', *Psychoanalytic Study of the Child*, vols 3 and 4, International Universities Press, 1949.
[8] Op.cit., note 6, ch.1.
[9] A. Storr, *Human Aggression*, Pelican Books, 1970, p.27.
[10] But *cf.* A. Storr, idem, pp 35-6.
[11] R.L. Conner and S. Levine, 'Hormonal Influences on Aggressive Behavior' in S. Garratini and E.B. Sigg (eds), *Aggressive Behavior*, Wiley, 1969.
[12] V. Mark and F. Ervin, *Violence and the Brain*, Harper and Row, 1970.
[13] M. Casey, et al, 'Sex Chromosome Abnormalities in two state hospitals for patients requiring special security', *Nature*, 5 February 1966, p.641; W. Price, et al, 'Criminal Patients with XYY sex chromosome complement', *The Lancet*, 1966, p.1.
[14] W. Price, et al, 'Behaviour Disorders and Patterns among XYY males identified at a Maximum Security Hospital', *British Medical Journal*, 1967, p.533. For a general critique see T. Sarbin and J. Miller, 'Demonism revisited: the XYY Chromosome Anomaly', *Issues in Criminology*, vol.5, 1970, p.195.
[15] A. Bandura, et al, 'Transmission of Aggression through Imitation of Aggressive Models', *Journal of Abnormal and Social Psychology*,

vol.63, 1961, p.575; A. Bandura and R.H. Walters, *Social Learning and Personality Development*, Holt, Rinehart and Winston, 1963; J.L. Singer (ed.), *The Control of Aggression and Violence*, Academic Press, 1971.

[16] C.E. Climent and F.R. Ervin, 'Historical Data in the Evaluation of Violent Subjects', *Archives of General Psychiatry*, vol.27, 1972, p.621. B. Steele and C. Pollock, 'A Psychiatic Study of Parents who abuse infants and small children' in R. Helfer and C.H. Kempe, *The Battered Child* (2nd ed.), University of Chicago Press, 1974.

[17] D. Owens and M. Straus, 'The Social Structure of Violence in Childhood and Approval of Violence as an Adult', *Aggressive Behavior*, vol.1, 1975, p.193.

[18] Idem, pp.195-6.

[19] S. Steinmetz, 'The Use of Force for resolving Family Conflict: the Training Ground for Abuse', *The Family Co-ordinator*, vol.26, 1977, p.19.

[20] Idem, p.25.

[21] R.R. Sears, E.E. Maccoby and L.D. Eron, *Patterns of Child Rearing*, Row Patterson, 1957.

[22] L.O. Walder and M.M. Lefkowitz, *Learning of Aggression in Children*, Little Brown, 1971.

[23] See *post*, p.22, 30.

[24] For some explanations see J. Feagin and H. Hahn, *Ghetto Revolts*, Macmillan, 1973, and I. Taylor in S. Cohen (ed.), *Images of Deviance*, Pelican Books, 1971.

[25] Genesis, ch.4.

[26] Livy, *The Early History of Rome* (translated A. de Selincourt), Penguin, 1960, p.40.

[27] R. Graves, *Greek Myths*, Penquin, (revised) 1962, no.105.

[28] See P. Sorokin, *Social and Cultural Dynamics*, vol.III, Allen and Unwin, 1937 and P. Calvert, *A Study of Revolution*, Clarendon Press, 1970. Nor is violence necessarily undesirable: many of today's accepted civil rights were only achieved after years of violent struggle. On the utility of violence see T. Gurr, *Why Men Rebel*, Princeton University Press, 1970, p.210.

[29] See J. Robottom in N. Tutt (ed.), *Violence*, HMSO, 1976, ch.III.

[30] See J. Walvin, *The People's Game*, Allen Lane, 1975.

[31] See E. Bishop, *Blood and Fire*, Longman, 1964 and see also *Beatty* v *Gillbanks* (1882), 9 Q.B.D.308 for a criminal prosecution which resulted out of one such confrontation.

[32] Report of the Commissioners on the Employment of Children in Factories, 1833, p.49.

[33] F. Davenport-Hill, *Children of the State*, Macmillan, 1868. See

T.C.N. Gibbons, *The Guardian*, 14 November 1967.

[34] R. Roberts, *The Classic Slum*, Manchester University Press, 1971, p.45.

[35] Discussed in I. Pinchbeck and M. Hewitt, *Children in English Society*, vol.II, RKP, 1973, pp 614-7.

[36] See the *Monckton Report*, Cmd. 6636, May 1945. J. Packman, *The Child's Generation*, Blackwell and Robertson, 1975, pp 168-9.

[37] *Oliver Twist* and *North and South* are two examples. See also F. Basch, *Relative Creatures*, Allen Lane, 1974.

[38] See *post*, p. 19. The latest NSPCC study suggests 110 fatalities a year (S.J. Creighton and P.J. Owtram, *Child Victims of Physical Abuse*, NSPCC, 1977). See, further, p.37, n.75.

[39] P. Bohannan, *African Homicide and Suicide*, Princeton University Press, 1960.

[40] A. Schlegel, *Male Dominance and Female Autonomy: Domestic Authority in Matrilineal Societies*, Hraf Press, 1972. See also, M. Straus, 'Societal Morphogenesis and Intrafamily Violence in Cross-Cultural Perspective' in *Annals of the New York Academy of Sciences*, vol.285, 1977, p.717.

PART I

CHILD ABUSE

2 Child abuse

A girl of four 'roasted' in front of an open fire by her father because she could not remember what she had eaten for her school lunch, [1] a boy of 20 months whose feet were deliberately burnt by his mother with a lighted cigarette end, [2] a six-week-old baby girl whose leg was bent backwards until it snapped and who also had severe head injuries, [3] a girl of eight months who died of brain damage caused by her mother's violent shaking of her, [4] are just four reported instances of child abuse in Britain today. There are better known cases, of course: Maria Colwell, [5] Lisa Godfrey, [6] Simon Peacock, [7] Steven Meurs, [8] are just a few of the tragic instances of children whose deaths in the 1970s fired the public imagination. This chapter examines what we mean by child abuse and what we understand of its causes. Subsequent chapters appraise the various strategies adopted in this country and others to tackle the problem.

What is child abuse?

It is difficult to define 'child abuse'. Much depends on the purposes for which the definition is being sought. A definition for a reporting law or for management guidance has very different functions from one developed for operational research. Thus Delaney can write, [9] from the perspective of the law, that 'the concept of child abuse and neglect is very much akin to the concept of negligence . . . One dictionary defines negligence as failure to exercise the care that the circumstances justly demand. This same simple concept is equally applicable to child abuse and neglect; each is a failure to provide the child with the care the circumstances demand'. Something more precise is required here. One difficulty is that physical assaults upon children by parents, caretakers, teachers and others are sanctioned in our culture, so that we have to distinguish abuse from legitimate corporal punishment. Another problem concerns the perspective from which the subject is approached. Is one concerned with the effects of an attack upon a child or with the behaviour of the attacker and, if so, how important is his motivation? Most writers agree to focus attention on the attacker's behaviour and to stress its non-accidental nature. But it is not always easy to distinguish intentional behaviour from that which

11

is accidental. Some children suffer injury when placed in a situation in which 'accidental' injury occurs.

If we include intentional acts, then deliberate omissions can hardly be ignored. But what of neglect? What of nutritional or emotional deprivation? What of children who fail to thrive [10] or show the even more severe 'deprivation dwarfism' syndrome? [11] The consequences of rejection may be every bit as traumatic as those of physical abuse. Martin has noted [12] that 'maltreatment of children is a spectrum. Physical assault, neglect and nutritional or emotional deprivation are points on that spectrum and overlap considerably'. Gil has estimated [13] that one-third of abusing parents also neglect their children. This is thought to be an exaggeration, for there are usually clear distinctions between parents and others who abuse and those who neglect their children. As will be shown, a parent who abuses his child has much more of an emotional investment in the child than one who neglects it. Physically abused children are often immaculately turned out so as not to let the parent down. Abuse and neglect can thus be distinguished. Physical and emotional abuse need to be kept separate if only because, as Gelles has observed, [14] 'while broken bones can be identified by X-ray, how can we identify a mental injury'. Mental health, furthermore, is not a value-free concept and is consequently subject to diverse cultural interpretations. This is also true to an extent of physical abuse. American Indians do not approve of physical chastisement of children and would presumably, therefore, understand as 'child abuse' behaviour which we would not so designate.

With these problems in mind the emphasis in this book is on physical abuse. Gil's definition of this is more useful than most. He defines it as 'the intentional, non-accidental use of physical force, or intentional non-accidental acts of omission, on the part of a parent or other caretaker interacting with a child in his care, aimed at hurting, injuring or destroying that child'. [15]

The 'discovery' of child abuse

The physical abuse of children has always existed [16] and there is less now than in the past. Its recognition as a social problem is, however, a relatively recent phenomenon. Its discovery is not attributable to any escalation in the abuse itself. [17] Assertions such as that by Skolnick and Skolnick [18] that increased nuclearisation of the family has led to an increase in victimisation of offspring cannot be substantiated.

A number of factors impeded the recognition of child abuse. [19]
Doctors were unaware of the possibility of abuse as a diagnosis. In
the 20th century the mechanics of diagnosis have been improved by
scientific progress, notably by the development of X-ray techniques.
The decision to X-ray, however, requires the doctor initially to doubt
the parent's word and many doctors could not bring themselves to do
this. The unwillingness of the medical profession to believe that
parents could inflict the injuries was, therefore, yet another barrier to
recognition of abuse as a social problem. A third impeding factor was
enmeshed in the organisational ethics of the medical profession: the
norm of confidentiality acted as an impenetrable shield protecting the
parents. Finally, the medical profession was understandably reluctant
to become involved in a criminal process that was time-consuming,
likely to achieve little of value and over which they had no control. It
also undercuts rapport with the patient by becoming what Rosenfeld
and Newberger have called 'coercive' [20].

It was the radiologists who 'discovered' child abuse. As a marginal
medical group they had a lot to gain. As Friedson has written, [21] it
is 'one of the greatest ambitions of the physician . . . to discover or
describe a "new" disease or syndrome'. Of the barriers referred to only
the last really affected them. But the potential for increased prestige,
role expansion and coalition formation with psychiatry and
paediatrics more than compensated for the sacrifice involved in
becoming a party to criminal processes. Further, as Pfohl has put it,
[22], 'the discovery of abuse as a new "illness" reduced drastically the
intraorganizational constraints on doctors' "seeing" abuse . . .
Problems associated with perceiving parents as patients whose
confidentiality must be protected were reconstructed by typifying as
patients who needed help . . . The maintenance of professional
autonomy was assured by pairing deviance with sickness'.

The fact that child abuse was 'discovered' by the medical profession
has left an important legacy. Other professions, social work and law
pre-eminently, have taken on the medical model. [23] What Kittrie
calls 'the therapeutic state' [24] has taken over. But though the
medical label may protect the patient from punitive measures, it may
also 'submit him to interminable instruction, treatment and
discrimination, which are inflicted on him for professionally presumed
benefit.' [25] Friedson's comment is particularly valuable: 'medical
definitions of deviance have come to be adopted even where there is
no reliable evidence that biophysical variables "cause" the deviance or
that medical treatment is any more efficacious than any other kind of
management.' [26]

The first major contribution to the 'discovery' of the concept of

13

child abuse was made by the radiologist Caffey in 1946. [27] But he did not recognise that the injuries he detected might have been deliberately inflicted. In 1951 another radiologist, Silverman, stated that 'individuals responsible for the care of infants and children . . . may deliberately injure the child and deny it.' [28] At this time there was growing uneasiness. The cases, however, continued to be noted in the literature as a syndrome of unknown aetiology, usually as chronic subdural haematoma, [29] or as a condition of increased metaphysical fragility of infancy. It was Woolley [30] who, in 1955, concluded that the syndromes described by Caffey, Silverman and others were different manifestations of the same basic process of repeated inflicted injury. Woolley, a paediatrician, based his conclusions on a ten-year retrospective study of injured children attending his hospital. He emphasised how important it was to accept the evidence of X-ray findings even where the parents denied abuse.

It was at a symposium organised by Dr Henry Kempe at the American Academy of Paediatrics in 1961 that the phenomenon of the abused child first attracted major attention. A year later Kempe [31] published his now classic article on the clinical, radiological and psychiatric manifestations of serious injuries to children inflicted by parents and other caretakers. He coined the phrase 'battered baby syndrome' to refer to the phenomenon. This term remained in current usage for a decade.

Kempe had studied 749 incidents reported by 71 hospitals and 77 district attorneys from all over the USA. He estimated that 10.4 per cent of the children had died and another 15 per cent were left with permanent residual damage as a result of parental attacks. 'A marked discrepancy between clinical findings and historical data as supplied by the parents', he noted, 'is a major diagnostic feature of the battered-child syndrome'. [32] Most of the children, he stated, were under three years of age and most of the parents came from a low socio-economic background. As far as causes were concerned Kempe hypothesised that 'psychiatric factors are probably of prime importance in the pathogenesis of the disorder'. The parents were often of 'low intelligence . . . Alcoholism, sexual promiscuity, unstable marriages, and minor criminal activities are reportedly common amongst them. They are immature, impulsive, self-centered, hyper-sensitive, and quick to reach with poorly controlled aggression'. [33] This psychopathological model of child abuse has dominated the literature ever since. [34]

In Britain the first paper on the subject was published in 1963. [35] Three years later the British Paediatric Association published a memorandum. [36] It described the syndrome, detailed cases which might be missed, including those where there had been persistent neglect. 'While these cases are not strictly included under the heading "battered baby syndrome" ', it noted, 'much of what is recommended here applies also to such cases of persistent neglect'. [37] The memorandum made no attempt to discuss the aetiology of the syndrome.

In the 1960s interest in the problem spread to the social work profession and contributions to our understanding of it were made in the USA by Elizabeth Elmer, Leontine Young and others. Young's *Wednesday's Children* [38] was a particularly influential book. It was the first major documentary study made of children abused or neglected by their parents. She drew on case records of public child welfare agencies. Although this methodology has inevitable biases Young did draw attention to the fact that abuse occurs across socio-economic lines. She also drew attention to the problem of the other parent, the passive, non-abusing one. They behaved, she commented, 'as if they were prisoners of the other marriage partner, hopelessly condemned to a life sentence . . . [T]heir role appeared more as another and more competent child in the family than as a parent.' [39] She also noted an interrelationship between child and spouse abuse. 'The parent who abused the children also abused his marital partner. Sometimes that abuse was physical, more often it took a less gross but even more deadly form.' [40] The profile of the families in the survey stressed poverty, inadequate housing, sporadic employment, and large numbers of children. Young also commented on the prevalence of alcoholism and chronic drinking, promiscuity, psychosis and mental retardation. She conceded that 'lack of economic resources tends to make deviant behaviour more visible to the outside community'. [41] Nevertheless, she saw the problem as principally one found in lower-class families.

Although she admitted that '[n]o one really knows the cause' [42] her own views inclined to psychodynamic determinism. Thus in discussing one (middle-class) abusive father she commented on 'the perverse fascination with punishment as an entity in itself, divorced from discipline and even from the fury of revenge. It is the cold calculation of destruction which in itself requires neither provocation nor rationale . . . The one invariable trademark of the abusing parent regardless of economic or social status is this immersion in the action of punishing without regard for its cause or its purpose'. And, describing a brutal incident, she remarks '[t]his was not punishment for something the child had done. It was punishment as an end in itself, without rational reason or purpose — not punishment to fit the crime but punishment without crime.' [43]

Elizabeth Elmer's *Children in Jeopardy* [44] advanced our knowledge, particularly of the abused children themselves, a little further. It was a retrospective study of 50 child patients of the Pittsburgh Children's Hospital with suspected or known non-accidental injuries. She noted that, although young on admission, almost one-third had records of previous hospital admissions. There was a high correlation with low birth-weight and a number of the children was illegitimate. Nearly half the children were mentally retarded though in many of the cases this was attributable to head injuries. The study also contains some comment on the constant stress under which the families lived, with economic hardship, isolation and marital and psychological difficulties.

By the end of the 1960s the problem had begun to be noticed in other parts of the world and case histories were flooding the periodical literature. Gil in the USA had attempted to discover the true incidence rates. [45] Kempe and Helfer had published their first collection of essays [46] (a second edition and two more books were to follow). All the states of the USA had passed, often as panic measures in response to Kempe's revelations, reporting laws [47] and questions were being raised about whether Britain needed a reporting law too. [48] 1969 saw the first NSPCC study [49] and by 1970 the government had issued its first memorandum designed to increase awareness of battering among social workers and doctors. [50] It quoted the 1967 Registrar-General's figures of 71 deaths to children under five years of age due to homicide and injury purposely inflicted and suggested that there were 40 infant deaths from this cause annually in England and Wales. 1970 also saw a law professor [51] devote his inaugural lecture to the subject of child protection, something which would have been unheard of only a few years earlier.

Child abuse had been discovered. It had come to be realised that children of all ages, and not just babies, suffered. The term 'battered babies' gave way to 'abused children'. In Britain the term 'non-accidental injury' is now used. The term is less emotive and more accurate. Much violence to children does not consist of battering. Burning, for example, is a common form of abuse. Some children injure themselves in situations in which this was to be expected and where it may even be intended that they should. It is not stretching language unduly to say these children have suffered non-accidental injuries or have been abused. Furthermore, references to a 'syndrome' are no longer current for it is recognised that this, with its implication of a unitary causal process, is misleading.

The size of the problem

We do not know how many children are killed or injured by their parents or other caretakers. Various estimates have been made. The most serious attempt to measure the problem has been made by David Gil in the USA. [52] He tackled the question by conducting a nationwide survey on opinions and attitudes. Of 1,520 respondents 58.3 per cent believed that 'almost anybody could at some time injure a child in his care', [53] 22.3 per cent thought they could at some time injure a child, [54] and 15.9 per cent admitted they had come close to perpetrating child abuse. [55] Only 0.4 per cent admitted having physically injured a child in their care. [56] Gil rightly believes both the final two statistics to represent the lowest possible estimate for they involve the admission of a criminal act or something close to it. He found that 3 per cent of the sample personally knew families involved in incidents of child abuse in the preceding year. He extrapolates from this that '2.53 to 4.07 million adults throughout the United States knew personally families involved in incidents of child abuse during the year preceding the October 1965 survey'. [57] This, he concedes, is an upper limit, for commonsense dictates that some of the abusing families are likely to be known to more than one person. Nevertheless, the upper limit for the year ending October 1965 was between 13.3 and 21.4 incidents per 1,000 persons. Gil's figures are regularly cited though more recent American estimates put upper limits as perhaps only one-quarter of the two million incidents reported in his survey. [58]

The 'true' incidence will never be known. In this country it has been suggested that between 2,400 and 4,600 children are seriously injured every year. Some 450 may be physically incapacitated for life. A large number die each year as a result of injuries inflicted upon them. The figure of two a day or 750 a year picked up by the press and repeated solemnly and uncritically [59] is almost certainly inaccurate and grossly exaggerated. MacKeith [60] speculates that there may be 400 new cases every year of brain damage severe enough to cause lasting incapacity. He suggests that this figure may account for some of the cases of cerebral palsy and mental handicap for which there seems no other satisfactory explanation.

It has been argued that the information required to establish the extent of death attributable to non-accidental injury can be readily extracted from the Registrar-General's Statistical Reviews. [61] These contain analyses of the registered causes of all deaths in England and Wales each year. In 1972, 80 deaths of children under five were registered as due to 'homicide and fatal injury purposely inflicted'. A

17

further 21 were registered as 'fatal injury undetermined whether purposely or accidentally inflicted'. The remainder (13,000) were attributed to various diseases. [62] There are, of course, dangers in regarding official statistics as simple reflections of the phenomena to which they refer. As Cicourel puts it: 'demonstrating how socially organised activities produce such outcomes as rates . . . parallels the transformations that occur in everyday events when members transform vague and disconnected pieces of information into an ordered "happening" '. [63] The statistics in question are part of a social process in which doctors, courts and coroners participate. [64] Coroners reach a large number of 'open' verdicts [65] and these cases would not, of course, appear in the Registrar-General's figures for 'homicide and fatal injury purposely inflicted'. Some at least of these deaths will be attributable to non-accidental injury as will a number of the 'sudden deaths (cause unknown)' category which will contain cot deaths, some of which are thought to be the result of undetected non-accidental injury. A further problem is that the Registrar-General classifies causes of death according to the International Classification of Disease. A death may be classified as due to pneumonia although the deceased child had contracted the disease whilst suffering from the effects of a non-accidental injury, for his injuries have not directly caused his death.

Other attempts to estimate the incidence of child abuse have been made by examining mortuary and hospital emergency department statistics. Simpson, the Home Office Pathologist, suggested in 1967 [66] an annual figure of 200-300 deaths for the Greater London area alone. He based his hypothesis on cases coming to mortuaries. If he were right the problem would be even more horrendous than it anyway is. His figures are unlikely, however, to be accurate. More credibility has been given to the figures by Hall in Preston [67] but they, equally, are a distortion of the truth.

On the basis of his experience in the Emergency and Accident Department of Preston Infirmary, Hall reported that in the years 1970-72 'definite' cases, including five deaths, were seen. He proceeded then to estimate national incidence on the following basis: the average number of cases in the Preston Infirmary for the years 1970-72 is 9.6 and 17.2 per cent of these are deaths. Fifteen million patients are treated annually in hospital emergency departments. In 1972, 34,000 patients were so treated in Preston. 'The incidence of these cases is 1 in 3,400 of the attendances at the Preston Emergency Department. If this is related to a national figure of 15 million attenders *per annum*, then it might be expected that 4,400 such children would be seen throughout the country every year. A mortality rate of 17.2 per cent would give 757 as the annual number of deaths to be expected in the whole population.' [68] These figures, the source for the oft-quoted 'two children a day killed by parents' already referred to, are misleading, for while the Preston statistics are based on 'new' attendances at the emergency department, the figure of 15 million (the national figure) takes in 'all' attendances at casualty departments. [69] There are about 8.5 million 'new' patients at casualty departments each year. Extrapolating from Hall's findings this would suggest 2,500 'definite' cases of which 430 would be fatal. Hall also identified seven cases a year in which there was a strong suspicion of non-accidental injury but insufficient evidence to justify measures apart from supervision. Extrapolation nationally would suggest that a further 1,750 cases would come into this category. Hall tells us nothing about the ages of the children nor about the severity of their injuries save to inform us that most were relatively minor ('only one example of the full-blown battering syndrome' was seen).

Another estimate has been made by Mounsey, a policeman, on the basis of cases brought to the notice of the police in Lancashire in 1972. [70] Crimes reported to the police are a notoriously unreliable measure of offences committed. [71] Mounsey's figures are not particularly helpful because we are not told what criteria were used for deciding whether or not an injury was non-accidental. We are also, surprisingly, not informed as to the outcome of the cases. A useful piece of information which we are given concerns the sources of the police information: most of the reports emanate from neighbours and close relations and relatively few from doctors, the social services etc. Mounsey includes all cases of injury, no matter how slight, cases of neglect and cases 'where children were felt to be at risk from birth up to and including the age of 13 years'. [72] The police received information about 105 suspected cases of child abuse involving 166 children. Twenty-six died, 36 were seriously injured and 13 were slightly injured. Seventy-five were neglected and 16 were considered to be at risk. Extrapolating nationally Mounsey's figures would suggest 1,600 cases coming to the notice of the police, of which 250 would be fatal, 350 seriously injured and 130 slightly injured. These figures are bound to be low estimates of true incidence, as feelings that the criminal law is a blunt instrument and desires to help the parents and rehabilitate the family, mean that comparatively few cases are likely to be brought to the attention of the police. This much was admitted in the memorandum submitted to the House of Commons Select Committee on violence in the family by the Metropolitan Police CID. 'The police see', it wrote, 'only the tip of the iceberg and any figure we produced could not reflect a true picture because unfortunately it

19

has been found that social workers, doctors and teachers are loath to inform us of this type of crime.' [73]

Another estimate of the extent of non-accidental injury has been made by Oliver et al. on the basis of a study in North-East Wiltshire. [74] They report that, after a year of educative activity with the professions involved, 22 children under the age of four were ascertained as having been severely injured during an 18-month period. From this work a national figure 3,500 cases a year of non-accidental injury may be worked out. Further, on the basis of the 10 per cent mortality rate which Oliver found in studying earlier years, some 350 deaths of children under four might be expected annually.

It is difficult to draw satisfactory conclusions from a plethora of unconnected surveys which differ in the definitions they apply to non-accidental injury (if they specify them), in the ages of the children under consideration and in their methodology. But together they suggest that workers in the field suspect that between 3,500 and 4,500 children suffer non-accidental injury at the hands of their parents or parent-substitutes and that between 250 and 450 children die [75] as a result of injuries inflicted upon them by such caretakers.

Perhaps, however, our greatest chance of discovering something like the true incidence of child abuse lies in systematic reporting and registration of suspected cases. In this country registers are a very recent phenomenon. Agencies such as the NSPCC have kept registers for some time and since 1974 under Department of Health and Social Security direction local organisation area review committees have established central registers. [76] But in the USA where reporting to central registers has been mandatory in all states since 1968 the legal requirement to report by no means eliminates uncertainty as to the relationship between those cases reported and the true incidence of abuse. Some doctors are unwilling to report or unaware of the laws or the clinical condition. [77] Sussman [78] suggests this is the case particularly with private doctors. In the USA reporting from non-medical sources constitutes a high percentage of the cases, just as references to Dutch medical referees come in large part from outside the medical profession. [79] In the looser system of communication which operates in this country a larger number of cases is likely to fall through the net. In February 1976 the Department of Health and Social Security was nonetheless able to report that 97 English authorities, accounting for about 90 per cent of the child population, had recorded some 5,700 cases, 40 of them fatal, of known or suspected non-accidental injury coming to their notice during the last three quarters of 1974. [80]

A more detailed report is that by the NSPCC on the registers they

maintain in their special units in Leeds and Manchester. [81] The
Society estimates on the basis of this study that some 3,360 children
under four suffer non-accidental injury each year, of whom 1,300 are
seriously injured and 27 die as a result of their injuries. This 'assumes
that the level of professional skill nationally approximates to that in
those areas where Special Units are operating'. [82] The presence of
a unit, however, reflects a heightened awareness of the problem of non-
accidental injury. The NSPCC's finding on the number of fatalities is
not particularly valuable for, as it states, 'non-reporting of cases of
death . . . may be due to dead children no longer being considered
"at risk"; or due to the fact that the legal proceedings ensuing on the
death of a child might imply to a notifying agent that a decision as to
the cause of death should be deferred until after an inquest or
possible prosecution.' [83] Its estimate of cases of injury is consistent
with the other research discussed in this section.

Whatever the exact number, and a 'dark' figure of hidden abuse will
always remain with us, there is no doubt that we are faced with a
problem of considerable dimension and seriousness. [84]

The causes of child abuse

There is no one cause of child abuse and a multidimensional
explanation must be sought. The most basic question is whether caretakers abuse children because they are driven by environmental
pressures so to do or because they are predisposed to violent behaviour
by psychological forces at work from within. In the final analysis it
may be that both of these factors play a part so that neither can be
ignored. Other considerations of a more structural and ideological
nature are also contributory factors and cannot be left out in our
considerations of the aetiology of child abuse. A number of models
has thus been constructed; the remainder of this section considers
each in turn.

The psychopathological model

A terse and accurate summary of this model is found in Gelles's
critique of it. [85] He states:

> Throughout the literature there runs a common theme:
> 'Anyone who would abuse or kill his child is sick.' This theme
> has become synonymous with a cause-and-effect relationship:
> that is, it is suggested that there is a psychological pathology

21

or sickness which accounts for child abuse. The notion of mental illness is the major explanatory tool of the psychopathological model of child abuse. Closely related is the assumption that child abusers tend to have distinctive personality traits which are typical of the psychopathic personality. The model assumes, furthermore, that the sickness is manifested in the form of a 'transference psychosis'. The final assumption of the model is that the cause of the psychopathy can be traced to the parent's early childhood, in which he or she was abused as a child.

Some, for example Justice and Justice, [86] would see here a fusing of two relatively distinct explanations: what they call the 'psychodynamic model' and the 'personality or character trait model'. They admit the essential similarity of the two but point out that the personality model pays less attention to the factors which underlie the traits of the person in question. While there is certainly some literature which is deficient in this way, the better psychological explanations make the sort of synthesis which Gelles describes. The models are, therefore, treated as one here.

One of the most authoritative and widely quoted of psychiatric studies of abusive parents is that of Steele and Pollock. [87] They studied intensively 60 families in which significant abuse of infants or small children had occurred. Excluded were murder cases and families where the abuse began when the children were older. They regard both these as examples of a different phenomenon. Their method of study was clinical, though it was supplemented by interviews and home visits by a social worker. The patients were a cross-section of the white population, all socio-economic strata being covered. The authors also note that 'in respect to psychopathology they were equally heterogenous.' [88] Their explanation of why their subjects abused their small children falls into the pattern set out by Gelles.

There is a wide spread of emotional disorders but 'instead of trying to associate child abuse with a specific type of psychiatric disorder or a commonly accepted character-type description' the authors 'searched for a consistent behavior pattern which can exist in combination with, but quite independently of, other psychological disorders' [89] They found the abusive parents

> expect and demand a great deal from their infants and children. Not only is the demand for performance great, but it is premature, clearly beyond the ability of the infant to comprehend what is wanted and to respond appropriately. Parents

deal with the child as if he were much older than he really is. Observation of this interaction leads to a clear impression that the parent feels insecure and unsure of being loved, and looks to the child as a source of reassurance, comfort and loving response. It is hardly an exaggeration to say the parent acts like a frightened, unloved child, looking to his own child as if he were an adult capable of providing comfort and love. [90]

Furthermore, '[w]ithout exception . . . , there is a history of having been raised in the same style which they have recreated in the pattern of rearing their own children'. The abusive parents themselves had been deprived of 'basic mothering'. [91] Many had themselves been abused as children.

Steele and Pollock also list other secondary elements of parental psychopathology: intense, unresolved sibling rivalry, an obsessive, compulsive character structure, and unresolved Oedipal conflicts with excessive guilt. [92] Further, they believe that the attacked child may innocently and unwittingly contribute to the attack unleashed upon him. 'Characteristics presented by the infant', they note, 'such as sex, time of birth, health status and behavior are factors in instigating child abuse.' [93]

A further example of the psychopathological model is the detailed study of 25 families who were referred to the NSPCC's Battered Child Research Department. [94] The authors concede that '[g]iven the small size of the samples employed . . . no absolute generalisations can be made regarding the psychosocial pathology of child batterers'. [95] They content themselves with listing 'suggestive pointers'. [96] They refer to 'immaturity, impracticality and a tendency to flee into fantasy in the face of real problems.' [97] The fathers are said to have 'introverted schizoid personalit[ies].' [98] The authors explain the mothers' role reversal in this way. 'If the father cannot support the mother at her time of need, it is no great mystery that she turns to her child for emotional replenishment, illogical as this may be'. [99] The authors do not ignore what they call 'social predisposers'. [100] Indeed, one of them [101] in a separate article explains the fact that 'we are seeing the great number [of battering parents] from the lower-economic groups' in terms of the 'greater social stress and . . . fewer avenues of relief' of such families. Another explanation of this over-concentration is put forward later in this chapter. [102]

Neither in Steele and Pollock nor the NSPCC study are battering parents found to be psychotic. Indeed, the general consensus among writers who subscribe to the psychopathology school is that psychotic sadistic battering parents are uncommon. [103] Smith's finding [104] that 8 out of 35 self-confessed baby batterers had abnormal electro-encephalogram patterns does not seem to be supported by other research, though no other research has examined specifically batterers' organic conditions. His finding that over 50 per cent of battering parents were of borderline ability [105] is also not supported else-where and may be explained partially in terms of his sample drawn as it was from an area of high immigrant concentration. [106]

A number of attempts has been made by supporters of the psycho-pathological approach to group distinct clusters of personality characteristics so as to form a typology of the abusing parent. The best known is that of Merrill. [107] He identified three distinct clusters and a fourth category that he found true of abusing fathers only.

One group of parents are beset with a continual, pervasive hostility and aggressiveness, sometimes focused and sometimes directed at the world generally. It is not controlled anger and needs the stimulation only of daily difficulties. Merrill conceived this anger to stem from conflicts within childhood and to be rooted in early childhood experiences.

A second group suffer from rigidity, compulsiveness, lack of warmth, lack of reasonableness and lack of pliability in thinking and belief. Such parents defended the right to act the way they did.

His third category showed strong feelings of passivity and depen-dence. They manifest strong needs to depend on others for decisions. These are particularly the parents who compete with their own children for the love and attention of their spouses. Many of these show signs of immaturity.

A fourth grouping included a significant number of abusing fathers. They are young and for one reason or another, often physical disability, are unable to support their families. Mother works and father stays at home, caring for the children. The frustrations that this engenders lead to angry, rigid discipline, and swift and severe punish-ment.

Merrill's typology is useful if only for showing that, within the psychopathological framework, there is more than one 'type' of abusing parent and not one single motivational factor.

The psychopathological model represents what the ordinary man in the street thinks of the parents of battered children. It is also the mainspring for much of our social policy on the question. That we should want to think of abusing parents as 'sick' may tell us something about ourselves. Gil certainly thinks so and his reasoning is most persuasive. He writes: [108]

is it possible that the illness-as-cause hypothesis is accepted readily because it soothes society's conscience, as well as the conscience of individual parents who may be subject to abusive impulses? Society is absolved from guilt by this interpretation, for if child abuse is the result of the emotional illness of the perpetrators, social conditions need not be blamed, society is justified in the self-righteous prosecution of individual perpetrators, and it need not examine the social circumstances and cultural trends which may be major factors of child abuse. Individual parents, too, may derive gratification from the sickness-as-cause interpretation, since it may fill them with a sense of security. For if abusive behaviour were a function of sickness, most parents could view themselves as free from the danger of falling prey to it, since they do not consider themselves sick.

The labelling of abusive parents as deviants is an important functional mechanism for the rest of us. [109]

There are, as Gusfield has demonstrated, different ways in which society can view deviants. [110] He has distinguished between assimilative reform, which seeks to improve individuals, and coercive reform, which seeks to force individuals to act in the desired way. He argues that when the reformer's own social status and way of life are secure, he will see the violator of rules as a 'deviant' deserving help. But when threatened he is more likely to view the violator as an 'enemy', a challenger of the legitimacy of the norm who cannot be reformed but must instead be subdued. Abusive parents are only rarely seen as enemies and then when a crime of peculiar horror has been perpetrated. William Kepple, responsible for Maria Colwell's death, is for many the stereotype of the 'enemy' deviant. But, if we determine categories according to the way we read the deviant's attitude, as Gusfield suggests, [111] then even the Kepples of this world are more likely to be perceived as 'sick' deviants or 'repentant' deviants than 'enemy' deviants for they are most unlikely to be seen as attacking the legitimacy of the norms they break.

How useful an explanation is the psychopathological model? Spinetta and Rigler, in a wide-ranging and perceptive review article, have made the following useful criticisms. [112] Most of the studies do not test specific hypotheses. 'Many start and end as broad studies with relatively untested commonsense assumptions'. [113] They tend to use samples that are not truly representative. Furthermore, practically all the psychological research in child abuse is *ex post facto*. They comment: '[w]hat is left unanswered and still to be tested is whether one can determine prior to the onset of abuse which parents are most likely to abuse their children, or whether high-risk groups can only be defined after at least one incident of abuse has occurred.' [114]   Each of these criticisms may be developed further.

The model is unduly narrow. It cannot 'account for the majority of cases of child abuse because it posits a single causal variable . . . and ignores other factors. [115] It does not explain why, for example, a parent himself abused as a child should express this experience in child abuse as opposed to other forms of dysfunctional behaviour. It does not explain why many people who are immature or impulsive or possessed of other character traits which psychologists impute to child abusers do not act violently towards their children. It assumes an act of abuse cannot occur unless the psychological potential is present. [116] It would thus seem to account for both too much and too little abuse. There is also 'an inability to pinpoint the personality traits which characterize the pathology . . . . [T]here is little agree-ment as to the make-up of the psychopathy.' [117] Gelles, having studied a representative selection of the writings, noted that 19 traits were referred to, but only four figured in the diagnoses of more than two authors. Nor are proponents of the psychopathological model always consistent within themselves. Thus Steele and Pollock, in a study already described, [118] excitedly announce that their first case was a 'goldmine of psychopathology' [119] and then tell us that their patients were a 'random cross-section of the general population' who 'would not seem much different from a group of people picked up by stopping the first several dozen people one would meet on a downtown street.' [120]

Further, because 'the analysis of the behaviour takes place after the fact, little analytic understanding of the genesis of the behaviour is offered.' [121] Thus to tell us that an abusive parent lacked control is not to tell us very much when we know that that parent has just beaten his child to death. The behaviour is not distinguished from its explanation, with the result that little predictive power is offered.

Finally, the evidence is largely assembled by clinicians using data constructed out of interviews with patients. But not all child abusers find their way to clinics so that the samples are biased. We need to know much more about how abusive parents get referred, or refer themselves, to psychiatrists, clinical psychologists and allied professionals. Nor is there any attempt to compare samples of their patients with any comparative group of non-child abusers. Certain individuals are more likely to be defined as 'abusers' than others. The greater the social distance between the typer and the person singled out for typing, the more quickly the typification may be applied. [122]

Once the label of 'abuser' has been attached it is difficult to remove it. When a parent comes to a psychiatrist as an abuser the psychiatrist is thus apt to engage in what Schur calls 'retrospective interpretation' of facts. [123] 'The *present evil* of current character must be related to *past evil* that can be discovered in biography'. [124] Goffman points out that the actual function of case records is geared to support current diagnoses. Writing of mental illness, he states: '[o]ne of its purposes is to show the ways in which the patient is "sick" and the reasons why it was right to commit him and is right currently to keep him committed, and this is done by extracting from his whole life course a list of those incidents that have or might have had "symptomatic" significance'. [125] The pathological model requires that parents be studied in terms of what is 'wrong' with them. [126] And it requires exceptionalist solutions, for their 'problems are unusual, even unique, they are exceptions to the rule, they occur as a result of individual defect, accident or unfortunate circumstance and must be remedied by means that are particular and . . . tailored to the individual case.' [127]

Sociological models

Even within psychopathological explanations of child abuse there are considerable sociological data though their analytical implications are glossed over. Sociological explanations, on the other hand, tend to focus attention on environmental stress. And whereas psycho-pathological models, like other forms of positivistic criminology, see the problem as located within the deviant parent, sociological theories of child abuse see the problem in terms of interaction between parent and child and interplay between the family and its social context.

The leading advocate of environmental stress as the cause of child abuse is Gil. [128] He argues that a major cause of child abuse is the stress and frustration which result from 'multi-faceted deprivations of poverty and its correlates, high density in overcrowded, dilapidated, inadequately served neighbourhoods, large numbers of children, especially in one-parent, mainly female-headed households, and the absence of child-care alternatives', as well as poor education and 'alienating circumstances in most work places.' [129] But Gil does not suggest that poverty in itself is a direct cause of child abuse; rather that it operates through an intervening variable, *viz.*, 'concrete and psychological stress and frustration experienced by individuals in the context of culturally sanctioned use of physical force in child rearing'. [130] Gil's thesis does not answer the question as to why some parents in stressful circumstances abuse their children while others under the same conditions do not.

Gil himself believes that child abuse is largely concentrated in the lower socio-economic classes. He bases this conclusion on his nation-wide survey of cases reported by child welfare departments and other public agencies. Children are subject to abuse in homes where material standards are good (Gil, indeed, found in an earlier pilot study that over one-third of the abusing families involved came from 'comfortable' homes [131]), but higher-income families have the resources to conceal abuse. Furthermore, because characteristics identified with child abuse are frequent concomitants of poverty, the poor are more likely to be perceived as abusive towards their children. The well-off are not expected to abuse their children, so that their explanations that 'the child has had an accident' are more readily believed. But if economic and related stress 'triggers' child abuse, why does the problem occur at all in higher-income families and why does it not occur even more commonly in families who suffer multiple deprivation and stress? These questions are not answered satisfactorily by proponents of the environmental stress model. Nevertheless, it is worth investigating the evidence of deprivation.

We note the parents tend to be poor. Most are very young. [132] Gil did not find this but he did find that parents under 25 were much more likely to inflict severe injuries. [133] The father is likely to be unemployed. Skinner and Castle and Castle and Kerr in two NSPCC reports found a significantly high rate of unemployment amongst a sample of battering fathers. [134] Much of the research stresses how, in a mobile society, the parents are often socially isolated. Jobs and accommodation are changed frequently to the point 'where they might be labelled nomadic'. [135] Many have accommodation problems. Some move constantly to avoid the limelight when their battering is exposed. It is common to find fathers with a criminal record. Their absence leaves mothers to cope alone. Many mothers were pregnant or recently confined at the time of the abuse. Many of the children abused are the products of unwanted pregnancies. A substantial percentage of the parents are not married, at least not to each other. Although both mothers and fathers abuse children, research shows that the sex of the abuser is more often female. In the NSPCC study of 78 cases mothers were responsible on 42 of the occasions. Steele and Pollock found that in 50 of their cases the mother was the abuser and in only 7 the father. [136] Gil's analysis of cases found the mother abused children 50 per cent of the time while the father abused children 40 per cent of the time. [137] His cases did, however, have a predominance of female-headed households and where the homes were headed by fathers, the father was the abuser two-thirds of the time. Gelles has explained why women who, given the culturally defined passive role in our society might be expected to be less aggressive, are found to be more abusive than men in terms of 'the child threaten[ing] or interfer[ing] with the mother's identity and esteem more than it does the father's'. [138] He quotes a case cited by Galdston [139] in which a mother had to leave work as a result of pregnancy and her husband's desire to return to work: 'forced into closer contact with her ten-month-old child, she subsequently beat him because she found his cries "so demanding" '.

The child himself is an important variable. Some children are particularly at risk. No one characteristic can be isolated as a pre-disposing factor but certain features do recur with a frequency which suggests that children who possess them are more likely to be subjected to abuse. Almost all the research shows that young children under five are at greatest risk of serious injury and death. [140] Most vulnerable are infants under one year and toddlers between two-and-a-half and three years. The NSPCC studies of 1969 and 1972 found that 78 per cent and 62 per cent respectively of the children abused were under two years. Gil, on the other hand, found that 75 per cent of his cases of child abuse were over two years old; almost 50 per cent were over six; and 20 per cent were in their teens (the majority of these were girls). [141] How is one to explain the disparity between Gil's findings and those of other researchers? The fact that Gil's figures are drawn from a national survey whereas those of the NSPCC consist of cases referred to it may be a partial explanation. [142] Older children are more resilient, less vulnerable to physical damage, and thus less likely to form the basis of referrals to welfare or medical agencies. Gil did find that the younger children were the most severely injured.

Child abuse can be explained as a phenomenon which affects the under three-year-olds very largely. Such a child is physically the most vulnerable; least capable of meaningful social interaction and this may frustrate the parent who reacts by physically assaulting him; and his birth may have caused economic hardship or interfered with parental plans in some way. [143] All this is true and yet Gil's figures remain, and remain convincing. Because physical punishment of children is culturally accepted and known to be widespread, [144] abuse may also be expected. It is likely then that parental abuse is not a function of the child's age and that the data which suggest this are unrepresen-tative of the true incidence of abuse and are the result of a selective gathering of cases that might be expected from medical and welfare sources. Older children may be abused less because they can contra-dict their parents' explanations and hold off attacks. [145]

The environmental stress view of child abuse finds some support in Garbarino's research in New York State. [146] He found that socioeconomic stress exacerbated by the unavailability of support systems for the family from the community is directly associated with the rate of child abuse. It accounted for 36 per cent of the variance in rates of child abuse across New York counties: economic conditions more generally affecting the family account for 16 per cent of the variance. One must exercise caution in examining these results for the data were derived from public agency sources where lower socio-economic classes were over-represented. Another valuable multi-factor approach is Light's re-analysis of Gil's original findings. Light's analysis allows for comparisons with non-abusing families. Of all the variables Light found that family stress due to father's unemployment is most closely related to child abuse. [147]

What the environmental stress model does not explain is why not all parents in stressful situations abuse their children, and why, furthermore, one father will abuse his child, another assault his wife and a third let out his frustration at a football match. Part of the answer to this may lie in an understanding of social learning. [148] There is evidence in both the psychopathological and environmental stress literature that abusive parents were themselves abused as children. Steele and Pollock point this out and so do the NSPCC studies. Their conclusions have already been referred to. Similarly, Gil found that 11 per cent of parents (14.1 per cent of mothers and 7 per cent of fathers) who abuse their children were victims of abuse during childhood. [149] That violence begets violence is also strongly suggested by Oliver and Taylor's report of five generations of abused children in one family pedigree. [150] How is this phenomenon to be explained? It is suggested that the key may lie in patterns of child socialisation, that a child who grows up in an environment where he learns that violence is a major resource in tackling life's problems resorts to similar techniques himself. Gelles puts it this way: [151] '[a] parent who was raised by parents who used physical force to train children and who grows up in a violent household has had as a role model the use of force and violence as a means of family problem solving. The parent who recreates the pattern of abusive child rearing may be doing this because this is the means of child rearing he learned while growing up. It is the way he knows of responding to stress and bringing up his child.' Gil also draws attention to this when, in explaining why the poor abuse their children more than the wealthier sections of the population, he notes as 'an additional factor' the 'tendency toward more direct, less inhibited, expression and discharge of aggressive impulses, a tendency *learned* [152] apparently through lower-class

30

mores and socialization.' [153] But Gil does not bring out the importance of social learning sufficiently.

Culture and structural models

'To gain understanding of any social problem one needs to view it in the total societal context within which it evolves.' [154] So argues Gil in his most recent and provocative paper on the aetiology of child abuse. In this he argues that child abuse manifests itself on three levels: in the home by parents and other caretakers; in institutions [155] such as day care centres, residential child care settings, schools and foster care; and in the 'destructive conditions' associated with the multifaceted deprivations of poverty. Child abuse, he argues, consists of 'acts or inactions of individuals, on their own or as institutional agents, whose behaviour reflects societal forces mediated through their unique personalities.' [156] Its cause is to be sought in:

> a cluster of interacting elements, to wit, a society's basic social philosophy, its dominant value premises, its concept of humans; the nature of its social, economic and political institutions, which are shaped by its philosophy and value premises, and which in turn reinforce that philosophy and these values; and finally, the particular quality of human relations prevailing in the society, which derives from its philosophy, values and institutions. [157]

He sees the dominant social philosophy in American society as non-egalitarian and competitive. Closely related to this is the 'social construction, or definition, of childhood prevalent in a society'. [158] Social policies which 'sustain different levels of rights for children from different social and economic backgrounds are', Gil claims, 'a major, direct cause of the many forms of child abuse on the societal and institutional levels, and an indirect cause of abuse on the family level'. [159] So is society's attitude towards the use of force as a legitimate means of achieving ends particularly in imbalanced, inter-personal relations. He notes that a non-egalitarian philosophy is far more likely to approve of the use of force than is an egalitarian one, for the use of force in relationships symbolises inequality. Violence against children, he had remarked in his earlier book, 'may . . . be a functional aspect of socialization into a highly competitive and often violent society.' [160] To these causes he adds factors relating to environmental stress and 'expressions of intrapsychic conflicts and psychopathology which, in turn, are rooted in the social fabric.' [161] So he ignores neither of the earlier models, though he seeks the root

31

causes of child abuse in pathogenic aspects of the social order rather than in individual pathology.

Gil purports only to describe American society but the conclusions he draws are equally applicable in a British context. Basically what he is saying is that violence against children is *normal* in our cultures. It did not surprise Gil, nor need it surprise us, that his public opinion survey revealed that 58.3 per cent of adult Americans thought that 'almost anybody could at some time injure a child in his care'. [162] Abuse, seen in these terms, is merely the unacceptable outcome of legitimate child-rearing practices. Middle-class parents may use corporal punishment less than working-class or ethnic minority parents but it must not be forgotten that a life of poverty or in the ghetto tends to generate the sort of stressful experiences that trigger child abuse by weakening the parent's psychological mechanisms of self-control. It is Gil's conclusion that violence against children is not the major social problem; it is rather 'the poverty, racial discrimination, malnutrition and inadequate provisions for medical care and education.' [163] The eradication of child abuse depends, in Gil's terms, on a complete social revolution.

Some concluding comments

Child abuse cannot be understood in terms of one specific causal dimension. [164] It is a complex problem and requires an understanding of the interaction between environmental stress and strain and malfunctioning personalities; and it necessitates a location of this interplay in the wider structure and culture of society. None of the models in themselves explains child abuse; a multidimensional approach is required. But, as will be seen in the next chapters, strategies geared towards the management and prevention of child abuse tend to have assumed that the explanation is to be sought in psychopathology. As a result they have individualised the problem. They are designed to pick up the pieces but rarely to forestall the incident.

The effects of child abuse

What happens to children who are abused? A minority die. Many of the remainder are abused again: Gil found that at least half the children in his sample of abused children had been victims of physical abuse before the incident reported in 1967. [165]

Little is known of the long-term consequences of abuse on

children. [166]   There is evidence of neurological impairment, including spasticity, paraplegia and blindness. [167]   A high incidence of mental retardation is reported by a number of authors. [168]   The Royal College of Psychiatrists, in its evidence to the House of Commons Select Committee, estimated that between 2 and 4 per cent of children in subnormality hospitals are brain-damaged following assaults by their parents. [169]   The Committee commented upon the cost of this. [170]   Other authors have detected language retardation. [171]   There is evidence that abused children later commit acts of juvenile delinquency [172] and many of the most notorious murderers have been found to be the victims of abuse when children. [173]   Many themselves grow up to abuse their own children. It has been suggested that abused children tend to lack trust and to be loners. Morse [174] found that 70 per cent of his study population in a three-year follow-up exhibited behaviour outside the normal range in social and motor development.

Some caution must be applied to many of these findings for the various impairments may have preceded the abuse and may be the results of other trauma. Nevertheless, a conservative estimate of the outcome of physical abuse on children is quite horrifying.

Notes

[1]   *The Times*, 27 October 1973. The father was jailed for three months.
[2]   *The Times*, 13 June 1974. The mother was jailed for three years.
[3]   *The Times*, 1 February 1974. The mother, an American, returned home before any steps were taken to prosecute her. The inquest jury asked if the USAF (her husband was a USAF sergeant) could make sure the mother got psychiatric help.
[4]   *The Guardian*, 3 April 1976. The mother was sentenced to fifteen months' imprisonment suspended for two years.
[5]   See *Report of the Committee of Inquiry into the Care and Supervision Provided in Relation to Maria Colwell*, DHSS 1974 and East Sussex County Council, *Children at Risk*, 1975.
[6]   *Report of Joint Committee of Inquiry into Non-Accidental Injury to Children with particular reference to the case of Lisa Godfrey*, London Borough of Lambeth, 1975.
[7]   *Report of Committee of Inquiry into Welfare of Simon Peacock*, Suffolk and Cambridgeshire Councils, 1978.
[8]   *Report of the Review Body appointed to enquire into the case of Steven Meurs*, Norfolk County Council, 1975.

[9]   J. Delaney, 'New concepts of the Family Court' in R. Helfer and C.H. Kempe (eds), *Child Abuse and Neglect — the Family and the Community*, Ballinger, 1976, p.335, 344.

[10] See M. Togut et al. in *Developmental Medicine and Child Neurology*, vol.11, 1969, p.601.

[11] See D. MacCarthy,'Maternal Rejection and Stunting of Growth' in DHSS, *The Family in Society*, HMSO, 1974, p.86.

[12] H. Martin, 'The Child and His Development' in C.H. Kempe and R. Helfer, *Helping the Battered Child and his Family*, Lippincott, 1972, p.100.

[13] D. Gil, *Violence against Children*, Harvard University Press, 1970, pp 128-9.

[14] R. Gelles, 'The Social Construction of Child Abuse', *American Journal of Orthopsychiatry*, vol.45, 1975, p.365.

[15] Op.cit., note 13, p.6. On intentionality see H. Kelley, *American Psychologist 28*, 1963, p.107.

[16] See S.X. Radbill, 'A History of Child Abuse and Infanticide' in R. Helfer and C.H. Kempe (eds), *The Battered Child*, 2nd ed., University of Chicago Press, 1974 and L. de Mause, *The History of Childhood*, Souvenir Press, 1976.

[17] J. Eads, *Stanford Law Review*, vol.21, 1969, p.1129.

[18] A. Skolnick, *The Family in Transition*, Little Brown, 1971.

[19] There is a good discussion of these in S. Pfohl, 'The Discovery of Child Abuse', *Social Problems*, vol.24, 1977, p.310.

[20] A.A. Rosenfeld and E.H. Newberger, 'Compassion versus Control', *Journal of the American Medical Association*, vol.237, 1977, p.2086.

[21] E. Friedson, *The Profession of Medicine*, Dodd & Mead & Co., 1970, p.252.

[22] Op.cit., note 19, p.319.

[23] A point also made by E.H. Newberger and R. Bourne 'The Medicalization and Legalization of Child Abuse', paper presented to Second World Congress of International Society of Family Law, Montreal 1977, p.13. See also R. Bourne and E.H. Newberger, 'Family Autonomy' or 'Coercive Intervention' in *Boston University L. Review*, vol.57, p.670, 1977.

[24] See N. Kittrie, *The Right to be Different*, John Hopkins Press, 1971.

[25] *Per* I. Illich, *Limits to Medicine*, Penguin Books, 1977, p.98.

[26] Op.cit., note 21, p.328.

[27] J. Caffey in *American Journal of Roentgenology*, vol.56, 1946, p.163.

[28] F.N. Silverman in *American Journal of Roentgenology*, vol.69, 1951, p.413.

[29] That is blood clots under the skull.

[30] P.V. Woolley in *Journal of the American Medical Association*, vol.158, 1955, p.539.
[31] C.H. Kempe in *Journal of the American Medical Association*, vol.181, 1962, p.17.
[32] Idem, p.18.
[33] Idem.
[34] See R. Gelles in *Amercian Journal of Orthopsychiatry*, vol.43, 1973, p.611 and J. Spinetta and D. Rigler in *Psychological Bulletin*, vol.77, 1972, p.296.
[35] By D.L. Griffiths and F.J. Moynihan, *British Medical Journal*, no.5372, 1963, p.1558.
[36] British Paediatric Association, 'The Battered Baby', *British Medical Journal*, 5 March 1966, p.601.
[37] Idem.
[38] L. Young, *Wednesday's Children*, McGraw-Hill, 1964.
[39] Idem, pp.49-50.
[40] Idem, p.67.
[41] Idem, p.81.
[42] Idem, p.75.
[43] Idem, pp.44-5.
[44] E. Elmer, *Children in Jeopardy*, Pittsburgh University Press, 1967.
[45] D. Gil, 'Incidence of Child Abuse and Demographic Characteristics' in R. Helfer and C.H. Kempe (eds), *The Battered Child*, University of Chicago Press, 1968; *Violence Against Children*, Harvard University Press, 1970.
[46] R. Helfer and C.H. Kempe (eds), *The Battered Child*, University of Chicago Press, 1968, 2nd ed. 1974. They later published *Helping the Battered Child and his Family*, Lippincott, 1972, and *Child Abuse and Neglect*, Ballinger, 1976.
[47] See *post*, p.95.
[48] J. Stark, *Public Law*, 1969, p.48.
[49] A. Skinner and R. Castle, *78 Battered Children: A Retrospective Study*, NSPCC, 1969.
[50] DHSS, *The Battered Baby*, 1970.
[51] H.K. Bevan, *Child Protection and the Law*, University of Hull, 1970.
[52] D. Gil, *Violence Against Children*, Harvard University Press, 1970.
[53] Idem, p.55.
[54] Idem, p.56.
[55] Idem, p.57.
[56] Idem, p.58.

[57] Idem, p.59.

[58] See, for example, R. Light, 'Abused and Neglected Children in America: A Study of Alternative Policies', *Harvard Educational Review*, vol.43, 1973, pp 560-7.

[59] For example by J. Howells, *Remember Maria*, Butterworths, 1974.

[60] R. MacKeith in *Developmental Medicine and Child Neurology*, vol.16, pp 216-8.

[61] For example by C. Peckham and M. Jobling, *British Medical Journal*, 21 May 1975, Correspondence.

[62] Office of Population Censuses and Surveys, The Registrar General's Statistical Review of England and Wales for the Year 1972, HMSO, 1975, table 17.

[63] A. Cicourel, *The Social Organisation of Juvenile Justice*, Heinemann, 1976, p.27. He is discussing juvenile delinquency. Similarly, see J. Douglas, *The Social Meanings of Suicide*, Princeton University Press, 1967.

[64] *Cf* J.M. Atkinson, 'Societal Reactions to Suicide: The Role of Coroners' Definitions' in S. Cohen (ed.), *Images of Deviance*, Pelican, 1971, p.165-6. See also J.M. Atkinson, *Discovering Suicide*, Macmillan, 1978, pp 58-60.

[65] S. Smith and R. Hanson in *British Journal of Psychiatry*, vol.125, p.568, report that coroners reached 'open' verdicts in 5 out of 21 deaths in their study of 'battered' children. For an instructive example see R. Castle, 'Non-Accidental Injury — The Battered Child' in N. Tutt (ed.), *Violence*, HMSO, 1976, pp 112-3.

[66] K. Simpson in *Royal Society of Health Journal*, vol.3, 1967, p.168.

[67] Reported in 'A View from the Emergency and Accident Department' in A.W. Franklin (ed.), *Concerning Child Abuse*, Churchill Livingstone, 1975, pp 7-11.

[68] Idem, p.10.

[69] See NSPCC, *Registers of Suspected Non-Accidental Injury* (Report on Manchester and Leeds), 1976, p.13.

[70] J. Mounsey in A.W. Franklin (ed.), *Concerning Child Abuse*, Churchill Livingstone, 1975, p.127.

[71] See N. Walker, *Crimes, Courts and Figures*, Penguin Books, 1971, ch.1 and S. Box, *Deviance, Reality and Society*, Holt, Rinehart & Winston, 1971, ch.6.

[72] Op.cit., note 70, p.128.

[73] *Minutes of Evidence*, H.C. 350-ii, 1976, p.20.

[74] J.E. Oliver, et al, *Severely Ill-treated Children in N.E. Wiltshire*, Oxford Unit of Clinical Epidemiology, 1974. See also op.cit., note 73,

pp 159-62.

[75] Almost certainly an exaggerated estimate if any credence is to be given to the DHSS figures reproduced below. This view is now supported in the latest NSPCC study (S.J. Creighton and P.J. Owtram, *Child Victims of Physical Abuse*, NSPCC 1977). It is there suggested that some 8,000 children a year are non-accidentally injured, some 1,500 seriously and 110 fatally.

[76] See DHSS, Circular LASSL (74) 13, 22 April 1974.

[77] See B. Simons et al. in *New York State Journal of Medicine*, vol.66, 1966, p.2783.

[78] A. Sussman in *Family Law Quarterly*, vol.8, 1974, p.245.

[79] M.D.A. Freeman, *Family Law*, vol.7, 1977, p.53 and *post*, p.98.

[80] DHSS, LASSL (76) 2, para.33.

[81] See op.cit., note 69.

[82] Idem, p.14.

[83] Idem, p.15.

[84] A useful tabular summary of the research is in the *Minutes of Evidence* of the House of Commons Select Committee, pp 159-62. Accidental injury to children is far more frequent. See Court Report, *Fit for the Future*, 1977, Cmnd 6684, vol.1, p.42 (141,000 children admitted to hospital in 1972 and 1,800 deaths).

[85] R. Gelles, 'Child Abuse as Psychopathology: A Sociological Critique and Reformulation', *American Journal of Orthopsychiatry*, vol.43, 1973, p.611.

[86] B. Justice and R. Justice, *The Abusing Family*, Human Sciences Press, 1976, pp 38-42.

[87] B. Steele and C. Pollock, 'A Psychiatric Study of Parents Who Abuse Infants and Small Children' in R. Helfer and C.H. Kempe (eds), *The Battered Child*, 2nd ed., University of Chicago Press, 1974, p.89.

[88] Idem, p.94.

[89] Idem, p.95.

[90] Idem.

[91] Idem, pp 97-8.

[92] Idem, pp 112-4.

[93] Idem, p.114.

[94] NSPCC Battered Child Research Department, *At Risk*, RKP, 1976. The department is now called the National Advisory Centre on the Battered Child.

[95] Idem, p.194.

[96] Idem.

[97] Idem.

[98] Idem, p.195.

[99] Idem.
[100] Idem, p.196.
[101] R. Castle in N. Tutt (ed.), *Violence*, HMSO, 1976, p.115.
[102] *Post*, p.26.
[103] See C.H. Kempe et al. op.cit., note 31; G. Fleming 'Cruelty to Children', *British Medical Journal*, 1967, p.421; S. Wasserman, 'The Abused Parent of the Abused Child', *Children*, vol.14, 1967, p.175. See also S. Brandon in M. Borland (ed.), *Violence in the Family*, Manchester University Press, 1976, pp 1, 8-9.
[104] S.M. Smith, *British Medical Journal*, 1973, p.20.
[105] S.M. Smith, *The Battered Baby Syndrome*, Butterworths, 1976; and *New Society*, vol.26, 1973, p.393.
[106] On the effect of intelligence tests on racial minorities see K. Richardson and D. Spears, *Race, Culture and Intelligence*, Penguin, 1972.
[107] E.J. Merrill, 'Physical Abuse of Children: An Agency Study' in V. de Francis (ed.), *Protecting the Battered Child*, American Humane Association, 1962. Another example is S. Zalba, 'The Abused Child: A Typology for Classification and Treatment', *Social Work*, vol.12, 1967, p.70.
[108] Op.cit., note 13, p.17.
[109] *Cf* S. Box, *Deviance, Reality and Society*, 1971, Holt, Rinehart and Winston, ch.2.
[110] J. Gusfield, *Symbolic Crusade*, University of Illinois Press, 1963, chs 3-4.
[111] J. Gusfield, 'Moral Passage: The Symbolic Process in Public Designations of Deviance', *Social Problems*, vol.15, 1967, p.175.
[112] J. Spinetta and D. Rigler, 'The Child-Abusing Parent: A Psychological Review', *Psychological Bulletin*, vol.77, 1972, p.296.
[113] Idem, p.297.
[114] Idem.
[115] R. Gelles, 'Child Abuse as Psychopathology: A Sociological Critique and Reformulation', *American Journal of Orthopsychiatry*, vol.43, 1973, p.611.
[116] And that this is an 'all-or-nothing' consideration, whereas there are gradations in all traits.
[117] Op.cit., note 115, p.615.
[118] Op.cit., note 87.
[119] Idem, p.89.
[120] Idem, p.92.
[121] Op.cit., note 115, p.615.
[122] E. Rubington and M. Weinberg, *Deviance — The Interactionist Perspective*, 2nd ed., Macmillan, 1973, p.31.

[123]   E. Schur, *Labeling Deviant Behavior*, Harper and Row, 1971, p.52.

[124]   *Per* J. Lofland, *Deviance and Identity*, Prentice Hall, 1969, p.150.

[125]   E. Goffman, *Asylums*, Pelican Books, 1968, p.144.

[126]   See also J. Mercer, 'Who is Normal? Two Perspectives on Mild Mental Retardation' in J.E. Gartley (ed.), *Patients, Physicians and Illness*, 2nd ed. Free Press, 1972.

[127]   *Per* W. Ryan, *Blaming the Victim*, Vintage Books, revised ed. 1976, p.17.

[128]   D. Gil, *Violence Against Children*, op.cit., note 13; *Journal of Marriage and the Family*, vol.33, 1971; 'Unraveling Child Abuse', *American Journal of Orthopsychiatry*, vol.45, 1975, p.346.

[129]   D. Gil, *American Journal of Orthopsychiatry*, op.cit., note 128, p.352.

[130]   Idem.

[131]   D. Gil in R. Helfer and C.H. Kempe (eds), *The Battered Child*, University of Chicago Press, 1968.

[132]   In the NSPCC Study 74 per cent of the mothers were under 25. S. Smith, in *New Society*, vol.26, p.393, is also struck by the youth of the parents.

[133]   Op.cit., note 13.

[134]   A. Skinner and R. Castle, *78 Battered Children: A Retrospective Study*, NSPCC, 1969; R. Castle and M. Kerr, *A Study of Suspected Child Abuse*, NSPCC, 1972.

[135]   *Per* J. Renvoize, *Children in Danger*, Pelican Books, 1975, p.51.

[136]   Op.cit., note 87, p.93.

[137]   D. Gil in *Journal of Marriage and the Family*, vol.33, 1971, p.641.

[138]   Op.cit., note 115, p.617.

[139]   R. Galdston, 'Observations of Children who have been Physically Abused by their Parents', *American Journal of Psychiatry*, vol.122, 1965, pp 440, 442.

[140]   See P. Resnick, 'Child Murder by Parents', *American Journal of Psychiatry*, vol.126, 1969, pp 325, 327; E. Bennie and A. Sclare, 'The Battered Child Syndrome' idem, pp 975, 977.

[141]   Op.cit., note 13, p.105.

[142]   Similarly the evidence of Resnick, Bennie and Sclare is taken from patients.

[143]   So argued by R. Gelles, op.cit., note 115, p.618.

[144]   Where physical punishment of children is not sanctioned there appears to be less abuse.

[145]   Op.cit., note 135, p.39.

[146] J. Garbarino in *Child Development*, vol.47, 1976, p.178.

[147] R. Light in *Harvard Educational Review* reprint, *The Rights of Children*, 1974, p.198.

[148] *Cf supra*, p.3.

[149] Op.cit., note 13, p.114.

[150] J.E. Oliver and A. Taylor in *British Journal of Psychiatry*, vol.119, 1971, p.473.

[151] Op.cit., note 115, p.620.

[152] Emphasis mine.

[153] Op.cit., note 13, p.139.

[154] D. Gil, 'Unraveling Child Abuse', *American Journal of Orthopsychiatry*, vol.45, 1975, p.346. He expressed similar views in a paper he gave to the Second World Congress on Family Law in Montreal, June 1977. See further *post*, p.117.

[155] On institutional abuse see K. Wooden, *Weeping in the Play-time of Others*, McGraw-Hill, 1976.

[156] Op.cit., note 154, p.350.

[157] Idem.

[158] Idem, p.351.

[159] Idem.

[160] Op.cit., note 13, p.142.

[161] Op.cit., note 154, p.354.

[162] Op.cit., note 13, p.56.

[163] Idem, p.137.

[164] Recognised by the House of Commons Select Committee in its *First Report on Violence in the Family*, H.C. 329, 1977, para. 32.

[165] Op.cit., note 13, p.140.

[166] See, generally, Royal College of Psychiatrists, *Evidence to Select Committee on Violence in the Family*, H.C. 329-ii, 1977, pp 162-3, 175-6, and Q.281.

[167] S.M. Smith and R. Hanson, *British Medical Journal*, vol.3, 1974, p.666. '134 Battered Children: A Medical and Psychological Study'.

[168] E. Elmer, *Pediatrics*, vol.40, 1967, p.596; C.S. Morse, et al. in *American Journal of the Disabled Child*, vol.120, 1970, p.439; H. Martin in C.H. Kempe and R. Helfer (eds), *Helping the Battered Child and His Family*, Lippincott, 1972, p.93.

[169] Op.cit., note 166, pp 162 and 175-6.

[170] Op.cit., note 164, para.31.

[171] H. Martin, op.cit., note 168, and S.M. Smith, op.cit., note 167.

[172] See B. Steele in R. Helfer and C.H. Kempe (eds), *Child Abuse and Neglect*, Ballinger, 1976, pp 20-1.

[173] See N.F. Chase, *A Child is Being Beaten*, McGraw-Hill, 1975,

ch.9; and on Manson, see K. Wooden, op.cit., note 155, ch.4. See also C.H. King, *American Journal of Orthopsychiatry*, vol.45, 1975, p.134 and D.H. Russell in *Journal of Offender Therapy*, vol.9, 1965, p.55.

[174]   Op.cit., note 168.

3 Legal responses to the problem of the abused child

Mia Kellmer-Pringle writing in 1972 described our society as 'adult-orientated and not child-centred'. This is, she added, 'clearly reflected in our laws'. [1] In recent years rapid strides have been made in legislation and case law to put the best interests of children first. The 1975 Children Act has been hailed as a 'children's charter', [2] the judges in custody and adoption cases particularly have stressed the importance of emphasising the welfare of children. [3] Sometimes the interests of adults and children coincide. But, where they do not, the law often seems, as MacDougall has put it, [4] to reflect adult rather than children's interests. He compares the different attitudes taken to juvenile delinquency and child abuse:

> [w] e are all potential victims of juvenile delinquency. Many of us have been actual victims. We are effective in asserting our interest in protection from such anti-social behaviour. Child abuse is another matter. We are no longer potential victims. Any regulation in this area is likely to restrict our freedom, as parents, to deal with our children as we see fit or require us to take action (e.g. reporting our client or our neighbour) which we consider distasteful. And children, especially young children, do not have an effective voice in any of the authoritative conclaves of our society.

These different attitudes can be explained historically.

Some historical perspectives

The concept of childhood itself is a relatively recent development. [5] But, even before its emergence in the 16th century, two strands in the attitude of law and society towards children can be detected. First, children were 'non-persons'. True, the law recognised their legal personality: it may have turned a blind eye towards infanticide but the killing of a child was murder. [6] Second, family autonomy was something to be preserved at all costs and state intervention in the affairs of a family was deprecated. The two strands are linked, both were very much in prominence still at the latter end of the 19th century, and neither has completely disappeared even today.

The position of children in English law until well into the 19th century has been well described by Pinchbeck and Hewitt:

> Children were legally the property of their parents and were used by them as personal or family assets. Thus among the poor, the labour of children was exploited; among the rich their marriages were contrived; all to the economic or social advantage of the parents. [7]

Nineteenth century legislation to protect children in various industries was directed not least against the danger of exploitation by their parents. Reformist legislation had to fight against views of parental responsibility which identified this with family stability and through it the stability of society itself. The great factory reformer, Shaftesbury, was opposed to proposals for the compulsory education of children for they infringed the right of a parent to bring up his child as he saw fit. [8] One of the leading welfare agencies of the later 19th century (The Charity Organisation Society) opposed the introduction of school meals on the basis that it was better in the interests of the community to allow 'the sins of the parents to be visited on the children than to impair the principle of the solidarity of the family and run the risk of permanently demoralising large members of the population by the offer of free meals to their children'. [9]

We have spoken of parental rights but in law until 1886 it would be more accurate to speak of paternal rights. The legal and social structure of the family in England until late in the 19th century stressed the principle of paternal domination which was thought to be the will of God. Although Blackstone [10] could write of the power of the parent being derived from his duty, he himself admitted that parental duties were imperfect obligations since there was no power of enforcing duties of support, education and protection except through the Poor Law.

Attempts to give weight to duties to protect children against cruelty and neglect, which got under way in the late 1860s, had to counter opposition from a number of sources, not least from nascent feminist movements. When the Infant Life Protection Bill was introduced in 1871 (it was directed against baby-farming in the wake of the Waters Scandal [11]) The National Society for Women's Suffrage published a *Memorial* claiming that the Bill 'would interfere in the most mischievous and oppressive way with domestic arrangements' [12] and the Committee for Amending the Law in Points where it is Injurious to Women objected 'to the compulsion to be put on parents to employ none but those holding . . . licences' for '[t] he responsibility for the child in infancy . . . lies with them, and we emphatically deny that the State has any right to dictate to them the way it shall be fulfilled'. [13]   And Lord Shaftesbury, replying to a letter canvassing his support for legislation to protect children from parental cruelty wrote: '[t] he evils you state are enormous and indisputable, but they are of so private, internal and domestic character as to be beyond the reach of legislation'. [14]   But Benjamin Waugh, one of the founders of the NSPCC, knew 'how little sacredness of family life existed among the more depraved.' [15] Legislation had been passed to protect animals from cruelty in 1823. Yet in 1889 when what became the Prevention of Cruelty to, and Protection of, Children Act 1889 was in the House of Commons, the Attorney-General counselled against interfering with the 'legitimate conduct of parents and guardians with regard to children . . . and the reasonable earnings of children assisting their parents.' [16]   The riposte of the Bill's sponsor, Mr Mundella, was to state that he was 'anxious that we should give [children] almost the same protection that we give . . . domestic animals'. [17]   Opposition was overcome in 1889. The Act made ill-treatment and neglect of children a statutory offence, and enabled children who were ill-treated or neglected to be removed from parents and anyone else having custody and control and entrusted to a fit person. In 1894 the legislation was extended to cases of assault, and the power to commit a child to a fit person was applied to the various offences against children in the Offences against the Person Act 1861. There were further amendments of a minor nature before, in 1933, the law governing physical protection of children was placed on its present footing. [18]

But the ideological strands referred to, though severely battered, refuse to lie down. The unwillingness to remove children in danger and the over-hasty readiness with which they are returned to parents has been commented upon in the reports of the inquiries into some of the better known cases of abuse. [19]   An extreme critic like Howells can even claim that Maria Colwell was killed by a misplaced emphasis on the blood tie. [20]   Kellmer-Pringle thinks it necessary still to counsel against attitudes 'that a baby completes a family, rather like a TV set or fridge . . . that a child belongs to his parents like their other possessions over which they may exercise exclusive rights'. At most, she argues, 'he is theirs only on temporary loan . . . There needs to be a shift from stressing the importance of parental rights to an emphasis on parental duties.' [21]   Yet in some ways the Children Act is an over-reaction and, in improving the rights of foster parents and facilitating adoption, it has neglected the biological family unit in favour of psychological, substitute parenting. [22] The law today stands at a crossroads and it is difficult to predict which road it will take.

The physical protection of children under criminal law

The criminal law as a mechanism to protect children from abuse is ineffective. It is often extremely difficult to obtain a conviction: there are problems of evidence and proof. An acquittal may be seen by the parent as a vindication of the legitimacy of his behaviour and this in turn makes therapeutic intervention impossible. Successful prosecutions, on the other hand, which are few and far between do not act as deterrents but tend instead to confirm the parent in his 'negative self-image'. [23] There is also the danger that a parent who knows he may be prosecuted may neglect or delay to seek medical treatment for his injured child because of fear of the consequences. Furthermore, prosecutions may divide families. There is no doubt, though, that in really serious cases prosecutions must and do take place. [24]

Corporal punishment

The question is complicated by the fact that parents, and anyone *in loco parentis*, may administer reasonable corporal punishment to correct children. This right (it is more correct to describe it as a liberty or freedom [25]) is expressly preserved in the 1933 Act which states: '[n]othing in this section shall be construed as affecting the right of any parent, teacher or other person having lawful control or charge of a child or young person to administer punishment to him.' [26] In other words what would otherwise be assault or ill-treatment is rendered lawful when a parent or substitute punishes a child in a reasonable and moderate manner. Most case law and most critical discussion has centred on corporal punishment in schools. In England a Bill to abolish such punishment failed in 1973. [27] It did, incidentally, expressly preserve the rights of parents, foster and adoptive parents and guardians to use corporal punishment on their children. In the USA the Supreme Court has recently upheld the constitutionality of corporal punishment in schools. [28] It used to be thought that in England school teachers had the right to punish children because it had been delegated to them by parents. [29] The better view is that the right exists independently of any parental

45

delegation so that parents cannot lawfully forbid schools to punish their children. [30]

A useful statement of the law is found in a 1860 case. Cockburn J., having stated that a parent might inflict moderate and reasonable corporal punishment, proceeded to define the general limits of parental freedom:

> [i]f it be administered for the gratification of passion or of rage, or if it be immoderate and excessive in its nature or degree or if it be protracted beyond a child's power of endurance or with an instrument unfitted for its purpose and calculated to produce danger to life or limb, in all such cases, the punishment is excessive, the violence unlawful, and if evil consequences to life and limb ensue, the person inflicting it is answerable to the law. [31]

In this case a schoolmaster had dragged a boy he deemed to be obstinate out of bed and beaten him with a thick stick and skipping rope for two-and-a-half hours, by which time the boy was dead. He was found guilty of manslaughter. It is difficult to state definitively what constitutes reasonable chastisement. From the cases it seems that caning, provided it is not excessive, is permissible [32] whereas boxing on the ears [33] or beating the legs with a clothes brush [34] have been held to be unreasonable. Additionally, the child must be capable of appreciating the correction. With standards so vague it hardly makes sense for immigrant parents to be told that they must conform to the standard of behaviour acceptable in England but that is what a West Indian father was recently told by an English appeal court. [35] The court held it was not a defence to show that the standard of parental correction is harsher in the West Indies.

Criminal offences

This is not the place for, nor does space permit, a lengthy, detailed recital of all the criminal offences with which a parent may be charged. Suffice to say that a number of courses are open to the prosecution. [36]

Where the child dies the parent may be charged with murder, manslaughter or infanticide. The difference between murder and manslaughter lies in the *mens rea* accompanying the act.

Murder. If a parent attacks a child intending to kill him or cause him grievous bodily harm and death results the offence of *murder* has been committed. But the parent must actually have this intention; it

46

is not enough to impute the intention to him on the basis that a reasonable man acting as he did would have realised that death or really serious harm might result. This was not the law in 1956 when a man of subnormal intelligence who suffered with severe stomach ulcers shook his crying 14-month-old baby so violently that he died. His conviction for murder was upheld. [37] Today, that man would be relieved of his obligation to behave as a reasonable man. Additionally, provided he could prove a 'defect of reason resulting from a disease of the mind', the defence of diminished responsibility would be available, reducing his crime to manslaughter. [38] Although the presumption of intent is no longer conclusive, it will be for the accused parent to rebut the presumption that he intended the harm if all the evidence points that way. In addition to the defence of diminished responsibility, provocation will also reduce the offence to manslaughter. [39] Where the prosecution does not think it may be able to establish the necessary *mens rea* for murder it may charge the accused parent with the lesser [40] office. Sometimes, also, the prosecution is willing to accept a plea of guilty to manslaughter as an answer to a murder charge. It did in *Fitzgerald*'s case. [41] He repeatedly lost his temper with his two-year-old stepdaughter and punched her with his fist causing serious bruising and rupturing her spleen and liver, as a result of which she died. One comment of the Court of Appeal in this case is worth recording for it may be said to represent the dominant attitude of lawyers towards child abuse: 'the gravity of child killing is not lessened by describing it in terms of a syndrome'.

Manslaughter. There are a number of ways in which a *manslaughter* verdict may be reached. Several of these have emerged in the course of our discussion of murder. [42] More directly, manslaughter is constituted by gross neglect of a child which leads to his death, or unlawful behaviour towards a child which all sober and reasonable people would realise was likely to cause at least some harm and which does in fact lead to death. [43] Thus, where the parents of a three-year-old, who suffered serious injuries from scalding, did not call a doctor for three days though the surgery was three doors away, they were convicted of manslaughter by neglect. [44] This case was in 1959; a few years later the aetiology of the scalding might have been more thoroughly questioned than it appears, from the brief recital of facts in the law report, to have been. Manslaughter verdicts were also reached in the cases of *Adesokan* [45] and *Nuttall*. [46] Adesokan killed his two-year-old stepdaughter by beating her with his hand which was in plaster, causing areas of abrasion or bruising over the whole of her body and bleeding of the brain. Nuttall ruptured the liver, fractured the ribs, dislocated the neck and caused severe bruising to the 18-month-old child of a woman with whom he was living and then as a grotesque finale pegged the child to a clothes line. He was charged with murder but the jury returned a verdict of manslaughter. As these cases illustrate the line between murder and manslaughter is often thin and barely distinguishable.

Infanticide. Where a mother wilfully causes the death of her child who is under 12 months old she may be charged with *infanticide* if at the time of her act or omission the balance of her mind was disturbed because she had not fully recovered from the effect of giving birth to the child or because of the effect of lactation after the birth. The offence was introduced in 1938 [47] because juries were unwilling to convict mothers of murder. Theoretically, she may be sentenced to life imprisonment but in practice terms of imprisonment are rare and probation is common. [48] Glanville Williams has described the offence as 'an illogical compromise between the law of murder and humane feelings'. [49] It only applies to the mother, so that the stress felt by the father is ignored. More surprisingly it only applies if the mother kills the new-born baby, though in her mental distress she is equally likely to kill a difficult toddler or older child as the latest arrival. With the defence of diminished responsibility open to them most mothers who kill a child other than the most recently born whilst suffering the effects of birth or lactation are likely to be convicted of manslaughter rather than murder. [50] Indeed, the *Butler Report on Mentally Abnormal Offenders* in 1975 recommended that the special provision for the offence of infanticide should be abolished, arguing that diminished responsibility could cover infanticide cases. [51] The Criminal Law Revision Committee, however, has drawn attention to what it sees as certain advantages in retaining the separate offence. It believes it might not always be possible to avoid an initial charge of murder for evidence of the mother's disturbed state may be lacking at the earliest stages of the prosecution process. The Committee does, however recommend a reduced maximum penalty of two years' imprisonment. [52]

Offences where death does not result

Where the child does not die the parent may be charged with a large number of statutory offences. Offences are laid down in the Offences against the Person Act 1861 (common assault, [53] aggravated assault, [54] assault occasioning actual bodily harm, [55] unlawfully and maliciously wounding or inflicting grievous bodily harm, [56] unlawfully and maliciously wounding or casuing grievous bodily harm with intent to do grievous bodily harm. [57]   However, parents are seldom charged with any of these offences, so that they need not detain us any further.   The reason is that a specific offence of cruelty to children is provided for by s.1 of the Children and Young Persons Act 1933.   The 1861 Act, however, remains useful for a small, residual category of cases where the accused did not have custody, charge or care of the child, or where the child is over 16, or where, indeed, it is felt that the gravity of the offence is such that the parent ought to be charged with an offence carrying the potentiality of a heavier sentence than s.1. [58]

Children and Young Persons Act 1933 s.1

This section states:

> If any person who has attained the age of 16 years and has the custody, charge, or care of any child or young person under that age, wilfully assaults, ill-treats, neglects, abandons or exposes him, or causes or procures him to be assaulted, ill-treated, neglected, abandoned, or exposed, in a manner likely to cause him unnecessary suffering or injury to health (including injury to or loss of sight, or hearing, or limb, or organ of the body, and any mental derangement) that person shall be guilty of [an offence].

The maximum sentence is two years' imprisonment. [59]   It is this comprehensive offence, [60] specially tailored to deal with cases of child cruelty and neglect, rather than any of the more general offences, which forms the basis of the majority of criminal prosecutions in cases of child abuse short of homicide.   This is not to say that a parent cannot be charged under s.1 where the child has died. [61]   He can as *Hayles*'s [62] case, to which reference will be made, shows.   Thus, in 1976, 141 men and 135 women were charged with offences under this section.   Eighty-eight men and 100 women were found guilty.   A few (14 men and 4 women) were given immediate sentences of imprisonment.   Thirty-three more (16 men and 17 women) were given suspended sentences.   By far the largest number, however, were not given any form of prison sentence, probation orders and conditional discharges being common. [63]

The conduct must be 'wilful'. 'Wilfully' has been interpreted narrowly to mean deliberately and intentionally as opposed to accidentally or inadvertently. 'The mind of the person doing the act [must go] with it', the court said in the leading case of *Senior*. [64] But it does not matter that the parent did not foresee the consequences of his behaviour. [65]

The cruel conduct may take one or five forms but these are not mutually exclusive offences. The case of *Hayles* shows how the section may operate. Hayles's three-year-old son hurt himself in a fall. Hayles put him to bed without any medical attention or treatment for his injuries. He died next day. Hayles was charged with 'wilfully ill-treating' his son or 'causing or procuring him to be ill-treated.' He contended that he could not be guilty of ill-treatment because what he had done was to neglect his son. It was held, upholding his conviction, that the words 'assaults, ill-treats, neglects, abandons or exposes' in s.1 did not create separate and watertight offences. So, if the evidence could fairly be said to indicate 'ill-treatment' even though the same conduct might equally well be called 'neglect', it was immaterial that the judge directed the jury that they could regard neglect as sufficient to support the charge of ill-treatment. Whilst this decision must in general be welcomed it cannot be entirely correct for a charge of assault could surely not be substantiated by demonstrating neglect. [66]

'Assault' means either battery or its threat. [67] The main problem is drawing the line between lawful punishment and criminal assault. [68] 'Ill-treat', it has been suggested, means any course of conduct likely to cause injury to a child. [69] 'Neglect' has been held to be 'want of reasonable care — that is, the omission of such steps as a reasonable parent would take, such as are usually taken in the ordinary experience of mankind — that is, . . . provided that the parent had such means as would enable him to take the necessary steps'. [70] If the parent lacks the means he is still liable if he fails to take steps to procure their provision under welfare legislation. 'Abandons' means to leave a child to its fate. So *Whibley* [71] was not convicted when he took his five children to a juvenile court and left them there. He had not left them in a place which would expose them to injury for substitute care would obviously quickly be arranged. Bearing in mind s.1(3)(a) (which states that a person may be convicted notwithstanding that injury or likelihood of injury was obviated by the action of another person), the decision in *Whibley* is surprising. *Whibley*'s case may be contrasted with *Boulden*, [72] where five children were left in a dark house with little food and the NSPCC was telephoned to come. Boulden watched a WPC arrive from across the road and then headed for Scotland. The Court of Criminal Appeal was in no doubt that Boulden's intention was 'to clear out, leave these children to their fate and wipe his hands clean of them'. Often abandonment will be accompanied by 'exposure' (for example, the child may be left in a bus shelter) but there may be cases of exposure which do not involve abandonment as well. Bevan gives the example of depriving a child of shelter made available to both parent and child. [73]

It may not be easy to determine which of the parents is responsible. In cases of neglect a parent is guilty if he knows the other parent is neglecting the child. In cases of ill-treatment it may be particularly difficult to establish guilt if the parents stick together. [74]

So far reference has been made to parents but liability extends beyond them to cover any person over 16 who has 'custody, charge or care' of any child or young person under that age. It is thus wide enough to cover, for example, a baby sitter. The phrase 'custody, charge or care' is unduly complicated and is not made any easier by a set of elaborate presumptions found in s.17. Custody, it seems, does not mean actual custody but rather custody in its wider sense of guardianship. [75] This means that where a mother has care and control, a father who is living separately can be charged, for example, with neglect even if he sends the mother an adequate amount for the child's support if he knows she is neglecting the child. The presumption also states that a person who is 'legally liable to maintain' a child has custody of him. A step-parent who has treated a child as a child of the family [76] would come into this category. On separation, therefore, he could be held to be neglecting his stepchild even though granted neither custody nor care and control. A putative father against whom an affiliation order has been made is also presumed to have custody. [77] As for 'charge and care' one must agree with Bevan's comment that 'it is very difficult to know exactly what these terms mean'. [78] He suggests that they go hand in hand and that they may be simultaneously entrusted to more than one person. Liability, it is clear, extends very widely.

Prosecutions are usually brought by the police or the NSPCC [79] but a local authority may do so either as a local education authority [80] or a social services department. [81]

The attitude of the police towards prosecution is clear. Assaults upon children are criminal offences and should be treated as such. Thus, commenting on the failure of social workers to notify the police of cases of violence against children, the Metropolitan Police CID, in a memorandum submitted to the House of Commons Select Committee, notes their attitude to be 'contrary to the existing legislation and natural spirit of justice together with a direct challenge as to the right of the police to investigate'. [82] And the Metropolitan Police Force, in a separate memorandum, is concerned that case conferences make decisions about a child's future without any proper investigation of the criminal aspect. The Metropolitan Police stress that 'only Police have the training and experience to deal with this type of case'. [83] The British Association of Social Workers, in a memorandum to the same Committee, admit the 'key role' of the police. But, they add, 'police and the social services are exercising different functions. It is a duty of the police to apprehend persons suspected of having committed an offence and to bring them before a court. It is a duty of social workers to promote the welfare of children. It is not always in the interests of a child to prosecute his parents for ill-treating him — indeed, it can be contrary to his welfare.' [84] The tightrope that must be trodden between legal and therapeutic roles is also recognised by the NSPCC. In *At Risk* its Battered Child Research Department refers to a scheme whereby responsibility was divided up, the local authority taking legal proceedings and the NSPCC units assuming the role of primary therapeutic workers. Not surprisingly this did not work. Neither the NSPCC nor local authority social services are keen to initiate prosecutions and few take place. [85]

Manslaughter is normally prosecuted and it is in relation to this crime that certain sentencing guidelines have been developed in the appeal courts. [86] The courts are influenced by the degree and persistence of the violence shown. They approve of long sentences where the act is not an isolated incident but the final act in a continual course of violence. Thus, they approved a sentence of 10 years in *Nuttall*, [87] but in *Perkins* [88] reduced a similar sentence to 4 years. Perkins had never struck the child before so that his case was not one of 'that type of villainy which sometimes occurs in these cases'. *Blackburn*'s act was out of character and, as he was an immature 18-year-old, the court regarded a three-year sentence as proper. [89] Even with isolated incidents the courts feel they must give effect to public revulsion to the crime: so *Whitecombe* [90] got four years and *Sutton*, [91] an aunt who lost her temper and put a three-year-old in scalding hot water, received a five-year sentence.

The removal of children from
abusive environments

Granted the generally accepted ineffectiveness of the criminal law, the powers that exist to remove children from abusive parents are of the greatest importance. In this section the emphasis is on care proceedings (allied to which are 'place of safety' powers) under which the child is, subject to a limited exception, [92] involuntarily removed from his parents. But it should not be forgotten that many children who are at risk because of homelessness or unsatisfactory home conditions or the temporary or permanent absence of one parent are voluntarily received into care at the behest of parents. A later section discusses such children briefly.

Care proceedings

Care proceedings are governed by the Children and Young Persons Act 1969. They may be brought by the police, a local authority social services department or the NSPCC. The local authority for the area where the child lives (or is found) has a positive duty to make inquiries if it receives information suggesting that there are grounds for bringing proceedings, unless it is satisfied that inquiries are unnecessary. Information will usually come from relatives, neighbours, teachers or doctors. People do not want to get involved in what they perceive as other people's business so that many cases of undoubted cruelty do not come to the notice of the relevant authorities. Clearly, the sources of information would dry up almost completely were the authority to have to disclose its source of information in care or other proceedings. It has long been held that the identity of police informers may not be disclosed in a civil action, whether by process of discovery or by oral evidence at the trial. [93] In a recent case [94] an attempt was made to make the NSPCC disclose a source of information, which proved utterly false and may have been malicious, indicating that a 14-month-old baby girl was being ill-treated. After prolonged litigation the House of Lords held that the Society, and by implication local authorities as well, [95] should be immune from disclosure of the identity of informants in legal proceedings.

Care proceedings may be brought in respect of any child or a young person. [96] The child must be 'brought before the court' [97] though he may be asked to leave while certain evidence is being given. [98] Parents, if their whereabouts are known, must be notified of the proceedings as must any foster parents or any other person with whom the child has had his home for not less than six weeks, ending not more than six months before the application, provided whereabouts are known. [99] The provision about foster parents was introduced after the Maria Colwell case to remedy the situation under which Maria's uncle and aunt who had looked after her for six years had no right to be heard in the proceedings initiated by Maria's mother to discharge the care order. [100]

In spite of the nature of the proceedings the rules provide that the court must allow the parent to conduct the case on the child's behalf. [101] Until the Children Act 1975 the only exceptions to this rule were where the child or his parent was legally represented or where the proceedings were brought at the request of the parent. The 1975 Act enables the court to order that in relation to the proceedings the parent is not to be treated as representing the child or as otherwise authorised to act on his behalf, if there appears to be any conflict of interest between them. [102] Another provision in the 1975 Act (which at the time of writing has not been implemented) will require such an order to be mandatory on unopposed applications to discharge care or supervision orders unless the court is satisfied that it is not necessary to safeguard the child's interests. [103] Once an order has been made the court must also appoint a guardian *ad litem* for the child if it appears to the court that it is in the child's interests to do so. [104] It is intended to set up panels of experienced social workers and probation officers to act as guardians but this has not yet been done and currently the courts arrange for a suitably qualified person, who is independent of any authority which is a party to the proceedings, to represent the child.

The situation before the 1975 Act was indefensible but it is hardly much better today. *Justice*, the British section of the International Commission of Jurists, recommended in 1975 that in '*any* proceedings where the child or his rights might be adversely affected by the decision in the proceedings . . . he must be considered an indispensable party to the proceedings, with the right to separate legal advice and representation'. [105] Even when fully implemented the new provisions get nowhere near this ideal.

The juvenile court may make a care order, a supervision order or any of the other orders [106] specified in the 1969 Act provided the applicant proves one or more of seven primary conditions *and* that the child is in need of care or control which he will not receive unless the court makes an order. Civil rules of evidence apply so that both the parents and the child may be compelled to give evidence and the burden of proof is 'on the balance of probabilities'. [107] Of the seven primary conditions three are of particular relevance to the abused child. The first (a) states: '[h]is proper development is being avoidably prevented or neglected, or his health is being avoidably impaired or neglected, or he is being ill-treated'. Under this condition it is not necessary to prove that the parents have injured or neglected the child; nor is there any need to prove deliberate intention to harm him. Indeed, it is not necessary to point the finger of accusation at anyone. The provision is broad in that mental as well as physical development is covered. There are limitations. Thus the condition is phrased in the present tense. A child who *was* ill-treated some time ago probably does not come within its terms. This can cause difficulties. It means that a local authority which has received into its care a child who had been abused cannot retain that child in care by seeking a care order under this condition. [108] There are other ways in which it can, but to apply for a s.1 care order is tantamount to admitting that it, through a foster parent or children's home, is abusing the child. Further, if nothing yet has happened, condition (a) is also clearly inapplicable.

But two situations which might arouse suspicions of potential danger to a child are covered in the next two primary conditions. Thus, (b) states that it is probable that the conditions in (a) will be satisfied 'having regard to the fact that the court or another court has found that that condition is or was satisfied in the case of another child or young person who is or was a member of the [same] household'. This condition was interpreted expansively in *Surrey C.C. v. S.* [109] The Court of Appeal held that where a child had died (the father had been acquitted of murder) another child of the family could be taken into care under (b) even though (a) was never found in any adjudication in respect of the first child. It was under paragraph (b) that the Wood Green Juvenile Court in 1974 made a care order in respect of Maria Colwell's mother's eleventh child shortly after he was born. [110]

Condition (bb) states that it is probable that the condition in (a) will be satisfied 'having regard to the fact that a person who has been convicted of an offence mentioned in Schedule 1 [of the Children and Young Persons Act 1933] is, or may become, a member of the same household as the child'. This condition was added by the Children Act 1975. [111] Although often referred to as the 'Kepple clause' it would be more apposite to designate it the 'Auckland clause'. None of Kepple's previous convictions come within the schedule referred to, whereas Auckland, who killed his 15-month-old daughter, Susan, in 1974 had been convicted of manslaughter of his nine-week-old daughter, Marianne, in 1968. [112] The Schedule lists murder or manslaughter of a child and certain other assaults including cruelty to a child and sexual offences against children. Hoggett has expressed a doubt as to whether indecent assault is included. [113] The difficulty about this condition has been obtaining the necessary information from the police. Home Office Circular 140/73 only enables the police to release information to social service departments about prospective adoptive and foster parents. During the Report stage of the Children Bill a clause was moved to widen such releases but the civil liberty interest prevailed over that of child protection and the clause was rejected. [114]

The problem involved is well documented in a report commissioned by Surrey County Council [115] on the case of a man who raped a daughter and indecently assaulted a son and of a second son who himself was convicted of indecent assaults, while all three children were in the care of the council. The report comments that police information on the father was not forthcoming. 'This case demonstrates', the report notes, 'a gap in information which, in our opinion, should be made available'.

The problem has now, it is hoped, been solved by a joint DHSS-Home Office circular of November 1976. [116] It has been recommended to the police that they should make available to case conferences the details of any relevant previous convictions concerning a person involved in the care of a child who is the subject of a case conference. It is also the view of the Home Office that disclosure of convictions which are 'spent' under the Rehabilitation of Offenders Act 1974 to local authorities or other bodies assessing the suitability of a person to have care of children or young persons does not contravene s.9(2) of that Act. [117] So, if convictions are relevant, they ought, in the opinion of the government departments involved, to be disclosed. It is too early to assess how the new circular is working though, as no adverse comments have been forthcoming, one may view the situation with cautious optimism.

The other primary conditions may be listed briefly. Condition (c) states that the child is 'exposed to moral danger' (the case of *Mohamed* v. *Knott* [118] suggests that a pluralistic view of morality is adopted); condition (d) that 'he is beyond the control of his parent or guardian'; condition (e) that, being of compulsory school age, he is 'not receiving efficient full-time education suitable to his age, ability and aptitude' and (f) that 'he is guilty of an offence, excluding homicide'.

If one of the primary conditions is proved an order can still not be made unless the court is satisfied that the child is 'in need of care or control which he is unlikely to receive unless the court makes an order under this section in respect of him'. A good illustration of the working of this principle is the case of *Re D.J.M.S.* [119] A 12-year-old boy had been kept away from school because his parents disapproved of comprehensive education. Condition (e) was clearly satisfied. The juvenile court made a care order. The Crown Court reversed this decision. It said that, even if the care and control test had been satisfied and it thought it had not, this was not an appropriate case for a care order. The Court of Appeal allowed the local authority's appeal. To be in need of care the boy did not have to be neglected in his day-to-day emotional or physical needs. 'Care' included 'protection and guidance' [120] and depriving a child of education was depriving him of care in this sense. A child from an otherwise good home might, therefore, be said to be in need of care. The care and control test must not be considered a mere formality; it imports a very real discretion and the court must often weigh up alternatives. A child may be better off in a bad home with his parents than in a children's home.

There will be cases where criminal proceedings have been taken against parents and care proceedings are also envisaged. Conviction in the adult court can shorten and simplify proceedings in the juvenile court since it provides part of the evidence required. Thus if a prosecution is being brought it is useful to hold back the care proceedings pending the outcome of the criminal case. The child in the meantime may be taken into care on an interim care order or may be in hospital on a place of safety order (these orders are discussed below). Until it is known what is to become of the parent no definite plans for the child's future can be made. An acquittal of the parent does not necessarily mean that proceedings in the juvenile court will also fail. Convictions in child abuse cases are difficult to sustain for reasons which have already been given. In the juvenile court, however, the essential question concerns the child's situation and not necessarily who is responsible for causing it. 'The point at issue is the child's actual situation now and probable situation in the future, not the culpability *per se* of whoever did the damage'. [121]

If a case is proved under s.1 of the 1969 Act the court may make one of a number of orders. In most cases the choice lies between a supervision order, which does not give the local authority power to remove the child, and a care order which does. Before deciding what order, if any, ought to be made, the court is directed to consider the child's 'general conduct, home surroundings, school record and medical history'. [122] The court's choice may be influenced by the available resources. As the British Association of Social Workers remarked, in a memorandum submitted to the House of Commons Select Committee, 'the report of the Richard Clark inquiry shows how decisions about whether or not to remove children known to be at possible risk are influenced by the alternatives available'. [123] A paucity of potential foster parents prepared to take difficult children on a short-term basis and a shortage of residential places for children may circumscribe the court's choice.

If the court makes a *supervision order* the child usually remains with his parents. The court can require him to live with a named individual [124] but this provision is meant for the older child offender rather than the abused child. A supervision order places the child under the supervision of a local authority. It lasts for a specified period of up to three years. The supervisor's duty is to 'advise, assist and befriend' [125] the child. Rules require the child to submit himself to medical examination when requested so to do by the supervisor. [126] This is an important provision in this context but the position of the parents is not made clear. If they refuse to allow the child to be medically examined or, indeed, refuse the supervisor entry, the supervisor would have to seek a place of safety order or a warrant under s.40 of the 1933 Act, and ultimately apply for the supervision order to be discharged and replaced by a care order. The House of Commons in its first report on violence in the family, recommended that the supervisor be given additional powers to ensure the safety of a child. [127] The supervisor's duties are nowhere laid down with any clarity. Before a child can be boarded out with officially approved foster parents, regulations [128] provide for a stringent examination of them and their home. Yet, ironically, where a child is to be supervised in his own home where he is known to be at risk he is not accorded similar protection. The DHSS report into the Maria Colwell case commented upon this disparity critically: 'no harm could be done by assisting social workers concerned in their difficult task by laying down certain similar statutory criteria'. [129] Power to make regulations is now accorded the Secretary of State by the Children Act 1975; no regulations have yet been made. [130]

Where a child has been abused or is at risk a *care order* is more appropriate. This commits the child to the care of the local authority which must keep him in care as long as the order is in force 'notwithstanding any claim by his parent or guardian'. [131] A care order lasts until the child is 18, [132] though it may be discharged at any time. [133] But, as the DHSS Colwell report noted, 'when a child [is] taken into care the expectation [is] not that she [will] remain in care until the age of eighteen but that she [will] return to her own family when their circumstances [have] improved.' [134] Under the Children Act 1975 a care order must not be discharged if the child is under 18 and still in need of care or control, unless the court is satisfied that he will receive that care or control, whether through the making of a supervision order or in other ways. [135] Furthermore, it provides for separate representation for the child, where an application to discharge a care order is unopposed. [136]

The effect of a care order is to give the local authority the same 'powers and duties' [137] which a parent would have over the child were it not for the order. The local authority cannot, however, change the child's religion, [138] or agree to his adoption. [139] It probably cannot consent to his marriage under 18 or control his property but neither of these disabilities is clear. It can restrict the child's liberty [140] whereas parents cannot, at least once the child has reached what is quaintly called 'the age of discretion' (14 for boys, 16 for girls). The local authority may make such arrangements for the child's accommodation and maintenance as seem appropriate. In most cases the choice is between boarding the child out with suitable foster parents and placing him in a community home.

If the child is boarded out the foster parents are the agents of the local authority and they sign an undertaking to return the child to the authority when requested to do so. The child may be boarded out with a view to adoption (or, when it comes into effect, custodianship). [141] Parental agreement to adoption is still required, though in the case of serious abuse, it will readily be dispensed with. [142] Indeed, in such cases if rehabilitation is out of the question local authorities may be encouraged to place the children for adoption at the outset. When implemented the intermediate relationship of custodianship will also be available to foster parents who have had the child in their care for 12 months (with the parents' consent) or three years (without). [143]

The Children Act of 1975, in strengthening the foster parents' hands, has undoubtedly emphasised 'exclusive' fostering where parents are excluded from the child's life rather than 'inclusive' fostering where 'emphasis is placed on the children's need to retain a true sense of their present identity and past history within a framework of affection.' [144] Studies suggest that 'features associated with inclusive fostering are particularly related to fostering success'. [145] There is a high rate of breakdown of long-term fostering [146] and considerable emotional disturbance amongst long-term foster children. [147] There is also evidence that foster children in regular contact with their biological parents are the least disturbed. [148] From an emphasis on exclusive fostering it is only a short step towards adoption as the norm. Adoption may be desirable in some cases but once it becomes the normal solution (and it is cheap and convenient, for the adoption market is drying up) the tendency to avoid preventive and supportive work with parents will increase. [149] This in its turn may lead to more abused children — and more adoption.

Interim care orders

An interim care order places the child in the care of the local authority for up to 28 days. [150] It may be discharged earlier and on expiry a further interim order may be made. They are temporary measures for taking or keeping a child away from home pending the disposition of the case. If an interim order is made the powers and duties of the local authority are the same as in a care order. Interim orders can be made in a number of situations: [151]   statistically most are made when the court thinks it is not in a position to decide what order, if any, ought to be made. A number of interim care orders were made in respect of Maria Colwell's mother's baby by the Wood Green Juvenile Court in 1974 for this reason. It was not appreciated until recently that a parent might apply for an interim care order but the Divisional Court has held this to be so. [152]

Place of safety powers

Under a number of statutes there are emergency provisions which enable the authorities to remove children in danger or prevent their removal from hospital. [153]   The most important provisions are s.28 of the Children and Young Persons Act 1969 and s.40 of the Children and Young Persons Act 1933.

Under s.28(1) any person may apply to a single magistrate at any time and in any place. The applicant does not have to prove anything. He must merely satisfy the magistrate that he has reasonable cause to believe that any of the primary conditions in s.1(2) (except the offence provision) is (or would in the case of condition (b) or (bb) would be found by an appropriate court to be) satisfied in respect of the child or young person in question. The magistrate can then authorise the applicant to take the child to a place of safety (community home, police station, hospital, surgery, or any other suitable place the occupier of which is willing to receive a child temporarily), where he may be detained for up to 28 days. There is no right of appeal against the order although, if sought improperly, it could be quashed by *certiorari*. [154]   There is no power to renew it [155] but an application for an interim order may be made before it expires. Indeed, where a place of safety order has been made a parent may apply for an interim order in the hope that this application will fail and the child be sent home. [156]

There is evidence that the place of safety concept is being used to fill deficiencies which exist in the appeal procedure of other orders. The *Kesteven* case in 1976 is a good illustration of this. [157]   A care order had been made. The father applied for a discharge and substitution of a supervision order. Evidence tendered by the local authority to the effect that incest had taken place with other children was not admitted (wrongly, the Divisional Court held). The care order was discharged and social workers, alarmed at this, applied

60

three days later for a place of safety order. There is no appeal against discharge of a care order. The Divisional Court refused to listen to the parents' suggestion that the local authority was using s.28 for a purpose for which it had not been intended. The purpose of a s.28 order is that 'a child in actual danger should be speedily and effectively put into a place of safety' [158] said Lord Widgery and this was the purpose for which it had been used in the present case.

Section 28(2) allows a police officer to detain a child or young person if he has reasonable cause to believe that any of the primary conditions (except the education and offence conditions) is (or in the case of condition (b) or (bb) would be found by an appropriate court to be) satisfied. There is no need for any order. The case is referred to a senior police officer who makes inquiries and may then either release the child or arrange for his detention in a place of safety. The maximum period of detention is eight days; if the child has to be detained longer before care proceedings can be commenced an interim order must be sought. A child detained under this procedure has the right to apply immediately to a magistrate for his release. [159]

Important powers are also contained in s.40 of the 1933 Act. This provides that, where it appears to a magistrate through information on oath laid by a person who is acting in the interests of the child or young person, there is reasonable cause to suspect that the child or young person is being assaulted, ill-treated or neglected in a manner likely to cause unnecessary suffering or injury to health or where an offence mentioned in Schedule 1 of the 1933 Act has been or is being committed in respect of the child or young person, the magistrate may issue a warrant authorising a police officer to search for the child and, if suspicions are justified, remove him to a place of safety. He may also be authorised to arrest any offenders at the same time. The child can be kept in the place of safety for any specified period up to 28 days. Thereafter he must be released, received into care (presumably on the grounds in s.1 of the Children Act 1948, though this is not made clear [160]), or brought before a juvenile court which can then make an interim order or release him.

The emergency procedures described here are valuable weapons in the fight to protect abused children. It is vital that powers should exist to detain in hospital children suspected of being non-accidentally injured. [161] No statistics are available but the majority of place of safety orders are certainly sought in this context. The question must be raised, however, as to the extent to which parental civil liberties are infringed. Mistakes are made and some children do suffer from *osteogenesis imperfecta* (brittle bones). In *Re Cullimore* [162] a place of safety order on a baby with brittle bones was made in May

1975 and only discharged in wardship proceedings in March 1976. Cases of even greater delay are cited in the evidence of the National Council for Civil Liberties to the House of Commons Select Committee. [163] Delays can have extremely deleterious effects. The parents have no right of access to the child who anyway may be miles distant, making visiting if permitted impracticable and infrequent. If rehabilitation of the family is to be pursued as the ultimate goal, the preservation of ties between parents and the child is imperative, as are good relations between the parents and the social workers involved. Neither is likely to prosper in these circumstances. The elimination of delay is, therefore, of great importance and, for this reason, a procedure akin to that existing for an application for an injunction, as suggested by the NCCL, is worth consideration. [164] It would involve transferring cases to the County Court (ultimately, perhaps, to a family court [165]) but there is a strong case for seeing all care proceedings as civil matters and thus more appropriately dealt with outside a quasi-criminal structure. The injunction-type procedure would have the advantages of speed, could if necessary operate on an *ex parte* basis, and in most cases would give the parent a chance to state a case in court immediately. The suggestion did not meet with the approval of the House of Commons Select Committee but deserves further consideration.

The uses of wardship

In an address to the Association of British Adoption and Fostering Agencies Legal Group in January 1977, Norman Turner, the Official Solicitor, commented on the fact that local authorites were 'more inclined than they once were to make use of . . . wardship jurisdiction to supplement or in substitution for their statutory powers.' [166] Wardship is one of the most ancient of institutions in English family law. Its origins are in the feudal obligation of the Sovereign to protect his subjects, especially those not capable of looking after themselves. The jurisdiction is now exercised by the Family Division of the High Court. Until 1967 anybody could apply to make a child a ward of court. Now it is necessary to state a relationship to prevent abuse of the process of the court. [167] Recently, an educational psychologist attached to a local authority applied successfully to stop the sterilisation of a girl of 11 who suffered from Sotos Syndrome. [168] Wardship vests guardianship in the court as *parens patriae* and throws 'a ring of care' [169] around the child. The court may then issue orders concerning aspects of his upbringing. In theory the

Family Division retains custody and the real caretaker gets care and control. [170] The court can make very detailed orders for care and control and access and these can be supervised by the Official Solicitor. [171] The court has the power to grant injunctions and, as an ultimate sanction the power to commit for contempt of court. [172]

There is no doubt that in an appropriate case a local authority social services department may make a child a ward of court. There is a number of situations involving abused children or children at risk where a wardship application may be particularly valuable. Turner himself, in the address previously referred to, gave one striking example. 'In an alleged baby battering case', he said, 'a local authority having procured a place of safety order or interim care order may prefer to have the matter fully investigated . . . in wardship proceedings rather than continue in the Juvenile Court especially if there is disputed medical evidence.' [173] One advantage of this is that the child will be separately represented by the Official Solicitor.

Another situation where wardship proceedings may be advantageous is where there is cause for concern that a child may be at risk of serious abuse although grounds for seeking a place of safety order or bringing care proceedings either do not exist or cannot be substantiated because of lack of evidence. [174]

A third justification for making a wardship application is to fill the gaps in the appeal process. Thus, it is not possible for a local authority to appeal against the refusal of a care order; nor is it possible to appeal against discharge of a care or supervision order. These gaps may be explained partly by the dual role which care and supervision orders play: they are also used in criminal proceedings where appeals would be tantamount to allowing the prosecution to appeal against acquittal. In the *Kesteven* [175] case the local authority resorted to seeking a place of safety order. But another way of retaining the child in care would be to make him a ward of court. This has been done in at least one recent case. [176]

A fourth case for invoking wardship is in seeking the court's assistance to supplement its powers. A good illustration of this, though the application for wardship was in fact made by the child's grandmother, is *Re B.* [177] In that case the danger was that the child's stepfather, who had already been convicted of causing her actual bodily harm, might discover her whereabouts and attempt to molest her again. The grandmother wanted care and control but the court refused to interfere with the local authority's decision to place the child with foster parents. The court ordered that wardship should continue thereby enabling the local authority to have immediate recourse to the courts in the discharge of its duties. There would, the court opined, 'be no abandonment of, or derogation from, [the authority's] statutory powers and duties were [it] to seek guidance and assistance from the High Court in matters of difficulty as distinct from day-to-day arrangements.' [178] Lane J. stressed that an application could be made for an injunction restraining the stepfather from endeavouring to ascertain the whereabouts of the child, or from approaching within a specified distance of the place where she lives or making any contact with her. Further if there were any breach of such an order the court could commit the stepfather to prison for contempt of court. [179]

Wardship may also be used by parents to challenge the propriety and, in limited circumstances, the wisdom of decisions taken by local authorities in respect of children in their care. A good illustration of this is the case of *Re Cullimore*, [180] the 'brittle bones' case. According to Sir George Baker, the President of the Family Division:

> [m] any doctors had seen the child and gave different diagnoses. At least one paediatrician had changed sides . . . Social workers and others were apt to see the matter in black and white, and some could make no allowance in their own minds for the possibility that the parents were not at fault.
>
> The dilemma was that if the injuries were wrongly held to be non-accidental, the parents . . . could suffer unjustly and be held in hatred, odium and contempt and pilloried in public while the child would be deprived of the loving care of parents . . . If a diagnosis of 'brittle bones' was made and that was wrong the child was gravely at risk if allowed to continue living with brutal parents.

It was held, after a five-day hearing, that on the balance of probabilities the child was suffering from brittle bones. The place of safety order, which had been made, was accordingly discharged. The parents were granted care and control but the wardship order was continued to enable the Official Solicitor to act as the child's guardian *ad litem*.

An extended comment on *Re Cullimore* is appropriate as in many ways it is an ideal case for wardship. The issues involved were complex, the medical evidence conflicting, and it was clear that it would be lengthy to hear. In such circumstances the High Court is the only appropriate forum. A juvenile court is not a suitable tribunal to deal with cases where 'a prolonged investigation into disputed facts are called for or in which the court may have to give and enforce detailed directions as to the upbringing of children.' [181] Further, the use of the Official Solicitor and the continuation of wardship enabled the court, at least in theory, to keep the case under review. But most importantly, as Lowe has written, there is 'at least a suspicion that had not the child been made a ward the parents might have lost the case'. [182]

Adoption of abused children

As a response to child abuse adoption is a drastic remedy. It involves the transfer of a child from his biological family into a new family entity. The adoptive parents become his parents and all ties of biological parenthood are severed. [183] We have no knowledge of how typical a solution adoption is seen to be. If Brenda Clark is right [184] and adoption is to be seen as a normal way of dealing with family disorganisation, then it is a response to the problem of abused children that must be considered. It must be stressed, however, that severely abused children, particularly those who suffer brain damage or other mental or physical handicap, are not easy to place. [185]

Prima facie adoption requires the agreement of the parents. If this is not forthcoming it may be dispensed with on one or more of a number of specified grounds. There are six of these grounds and any of them could be relevant to a situation of abuse. [186] Until the passing of the Children Act 1975, agreement could only be dispensed with on the grounds of ill-treatment where the ill-treatment was persistent. The Children Act introduced a new ground of 'seriously ill-treating the child' though this ground does not apply unless, because of the ill-treatment or for other reasons, the rehabilitation of the child within the household of the parent is unlikely. [187] Re-habilitation of an injured child with his family is, as the Houghton Report noted, [188] often distinctly possible. But the new provision does encompass the case of the single brutal attack, in cases where re-habilitation does not appear to be likely. And it will not be likely where, for example, there have been care proceedings and the child has been removed from his parents. Rehabilitation may also be unlikely where the parents are in prison or homeless.

Agreement may also be dispensed with where it can be shown that a parent has abandoned or neglected the child. The courts have held that this connotes conduct which would render the parent liable to be prosecuted under the Children and Young Persons Act 1933. [189]

The most commonly used ground for dispensing with agreement is that the parent is withholding his agreement unreasonably. According to Lord Denning this is determined by examining whether 'it is reasonable or unreasonable according to what a reasonable woman in her place would do in all the circumstances of the case'. [190] Although the court must give 'first consideration' to the welfare of the child it has been held that this duty does not qualify the terms upon which agreement is dispensed with as being unreasonably withheld. [191]

Compensation for abused children

There is no state fund earmarked to provide compensation for children who suffer abuse at the hands of their parents or caretakers, though a strong case could be made out for setting up a children's fund to assist abused children. The case for compensating such children may be no greater or less than that for paying sums of money to children born with congenital injuries or other handicaps. The Congenital Disabilities (Civil Liability) Act of 1976 preserves the existing system of fault liability. [192] A child born disabled because of the wrongful act of another person can recover damages from that person. A child who cannot prove fault can recover no compensation from anyone. Furthermore, the child's mother is exempted from liability to her child for any ante-natal injuries which he suffers, unless she drives a car when she knows or ought reasonably to know she is pregnant and fails to take the same care for the child's safety as she has a duty to take for the safety of others under the general law.

Sir George Baker, the President of the Family Division, opposed the granting of a cause of action against the mother or father because 'it would give a new weapon to the unscrupulous spouse — and there are many.' [193] A child abused by his parent can, in theory, sue the parent in tort. But, unlike the situation where the child injured though parental negligence in a car crash sues the parent ostensibly but in reality his insurance company, there is little to gain in the vast majority of abused child situations.

The state non-statutory system of compensating those who suffer criminal injuries will also rarely assist the abused child. The scheme specifically excludes compensation where the victim and the offender were 'living together at the time as members of the same family'. [194] Each year a number of applications fail because of this exclusion. The exclusion is difficult to justify. It would be going too far to suggest that the state is responsible for the child's misfortune but it does not seem unreasonable to suggest that in cases of child abuse it should accept responsibility. [195] A report of an Interdepartmental Working Party has now recommended that compensation should become possible under the Criminal Injuries Compensation scheme. [196] Two things troubled the committee. First, it thought that there were cases where an award would not be in the child's interests. Thus, it recommends that 'if a child less than about 10 years old suffers an injury which has no lasting effect, compensation should not normally be paid.' [197] Second, it was concerned to ensure that the assailant should not benefit from an award. This is understandable. More dubious is the first consideration for, despite the committee's arguments, it is difficult to see how an award cannot be in the child's interests. It seems most unlikely that a parent will injure a child in order that the state should award the child compensation. [198] And, if a parent does so, it seems unfair to deny the child an award. It is to be hoped that the committee's recommendations will be implemented without this dubious limitation. Nothing has yet been done.

There remains one possible source of compensation hitherto un untapped in this country, i.e. the medical profession. Before serious abuse a child is often presented to a doctor or hospital out-patients' department with less serious injuries. Frequently that child is allowed to go home with his parents because the non-accidental nature of his injuries has not been spotted. No one in this country has attempted to rely on the law of negligence and sue the doctor or hospital concerned for negligence in failing to diagnose the injuries and report them to the proper authorities. In California the Supreme Court has recently upheld such a cause of action. In *Landeros* v. *Flood*, [199] an 11-month-old child with comminuted spiral fracture of the tibia and fibula of the right leg which gave the appearance of having been caused by a twisting force, as well as bruises, lacerations and a skull fracture was released by a hospital to her mother and her common law husband. Shortly afterwards she suffered permanent injury at their hands.

Justice Mosk held that the child's claim disclosed a potential cause of action. Whether it should succeed would depend on whether the doctor concerned had displayed the skill which a reasonable doctor in his position might have been expected to exercise. This, the judge held, could not be determined by lawyers; it was a question of fact and required expert testimony. [200] He further held that the defence that the damage was caused not by the doctor's omission but by a subsequent act of the mother was of no value as an intervening act did not amount to a superseding cause where it was reasonably foreseeable. There were other causes of action which turn on the wording of the California reporting law and these are not relevant to an English situation. The basic claim is. The categories of negligence are not closed and whether a duty is to be recognised is ultimately a question of policy. [201] Provided the English judiciary is prepared to recognise that abused children are entitled to protection there seems no reason why a similar claim to that in *Landeros* v. *Flood* should not succeed here too.

Notes

[1] M. Kellmer-Pringle, *Growing Up Adopted*, NCB, 1972, p.174.

[2] *Cf* M.D.A. Freeman, *The Children Act 1975*, Sweet and Maxwell, 1976, p.v.

[3] See *J.* v. *C.* [1970] A.C.668, *Re W.* [1971] A.C.682, *M.* v. *M.* [1973] 2 All E.R.81, discussed in M.D.A. Freeman, 'Child Law at the Crossroads', *Current Legal Problems*, vol.27, 1974, pp 165, 182-4, 191-2, 204-5 and *S (BD)* v. *S (DJ)* [1977] 1 All E.R.656.

[4] D. MacDougall, 'Children and the Law: The Limited Effectiveness of Legal Process' in *The Child and the Courts*, Ontario Institute for Studies in Education, Toronto, 1976, p.344.

[5] P. Aries, *Centuries of Childhood*, J. Cape, 1962.

[6] But commenting on the case of Anne Martin, sentenced in 1761 to two years' imprisonment for putting out the eyes of young children, I. Pinchbeck and M. Hewitt note: 'had it been the eyes of her own children possibly no notice would have been taken of the matter, for parents commonly treated their unhappy offspring as they chose'. See *Children in English Society*, vol.II, RKP, 1973, p.350.

[7] Idem, p.348. See also p.368.

[8] Idem, pp 357-8.

[9] Quoted in E.W. Cohen, *English Social Services — Methods and Growth*, Allen and Unwin, 1949, p.20.

[10] Sir W. Blackstone, *Commentaries on the Law of England*, T. Tegg, 1765, pp 449-51.

[11] There is a good description of this in I. Pinchbeck and M. Hewitt, op.cit., note 6, pp 614-7.

[12] Quoted idem, p.617.

[13] Idem, p.618.

[14] Idem, p.622.

[15] See G.M. Tuckwell, 'The State and its Children' in H. de B. Gibbins (ed.), *Social Questions of Today*, Methuen, 1891, p.127.

[16] *Hansard*, H.C. vol.337, col.227.

[17] Idem, col.229. It was at a meeting organised by the Society for the Prevention of Cruelty to Animals in 1882 that an appeal for a dogs' home was extended into an appeal for the protection of children. Developments in the USA bear striking similarities. In 1874 a nine-year-old child, Mary Ellen, was removed from her parents by the Society for the Prevention of Cruelty to Animals on the grounds that she was a member of the animal kingdom so that her case fell within the laws against animal cruelty. See V. Fontana, *Somewhere A Child is Crying*, Macmillan, 1973, pp 12-3.

[18] By the Children and Young Persons Act 1933.

[19] See Norfolk Enquiry into Meurs case, 1975; DHSS, Maria Colwell Inquiry, 1974.

[20] J. Howells, *Remember Maria*, Butterworths, 1974.

[21] M. Kellmer-Pringle, *The Needs of Children*, Hutchinson, 1975, pp 69-70.

[22] See M.D.A. Freeman, op.cit., note 2, pp v-vi.

[23] *Per* J. Court, 'Psycho-Social Factors in Child Battering', *Journal of*

[24] See generally, M. Paulsen 'Legal Protection against Child Abuse', *Children*, 1966, and in C.H. Kempe and R. Helfer (eds), *The Battered Child*, University of Chicago Press, 1972.

[25] *Cf* J. Eekelaar, 'What are Parental Rights', *Law Q.R.*, vol.89, 1973, p.224. See also P. Wallington in *Juridical Review*, 1972, p.124.

[26] S.1(7).

[27] Protection of Minors Bill 1973. See H.L. vol.347, cols 875-85, 893-965.

[28] *Ingraham* v. *Wright*, 430 U.S. 651 (1977). See I.M. Rosenberg, *Columbia L.R.*, vol.78, 1978, p.75.

[29] This view is found in Sir W. Blackstone and in *Cleary* v. *Booth* [1893] 1 Q.B. 465 and *Mansell* v. *Griffin* [1908] 1 K.B. 160.

[30] See, generally, P. Newell (ed.) *A Last Resort?* Penguin, 1972, and A. Samuels, 'Never Hit a Child', *Family Law*, vol.7, 1977, p.119.

[31] *R.* v. *Hopley* (1860) 2 F. and F.202.

[32] *Gardner* v. *Bygrave* (1889) 6 TLR 23; *R.* v. *Cheesman* (1836) 7 C. and P.455.

[33] *Ryan* v. *Fildes* [1938] 3 All E.R. 517.

[34] *Asquith* v. *Proctor, The Times,* 17 February 1967.

[35] *R.* v. *Derrivière* (1969) 53 Cr. App. Rep. 637.

[36] A fuller account is H.K. Bevan, *The Law Relating to Children*, Butterworths, 1973, ch.6. See also C. Low, 'The Battering Parent, the Community and the Law', *Applied Social Studies*, vol.3, 1971, p.65.

[37] *R.* v. *Ward* [1956] 1 Q.B. 351.

[38] Under s.2 of Homicide Act 1957.

[39] See s.3 of Homicide Act 1957.

[40] Since the abolition of the death penalty it makes little difference in practice of which offence the parent is convicted.

[41] *R. v. Fitzgerald* (1970) Crim. L.R. 357.

[42] Diminished responsibility, provocation and acceptance of a compromise guilty plea.

[43] *R. v. Church* [1966] 1 Q.B. 59.

[44] *R. v. Watson and Watson* (1959) Crim. L.R. 785.

[45] *R. v. Adesokan* (1970) Crim. L.R. 357.

[46] *R. v. Nuttall* (1968) Crim. L.R. 173.

[47] Infanticide Act 1938 s.1.

[48] In 1976, 6 women were convicted of infanticide. None was sentenced to an immediate term of imprisonment. One was given a suspended, 2 probation, 2 hospital orders under the Mental Health Act 1959 and 1 a supervision order.

[49] Glanville Williams, *The Sanctity of Life and the Criminal Law*, Faber, 1958, p.37.

[50] An Infanticide Bill in 1970 would have made the offence a summary one but it failed to get a second reading. See H.L. vol. 792, col. 433.

[51] *Butler Report on Mentally Abnormal Offenders*, Cmnd. 6244, 19. 22 – 19. 26.

[52] Criminal Law Revision Committee, *Working Paper on Offences against the Person*, HMSO, 1976, paras 65 and 66. Together with the James Committee, Cmnd 6323 (para. 121) it believes infanticide should continue to be tried on indictment only. This is criticised, rightly it is submitted, by P. English (1977) Crim. L.R. 79, 88.

[53] s.42.

[54] s.43.

[55] s.47.

[56] s.20.

[57] s.18.

[58] s.20 (GBH) carried 5 years; s.18 (GBH with intent) life.

[59] *Cf First Report from House of Commons Select Committee on Violence in the Family*, H.C. 329-1, 1977, para.115.

[60] B. Hoggett, *Parents and Children*, Sweet and Maxwell, 1977, p.102, says it can 'cover almost any deficiency in child care'.

[61] See s.1(3)(b).

[62] *R. v. Hayles* [1969] 1 All E.R. 34.

[63] Twenty-three were given conditional discharges and 59 were placed on probation.

[64] *R. v. Senior* [1899] 1 Q.B. 823.

[65] *R. v. Lowe* [1973] Q.B. 702.

[66] C. Low, op.cit., note 36, p.72.
[67] See *R. v. Hatton* [1925] 2 K.B. 322.
[68] *Supra*, p.
[69] See *R. v. Hayles*, op.cit., note 62. A useful case is *R. v. Thornton* (1965) Crim. L.R. 497.
[70] *Per* Lord Russell C.J. in *R. v. Senior* [1899] 1 Q.B. 291.
[71] *R. v. Whibley* [1938] 3 All E.R. 777.
[72] *R. v. Boulden* [1957] 41 Cr. App. Rep. 105.
[73] Op.cit., note 36, p.195.
[74] This problem is considered in *Marsh v. Hodgson* (1973) 3 Fam. Law 142.
[75] See *Hewer v. Bryant* [1970] 1 Q.B. 357, 373.
[76] See s.52 of Matrimonial Causes Act 1973.
[77] See *Butler v. Gregory* (1912) 18 T.L.R. 370; *Liverpool S.P.C.C. v. Jones* [1914] 3 K.B. 813.
[78] Bevan, op.cit., note 36, p.199.
[79] See S.I. No.1500 (1970), and B. Dickens, 'The Private Prosecutors', *New Society*, 19 February 1970.
[80] *Cf* A. Clegg and B. Megson, *Children in Distress*, Penguin, 1968.
[81] See B. Dickens, 'Discretion in Local Authority Prosecutions', (1970), Crim. L.R. 618.
[82] *Minutes*, p.21.
[83] Idem, p.37.
[84] Idem, p.231.
[85] NSPCC Battered Child Research Team, *At Risk*, RKP, 1976, pp 113-5.
[86] See D. Thomas, *Principles of Sentencing*, Heinemann, 1970, p.80.
[87] *R. v. Nuttall* (1968), Crim. L.R.173.
[88] *R. v. Perkins* (1968) Crim. L.R.337.
[89] *R. v. Blackburn* (1967), 51 Cr. App. R.368.
[90] *R. v. Whitecombe* (1971), Crim. L.R.51.
[91] *R. v. Sutton* (1968), 53 Cr. App. R.128.
[92] A parent may make a request to a local authority to take care proceedings in respect of a child beyond his control. (s.1(2)(d) of CYPA 1969).
[93] *Marks v. Beyfus* (1890) 25 Q.B.D.494.
[94] *D. v. N.S.P.C.C.* [1978] A.C.171, commented on by S. Maidment (1978), *Current Legal Problems* (forthcoming).
[95] The case for protecting local authorities is even stronger as they have a *duty* to bring proceedings.
[96] A child is a person under 14, a young person one between 14 and 17. For convenience succeeding references are to 'child' but,

unless otherwise stated, refer to young persons as well.

[97] Children and Young Persons Act 1969 s.2(9).

[98] Magistrates' Courts (Children and Young Persons) Rules 1970, r.18(1).

[99] Idem, r.14(3).

[100]   This was commented upon in the DHSS *Report of Committee of Inquiry into Care and Supervision of Maria Colwell*, HMSO, 1974, para.228.

[101]   Magistrates' Courts (Children and Young Persons) Rules 1970, r.17.

[102]   Children Act 1975 s.64, adding new section 32A(1) in CYPA 1969.

[103]   Idem, adding new section 32(A)(2) in CYPA 1969.

[104]   Idem, adding new section 32(B) in CYPA 1969.

[105]   *Parental Rights and Duties and Custody Suits*, Stevens, para. 54 and see J. Goldstein, A. Freud and A. Solnit, *Beyond the Best Interests of the Child*, Free Press, 1973, pp 65-7. A useful discussion of the problem of representation is B.G. Fraser, *Calif. Western Law Review*, vol.13, 1977, p.16.

[106]   Viz., a hospital or guardianship order under the Mental Health Act 1959, or an order requiring the child's parent or guardian to enter into a recognisance to take proper care and exercise proper control over him.

[107]   See the Canadian case of *Re B and Children's Aid Society of Winnipeg* (1976) 64 D.L.R. (3d) 517.

[108]   See M.D.A. Freeman, *Family Law*, vol.6, 1976, p.136, and *Justice of the Peace*, vol.140, 1976, pp 539, 556 and J. Eekelaar, *Modern Law Review*, vol.40, 1977, p.121.

[109]   *Surrey C.C. v. S.* [1974] Q.B.124.

[110]   See *The Guardian*, 17 April 1974. Also useful is *Daily Mirror*, 3 September 1974.

[111]   Schedule 3, para.67.

[112]   See *The Times*, 30 November 1974.

[113]   B. Hoggett, *Parents and Children*, Sweet and Maxwell, 1977, p.110.

[114]   H.C. vol.898, cols 1395-1407.

[115]   See *Social Work Today*, vol.8, no.27, 12 April 1977, p.2.

[116]   Quoted idem, p.3.

[117]   *Minutes of Evidence of Select Committee of H.O.C. on Violence in the Family*, pp 66-7.

[118]   *Mohamed v. Knott* [1969] 1 Q.B.1.

[119]   *Re D.J.M.S.* [1977] 3 All E.R.582.

[120]   See s.70(1).

[121] *Per* W. Cavenagh, 'Battered Baby Cases in the Courts', *Justice of the Peace*, vol.138, 1974, pp 30-1.
[122] Magistrates' Courts (Children and Young Persons) Rules 1970, r.20.
[123] Op.cit., note 117, p.230. This point was also stressed in the Birmingham *Howlett* report, p.12, conclusion 3 (City of Birmingham D.C. and Birmingham A.H.A.).
[124] s.12(1).
[125] s.14.
[126] Op.cit., note 125, Sched. Form 44.
[127] H.C. 329 paras 175-8 (1977).
[128] Boarding-Out of Children Regulations, 1955.
[129] Op.cit., note 100, para. 233.
[130] See schedule 3, para. 68, adding new section 11A to CYPA 1969.
[131] CYPA 1969 s.24(1).
[132] Unless the child is 16 when the order is made, in which case it lasts until he reaches 19 (s.20(4) CYPA 1969).
[133] CYPA 1969 s.21(2). Applications may be made by the local authority, child, child's parent or guardian or a visitor (see s.24(5)) acting on the child's behalf.
[134] DHSS, *Report of Committee of Inquiry into Care and Supervision provided in relation to Maria Colwell*, 1974, para. 42.
[135] Children Act 1975 Schedule 3, para. 69.
[136] Children Act 1975 s.64 (new section 32A(2) of CYPA 1969).
[137] CYPA 1969 s.24(2) *cf* 'rights and duties' in s.2 of Children Act 1948.
[138] Idem, s.24(3).
[139] The agreement of the parents is still required (s.12 Children Act 1975).
[140] CYPA 1969 s.24(2).
[141] Children Act 1975 s.33.
[142] See Children Act 1975 s.12(2)(e)(f) and *post.* p.65.
[143] Children Act 1975 s.12(2)(e) and (f), (5).
[144] *Per* R. Holman, 'The Place of Fostering in Social Work', *British Journal of Social Work*, vol.5, 1975, pp 3, 10.
[145] Idem, pp 11-12.
[146] V. George, *Foster Care*, RKP, 1970; R. Parker, *Decision in Child Care*, Allen and Unwin, 1966.
[147] H. Maas and R.E. Engler, *Children in Need of Parents*, Columbia University Press, 1959.
[148] S. Jenkins and E. Norman, *Filial Deprivation and Foster Care*, Columbia University Press, 1972.

[149]   See Brenda Clark, 'A Cause for Concern — Child Care Policy and Practice', *Social Work Today*, vol.8, no.43, 1977, p.7.
[150]   CYPA 1969, s.20.
[151]   Idem, ss.2(5), (10), 22, 28(6).
[152]   See *R. v. Lincoln (Kesteven) Justices exp. M*, [1976] Q.B.957.
[153]   See memorandum of Margaret Booth in *Minutes of Select Committee on Violence in the Family*, p.341.
[154]   Op.cit., note 152. See, generally, *Roberts v. Hopwood* [1925] A.C.578.
[155]   *Cf* op.cit., note 152, p.967.
[156]   Idem, pp 965-6.
[157]   Idem.
[158]   Idem, pp 962-3.
[159]   CYPA 1969, s.28(5).
[160]   *Cf* H. Bevan, *The Law Relating to Children*, Butterworths, 1973, p.58 (note 12). B. Hoggett, op.cit., note 113 expresses no doubt that this is so (p.122).
[161]   See NSPCC, *At Risk*, RKP, 1976, p.109.
[162]   *The Times*, 24 March 1976. For another example see P.H.R., 'Catch in the Child Care Court', *The Guardian*, 20 December 1974.
[163]   *Minutes of Evidence*, HC 350 1975-76, pp 265-8.
[164]   Idem, p.271.
[165]   There have been many proposals for a Family court. See, e.g. Finer *Report on One-Parent Families*, Cmnd 5629, 1974, sections 13 and 14.
[166]   N. Turner in *Adoption and Fostering*, no.88, 1977, p.34. The House of Commons Select Committee *First Report on Violence in the Family* also commented upon the trend (para. 179).
[167]   See *Re Dunhill* (1967) 111 Sol.Jo.113 and *Practice Direction* [1967] 1 All E.R.828.
[168]   *Re D.* [1976] 1 All E.R.326.
[169]   *Per* Lord Eldon in *Wellesley v. Beaufort* (1827), 2 Russ 1.
[170]   See *Re W.* [1964] Ch.202, 210.
[171]   *Re R.(PM)* [1968] 1 All E.R.691.
[172]   *Re B.(JA)* [1965] Ch.1112.
[173]   Op.cit., note 166.
[174]   A striking example of where wardship might have been valuable is the case of Wayne Brewer. See Somerset Area Review Committee, *Report of Review Panel*, 1977 where references are made to the danger in which the child was and to the fact that care proceedings were not thought likely to succeed. See also Appendix 47 of House of Commons *First Report on Violence in the Family*: 'in wardship proceedings a judge considers evidence by way of

relevance rather than admissibility' *per* East Sussex C.C.

[175]   *Kesteven* [1976] Q.B. 957.
[176]   *Re D.* [1977] 3 All E.R.481, *Re H* [1978] 2 All E.R.903.
[177]   *Re B.* [1975] Fam.36.
[178]   Idem, p.44.
[179]   Idem, p.43.
[180]   *Re Cullimore, The Times*, 24 March 1976.
[181]   *Per* The Hon. Mr Justice Cross, *Law Q.R.* vol.83, 1967, pp
200, 204.
[182]   R. Lowe, 'Wardship' in *The Child and the Courts*, Ontario
Institute for Studies in Education, 1976, p.124.
[183]   In exceptional circumstances continued access is allowed but
this would be out of the question in this context.
[184]   B. Clark, 'A Cause of Concern — Child Care Policy and
Practice', *Social Work Today*, vol.8, 1977, no.43, p.7.
[185]   J. Rowe and L. Lambert, *Children Who Wait*, ABAA, 1973.
[186]   Not discussed here are 'cannot be found or is incapable of
giving agreement'; 'has persistently failed without reasonable cause to
discharge parental duties'.
[187]   Children Act 1975 s.12(2)(f) and (5).
[188]   *Report of Departmental Committee on Adoption of Children*
(Houghton Report), Cmnd 5107, 1972, para. 219.
[189]   *Watson* v. *Nikolaisen* [1955] 2 Q.B.286.
[190]   *Re L.* (1962) Sol.Jo.611, said to be 'authoritative' in *Re W.*
[1971] A.C.682.
[191]   *Re P.* [1977] 1 All E.R.182 *cf* M.D.A. Freeman, 'First
Considerations in Adoption Law', *New Law Journal*, 1977, vol.127,
p.679.
[192]   On which see M.D.A. Freeman, 'Congenital Disabilities etc
Act 1976' in P. Allsop and H. Tate (eds), *Current Law Statutes
Annotated 1976*, Sweet and Maxwell, 1976, ch.28.
[193]   See Sir G. Baker in *Law Com.* no.60, para. 56.
[194]   For a good and typical example see para. 7 of the Scheme.
See Cmnd 6656.
[195]   *Cf* Lord Denning, H.L. vol.245, col.274 and see B. Downey
in *British Journal of Criminology*, 1965, vol.5, p.92 and S. Schafer,
The Victim and his Criminal, Random House, 1968, ch.3.
[196]   Home Office/Scottish Home and Health Dept., *Review of the
Criminal Injuries Compensation Scheme*, HMSO 1978. See further
post, p.181.
[197]   Idem, para. 7.20.
[198]   Idem, para. 7.15 (it was apparently the view of the DHSS and
Health Visitor's Association that the payment of compensation might

prove an incentive to unbalanced parents to injure children).

[199] *Landeros* v. *Flood* (1975) 551 P.22 389 commented upon by J. Clymer, *Washburn L.J.* vol.16, 1977, p.543. The problem is also discussed in L.B. Isaacson, *San Diego L.R.*, vol.12, 1975, p.743. An earlier case, *Robinson* v. *Wical* was settled out of court (*Time*, 20 November 1972, p.74).

[200] *Cf Roe* v. *Minister of Health* [1954] Q.B.66 and *Law Commission Report on Injuries to Unborn Children*, Cmnd 5709, para. 94. See also *Bolam* v. *Friern Hospital Management Committee* [1957] 2 All E.R.118: 'the test whether here has been negligence . . . is the standard of the ordinary skilled man exercising and professing to have that special skill' *per* McNair J.

[201] See Lord Denning M.R. in *Spartan Steel* v. *Martin* [1973] Q.B.27, 36 and Californian Supreme Court in *Dillon* v. *Legg* 441 P. 2d 912, 916. See also *Anns* v. *L.B. of Merton* [1977] 2 All E.R.492 *per* Lord Wilberforce (p.498).

4 Managing child abuse

The law described in the last chapter provides a framework for intervention. No law, however, can be better than its administration. And it is this which has been the subject of most criticism in recent years. This is not to suggest for one moment that the work of welfare authorities, the medical profession or even the police is limited to, or is expected to be limited to, implementing the statutory provisions which have been discussed. The principles of good casework cannot be reduced to any statutory formula, and it is attention to these, as much as to the law, which is likely to prevent child abuse and assist in its management. Above all it is co-ordination between the agencies which is essential, for failure to communicate and share information can prove fatal. Nor must this emphasis on professional agencies deflect our attention from the role which the general public itself can play. For, whilst the man in the street is quick to vent righteous indignation when a tragedy occurs, he is also likely to groan when money is levied from him to intensify social services and other welfare agencies.

This chapter discusses in turn the contribution of social work, the medical profession and the police as three agencies particularly concerned in the management of child abuse; it considers the problem of co-ordination through local area review committees, case conferences and registers; and it questions the need for a system of mandatory reporting such as exists in the USA and much of Canada. Throughout it draws on the reports of the enquiries held in the last five years to review cases of child abuse.

Social services

Social work is currently the subject of considerable self-questioning. The 1977 annual conference of the British Association of Social Workers chose as its theme: 'Who Needs Social Workers?' Research undertaken by Olive Stevenson [1] and Phyllida Parsloe [2] emphasises a 'yawning chasm' [3] between social work education and what actually happens in social services departments. Stressed particularly is the tension between organisational accountability and professional responsibility. To quote a leader from the Association's journal: '[h]ierarchies are more concerned about a few pounds spent under section 1 [of the Children and Young Persons Act 1963] than in giving formal support to the workers who carry the gravest burdens of responsibility for client welfare'. [4] And who can doubt that these tensions will increase as new recruits demand 'radical social work' and community action?

This self-searching follows a period of time when social workers have rarely been out of the public's firing-line. Every time a child is battered to death social workers take the brunt of the criticism even if other agencies and professions are not immune. Social workers must take enormous, calculated risks every day. They have to. As Geoffrey Banner, assistant director of residential care in Wiltshire told a Residential Care Association conference in 1974, '[i]f we attempt to create a system whereby all risk is eradicated we risk creating a system in which it is "death" to the kind of people we are trying to serve.' [5] Yet we do not expect the police to prevent every crime, nor do we blame them when they do not. Doctors, lawyers and other professionals also make mistakes.

Social work as a profession is still in its infancy. The idea that local authorities should concern themselves with child care goes back to the Curtis report of 1946. [6] Legislation followed in 1948. [7] The early concerns of children's departments were with rescuing children from deprived environments and, if adoption were not possible, [8] boarding them out with approved foster parents. The question of whether the deprivation might have been prevented was regarded by Curtis as 'of the utmost importance'. The report hoped that 'serious consideration [would] be given to it'. [9] It was not, however, their brief. By the mid-1950s most children's departments were actively engaged in preventing the admission of children to care and in working towards the rehabilitation of those in care with their families. In doing this they were following the pioneer work of the Family Service Units. [10] This impetus was stimulated by the Ingelby Committee's recommendation that children's departments should undertake preventive casework. [11] The 1963 Children and Young Persons Act encoded this recommendation in s.1. The impact of s.1 was such that by 1970 more than five times as many children were helped in their own homes as were admitted to care. [12]

The problem of juvenile delinquency proved the next catalyst of change. The 1969 Children and Young Persons Act absorbed delinquents into the 'mainstream of child care' and brought children's departments to an end. 'In order to create a "family service" that would underpin the new procedures in the juvenile courts and provide new treatments for offenders, the child care service was itself absorbed into . . . social services departments'. [13] This followed the recommendation of the Seebohm report of 1968 that 'a community based and family oriented' social services department should be established. [14]

Since April 1971 local authority social services departments have been generic. [15]   But there is a difference between a generic department and generic workers. [16]   Nevertheless, there has been a 'dilution of child care expertise' [17] which was probably inevitable in the reorganisation which took place. Many local authorities, probably in response to cases like that of Maria Colwell, are beginning to build in expertise in specific fields again and are allowing 'specialisations to be reintroduced almost'. [18]   The London Borough of Hammersmith and one or two other authorities are even appointing specialist social workers to deal with child abuse. [19]   On top of the Seebohm-modelled structural change (and other reorganisations [20]) social workers have had to cope with the changes in child care policy wrought by the Children Act of 1975. The move back to an emphasis on substitute care found in this legislation [21] was not, unlike some earlier reversals in child care social policy, engineered by the social work profession itself. And coming almost contemporaneously with the Finer report on one-parent families, [22] which emphasised prevention in a way that no earlier report had done, it seemed to many, including social workers, that Houghton [23] before Finer was the cart before the horse. The Children Act of 1975 was in part an over-reaction to the Colwell case; in the same way many of the administrative procedures now being used to fight child abuse seem hasty, ill-thought-out panic measures. [24]

One effect of Seebohm is that social services departments are now more accessible, decentralised and operate on an 'open-ended basis'. People no longer have to classify themselves and can approach a department with a problem as they see it, however difficult it may be to categorise it. This, together with a vast growth in legislation and an explosion of pressure groups pleading for their own interests, has increased the work of social services considerably. BASW's Code of Practice [25] instructs social workers that 'highest priority' should be given to children at risk of serious injury. A danger of this was pointed out by the Director of Social Services of the London Borough of Ealing in his evidence to the House of Commons Select Committee: 'the biggest problem . . . is the pressure for such cases to be dealt with as a matter of priority and the difficulty of balancing sometimes very slender resources between the demands for urgent attention in this sort of work and those in other sorts of work'. [26]   Neither resources nor manpower has increased at anything like the scale of the increased demand for services.

The result is that departments are woefully undermanned, the shortage extending to administrative and ancillary staff as well. [27] The percentage of fully trained professionals is increasing but is still as low as 40 per cent. [28] Many more will be partially trained and have considerable experience. Caseloads tend to be large. It is not uncommon for a social worker to be responsible for the problems of 50 families and some for very many more. [29] Yet a juvenile court in Somerset, on revoking a care order contrary to the advice of social workers, requested that 'supervision should be on the basis of three or four times weekly.' [30] The child in this case was killed 11 months later by his stepfather. Because of this case we know of the unrealistic demands made by magistrates but similar demands are probably not uncommon. There are also rapid turnovers in staff so that the same family can become the responsibility of a succession of social workers. A 'battering parent', writing in *Social Work Today*, spoke of working with her sixth social worker. [31] The House of Commons Select Committee has recommended that 'in planning for the future DHSS should regard the imposition of a statutory duty on local authorities to provide a 24 hour stand-by service as a priority'. [32] No recommendation is, however, made to increase manpower or improve salaries.

With these problems the temptation to close a case prematurely must be considerable. This virtually happened in the Auckland case where a convicted child-killer was left in sole charge of three small children. The social workers concerned did not believe a care order was necessary. Another child was killed within a couple of months. [33] Another temptation is over-anxiety which can lead to unnecessary entry of children's names on registers of risk with concomitant problems of labelling and dangers that the parent may indeed abuse his child.

In the NSPCC's *78 Battered Children: A Retrospective Study* the authors noted that 'actions which added to existing family tension precipitated further battering' and they commented that '[t]he rebattering incidence of 60 per cent in a sample of cases known to a protective agency does not compare favourably with the estimate that 25-30 per cent are rebattered in the absence of any intervention . . . The findings suggest that multiplicity of workers and overfrequent observation of battering families can increase family stress'. [34] Furthermore non-battering parents suspected of battering may come to abuse their children. [35] This process is graphically described in an address by Jordan to the British Association of Social Workers in 1975. [36] A case is reported to a social services department:

when the social worker goes to investigate . . . she often finds a family which is not significantly different at first sight from other families who refer themselves or are referred by other agencies for some form of material assistance. What a temptation there is to judge the issue of child abuse; never to state the precise purpose of the visit, the nature of the complaint . . .

More dangerously, if problems about child care do emerge, the temptation is to treat these as if they were requests for one of the range of provisions from the welfare pantry-day care, playgroups, holidays or priority on the housing list. And if the social worker really does begin to feel anxiety that the children are at risk, this process can insidiously be carried a stage further . . . The family can become a case, to be visited in a vague, supervisory way, to check up, for the social worker to cover herself. The danger here is that rather than helping, the social worker can instead become part of the client's nightmare. The situation is never defined; the reason for supervision is never brought into the open . . . These are the bases for the research finding [37] that, as applied to baby battering, anxious visiting by social workers of families actually increases battering. In the tragic cases we've all heard about, the clients were not new referrals who hadn't been investigated quickly enough, but cases known to the department for a considerable period.

Many criticisms are made of the social work profession's handling of cases of child abuse. [38] It is said (mainly by the police) that social workers are middle-class and have communication problems with working-class battering parents. Complaints are made that they do not know the law well enough, that they are over-protective of parental rights, that they lack investigative skills. Perhaps the most pervasive criticism has been its perceived over-concern with the functioning of the family as a unit, with rehabilitation of the child within his biological family the ultimate goal. [39] The Colwell case is a striking illustration of this philosophy at work. Maria's mother wanted her back from her aunt and uncle with whom she had been fostered for six years. There was never very much doubt in the minds of the social workers involved that ultimately this was the best solution, and the mother's application for Maria's care order to be discharged was unopposed by the local authority. Olive Stevenson, in a minority opinion attached to the DHSS report, blames 'the legal and social framework within which the social workers had to operate, in which it was assumed that a parent had a right to reclaim a child

81

if . . . she could prove [herself] to be [a] "fit person".' [40] But the ideology to which she refers has to a very large extent been fashioned by the social work profession itself, making her defence somewhat disingenuous. Certainly, when children's departments began a different philosophy prevailed. Children were deliberately fostered out of their own home areas to sever connections with their biological families. That this policy was reversed and more humane attitudes substituted is to be attributed to the initiatives taken and skills developed in children's departments in the 1950s and 1960s.

The medical profession

In the recent past doctors, both general practitioners and hospital staff, have received considerable blame for their failures to diagnose child abuse and, even where diagnosed, to do anything about it. Until recently there was little in the doctor's training or education to equip him to deal with the problem. Indeed, everything he had been taught encouraged him to deny the facts presented to him. Further, he had inbuilt inhibitions against suspecting the parent, especially if he had emotional ties with the family. The events of the last few years are likely to have improved the situation greatly on all these counts though it will be some considerable time before the effects of educating and training percolate the profession.

But some of the other problems remain. Notable among these is the doctor's ethical commitment to confidentiality. Doctors may not divulge information given to them by their patients unless given permission. Mandatory reporting laws circumvent this obstacle in the USA and in other countries which have them. [41] In Italy doctors and other auxiliary medical staff are required to refer cases that may reasonably be considered criminal offences to law-enforcement bodies or to the Attorney-General himself. [42] The Dutch have instituted the concept of a medical referee [43] to act as a go-between. The referee, or confidential doctor, is usually a paediatrician. Doctors, as well as friends and neighbours, social workers, the police, teachers, even one of the parents or the child himself can communicate their suspicions or knowledge to the referee and he can take further action. Most reports do in fact come from medical sources including the family's general practitioner. In this country ethical commitment remains and, although the veil of secrecy is often pierced, many cases still do not get beyond the general practitioner's consulting room.

The police

'The proper mission of law enforcement agencies relative to the child abuse phenomenon continues to remain unresolved'. So wrote Major Pitcher in his contribution to Kempe and Helfer's *Helping the Battered Child and his Family*. [44]   His assessment fits the current English problem well, as a reading of the minutes of evidence to the House of Commons Select Committee will show.   The police tend to be associated with law enforcement yet as early as Rowan and Mayne (Peel's first police commissioners) prevention of crime was laid down as a primary role of the police. [45]   Today sociologists refer to the dual role of the police as social support or peace-keeping and social control or law enforcement. [46]   Most police work is of a service nature. [47]   According to Chief Superintendent Keyte they are 'the oldest social workers', [48] a fact strengthened by the development of the community liaison concept.   The police unwillingness to get involved in domestic violence is notorious. [49]   But when it comes to violence against children, to many they seem over-anxious to play a full role. [50]   Thus the memorandum submitted by the Association of Chief Police Officers of England, Wales and Northern Ireland to the House of Commons Select Committee stressed that the police '*must* be involved in all cases of violence' against children. [51] And one of their biggest grievances is the fact that few cases are reported to them by social workers because of suspicion and mistrust, and in some areas they are excluded from case conferences. [52]

   Pitcher noted that '[t]he attitudes of the law enforcement profession on the handling of child abuse cases are continually changing toward favouring a less punitive approach. [53]   The position of the English police seems more equivocal.   In the memo-randum just referred to the Association of Chief Officers claim that to see the police as a punitive organisation 'shows a complete mis-understanding of the role of the modern-day Police Service'. [54] Similarly Commander Cass in his evidence to the House of Commons Committee insisted that the police were not 'out for punishment' but were 'fully conversant with the fact that the courts can deal with many cases sympathetically'. [55]   On the other hand the Metropolitan Police CID Memorandum called for stiffer penalties [56] and the Metropolitan Police Force Memorandum saw 'invest-igation, irrespective of a prosecution . . . as a positive deterrent . . . The fear of detection, a prerequisite of which is investigation, . . . as a preventive measure in respect of offences against children generally'. [57]
   The cases where prosecution can serve any useful purpose are

few. [58]   Once this is recognised by the police, and there are signs
that it is, the question becomes one of maximising police involvement
and setting out the specific functions which the police should perform
as participants in an efficient programme.   There is no doubt that the
police have expertise in investigation.   Bringing the facts into the open
is often the first step towards rehabilitation.   The use of senior police
surgeons as a liaison between the medical profession and the law is
particularly helpful.   Schemes using forensic physicians operate in
Northampton [59]   and Derby [60]   and both have been widely
praised.   Forensic expertise is particularly useful in cases which are
difficult to diagnose and skill is needed both in interpreting and
recording as well as in giving evidence in court should criminal or care
proceedings be thought necessary.   From what has been said the
admission of the police to case conferences is highly desirable,
particularly as the police are now prepared to co-operate in coming
to joint decisions.

The problem of co-ordination

Three agencies have been picked out for discussion.   Space does not
allow for a discussion of the many others involved ranging from the
NSPCC [61]   to family service units, [62]   probation to health visitors,
[63]   schools to the legal profession. [64]   All these institutions have
in varying degrees roles to play in the management of child abuse and
further references are made to them in subsequent discussion.   In this
section, however, the focus is on the problem of co-ordination of
work tasks.   If one common theme runs through the reports of
inquiries into child abuse it is that better co-ordination might have
saved innocent lives.   The Department of Health and Social Security
argued before the House of Commons Select Committee that co-
ordination was 'the key principle'. [65]

Co-ordination refers to the administrative mechanisms set up to
link and sustain liaison between two or more agencies.   It is in
Forder's language 'institutionalised co-operation' [66]   and involves
the systematic definition of roles and procedures to avoid conflicting
decisions and to enhance joint planning.   Co-ordination is now
generally believed to be beneficial in tackling child abuse.

Thus the House of Commons Select Committee noted that 'only by
collective discussion can adequate decisions be reached'. [67]   But
Howells has argued strongly for a sharpening rather than a broadening
of the sense of responsibility within the social services.   'Lack of
communication', he argues, 'is the supreme mechanism for white-

washing failure. Carried to its extreme it will result in large numbers of ignorant ineffectuals "co-operating". Nothing will happen except inconsequential talk'. [68]

Rein [69] has characterised the problems that hinder co-ordination as duplication, discontinuity and incoherence. Duplication is an overlap of similar services and occurs for abused children when the functions of individual workers or their policies are designed without reference to those of any other agency. Discontinuity occurs when services which are related to each other, but are required at different points in time, do not follow on consecutively; a transfer from the responsibility of one agency to another may not have been as smooth as it should. Incoherence is the failure of independent and specialised services to combine to solve a common problem.

The Maria Colwell case [70] exemplifies each of these faults. There was duplication between East Sussex County Council Social Services Department and the NSPCC; discontinuity in the changeovers of supervision as first Maria came under one authority and then another; incoherence in the failure of the social services to work with education welfare among other agencies. The defects are found also in the Auckland case. [71] Duplication occurred between social services and the health visiting service; discontinuity between probation and after care and other agencies; and incoherence in the failure of the social services and health visiting service to combine effectively in the period when Auckland was in sole charge of his three remaining children. And these defects are found to a greater or lesser extent in other cases as well.

Indeed, one common feature of the reports of inquiries is the constant assertion that, to quote the DHSS Colwell report, [72] it is 'a failure of a system compounded of several factors of which the greatest and most obvious must be that of the lack or ineffectiveness of communications and liaison'. And the report adds: '[a] system should so far as possible be able to absorb individual errors and yet function adequately'. Often noted is the failure to call a case conference. The failure to have a system of formal, regular case conferences had serious repercussions in the Piazzani case. [73] 'Had such a conference been in existence', the Inquiry Report noted, 'it might have brought matters to a head at an earlier date'. The Brewer report comments upon the inadequacy of informal case *discussions*, [74] as substitutes for case conferences.

Co-ordination, or integration, [75] can take place at a number of different levels. Carter, [76] using a model developed by Reid [77] to analyse co-ordination between agencies dealing with delinquents, suggests that co-ordination can take place on three levels:

[a] t the lowest level is 'ad hoc case co-ordination', where activities are generated by individual practitioners who work together to meet the client's need. The next level involves 'systematic case co-ordination', when in the interests of the individual case the services of two agencies are meshed together, as in the case conference. The third level, 'programme co-ordination', implies the development of joint programmes, mutual assistance, mutual modification of programmes and inevitably encompasses a larger part of the resources of each service. [78]

Each of these levels can be identified in the guide to the management of non-accidental injury issued by the Department of Health and Social Security in 1974.

The DHSS 1974 Circular [79]

The 1974 Circular was not the first guidance [80] issued by the Department but it is the most comprehensive. It strongly recommended the formation of area review committees as policy-making bodies. It recommended a case conference for every case involving suspected non-accidental injury to a child to minimise unilateral action and reach a collective decision. It stressed that a 'key worker' [81] should always be made responsible for co-ordinating the agreed treatment. The case conference was to retain overall concern for the management of the case and be prepared to reconvene at each successive development in it or when any professional worker was particularly worried about the family. It stressed that a central record of information in each area was essential to good communication between the many disciplines involved in the management of these cases. Good management of non-accidental injury was thus seen to involve local area review committees, case conferences and central registers.

Two years later the DHSS issued a local authority social services letter which reported the progress made in the handling of child abuse cases as of March 1975, and included some later information. [82] The letter set out guidance issued for the management of cases of non-accidental injury to children in Rochdale and Durham and those issued in Manchester [83] and Leeds [84] have been separately published.

The letter did not issue fresh guidance but concentrated on drawing attention to 'minimum standards or safeguards that are acceptable.' [85] It noted that all areas were now covered by an area review committee. Registers, however, were not universal. By July 1975

86

83 of the 102 area review committees had established central registers. [86] It noted also that in a few areas separate registers were kept by the area health authority and the social services department. It recommended that where such arrangements existed early amalgamation should take place to prevent fragmentation of effort and guarantee a uniform channel of information, and this was strongly endorsed by the House of Commons Select Committee. [87] It commented upon difficulties that had been experienced and suggested solutions. It also ducked some issues as, for example, the role of the police. [88]

Area review committees

The 'programme co-ordination', to which Carter referred, should be produced by the local area review committees. The circular directed that representation should be at a senior level and include representatives of the local authority, health services and other agencies including the police, probation and the NSPCC. It should meet three or four times a year (the later letter suggested quarterly [89]) and advise on local practices and procedures for cases, approve written instructions defining the duties of staff, review the work of case conferences, provide education and training programmes, collect information about the work being done in the area and collaborate with other area review committees, as well as advising on the need for inquiries into cases which had gone wrong and providing a forum for consultation between all involved in the management of child abuse.

The report on progress in 1976 noted that only 11 committees did not include a general practitioner and hoped that this omission would be remedied. It thought that representation of legal and administrative departments of local authorities and appropriate voluntary bodies was well justified. [90] It did, however, note that some reports suggested that membership of committees was so large as to make them 'unwieldy'. [91] This point was developed by the Association of Directors of Social Services in its memorandum to the House of Commons Select Committee. Describing the committees as 'cumbersome' and 'over-bureaucratised' [92] they pressed for a review of the 'elaborate structure'. The Select Committee was sympathetic to this viewpoint. [93] Membership on area review committees tends to consist of senior administrators rather than field workers. This is not surprising — the committees are policy-making bodies — but it tends to ignore the fact that the crucial decisions are made at field work level. [94]

There are limitations in the DHSS scheme, as Carter has shown. It tends to view co-ordination as 'the application of a set of static procedures, rather than as the negotiation of a dynamic process which is highly dependent for its definition on the accuracy of the perceptions of the professionals involved in the case'. [95] The perceptions and beliefs about child abuse which are held by workers in an agency will determine with which other services they will be prepared to co-operate. Co-ordination is not a technical procedure but a human process and as such involves values and choices. Different agencies have different goals: social workers may emphasise therapy or parental assistance, the police social control and criminal prosecution. A second limitation lies in the circular's assumption that it is an ideal world where the professionals involved act rationally, that is according to DHSS plans, and harmoniously, that organisations are efficient and responsive, resources are adequate and staff trained and experienced. Reality falls some way short of this ideal state. [96]

Case conferences

The objective of the case conference is to achieve 'systematic case co-ordination'. Case conferences are nothing new though recent events have brought them more to the fore and have undoubtedly formalised them. Nor are they uncontroversial. Many would argue that case conferences with their over-emphasis on administrative procedures divert social workers' attention from real issues of neglect and poverty that should concern them. The medical profession too, an editorial in *The Lancet* has argued, [97] may have greater priorities than attending case conferences. Castle's NSPCC study [98] and Martel's Family Service Unit Survey [99] provide us with some limited information. Castle's study is based on 777 case conferences attended by NSPCC officials in the three-month period from 1 March to 31 May 1976. Most (55.85 per cent) of these conferences were the first on the families concerned. Of these 57.14 per cent involved non-accidental injury to children. The majority of these case conferences were initiated by the social services (53.92 per cent), and the NSPCC (26 per cent). The police convened a handful. 72.33 per cent of the conferences were chaired by senior members of the social services; another 12.09 per cent by a hospital consultant, generally a paediatrician; on one occasion a senior police officer was in the chair. Most conferences were held in the social services department (55.85 per cent) or in a hospital (27.28 per cent); a few (2.83 per cent) took place in the general practitioner's surgery. The largest number of cases took between one and two hours (52.83 per cent); another 5.28 per cent took over two hours. GPs attended 26.89 per cent of conferences and hospital consultants 33.72 per cent. The police were present at 50.96 per cent of conferences. During the conference most of the children concerned were at home (58.58 per cent); another 19.93 per cent were in hospital. 12.18 per cent were already the subjects of care or supervision orders. 33 per cent of the initial case conferences resulted in court proceedings (only 11.81 per cent of these were criminal prosecutions). The social services department (55.12 per cent) and the NSPCC (37.80 per cent) were responsible for initiating the bulk of the juvenile court proceedings. The police, on the other hand, who initiated only 3.15 per cent of juvenile court proceedings, were the agency largely responsible for undertaking criminal prosecution (12 of the 17 cases, that is over 70 per cent). By contrast the social services department initiated only one prosecution.

The Family Service Unit survey consists of information compiled from replies to a questionnaire completed by 20 units covering 22 area review committee areas in January 1976. Most of the questions related to registers but two provide some information on the operation of case conferences. Only 9 area review committees had designated an officer to ensure that case conference decisions were implemented; 19 had a policy of designating a primary worker at the initial case conference. Martel comments on the lack of clarity in these answers. Some replies, she says, indicated that the key worker was the officer responsible for seeing that decisions were implemented. [100] It seems that the Family Service Unit assumed that the case conference has a decision-making role whereas its real function may often rather lie in giving guidance to whomever is concerned, the expectation being that the guidance will be followed. [101] Even so it must be recognised that agencies retain the right to act independently in accordance with their own policies.

The House of Commons Select Committee estimates that a typical hospital-based conference costs in the order of £130-150; [102] hospital-based conferences are not, however, typical. There is no information on the cost of conferences based on social services departments.

Castle made a number of criticisms of the operation of case conferences. They take too long; time is wasted because personnel involved have not prepared a resumé of their involvement and have to delve into large files at the meeting to extract relevant information. Key personnel are often missing. The absence of the general practitioner particularly is commented on. 'Medical personnel are more likely to attend if meetings can be held in a hospital or a G.P.'s surgery'. [103] Castle notes that the question of police involvement has not been fully resolved. There are difficulties particularly in some areas of London. The difficulty is one of competing ideologies. To the police, or at least some of them, the case conference 'represents an inquisition, self-appointed at that level, to decide yea or nay to whether a prosecution should ensue' [104] and this, they argue, is 'against the natural spirit of justice'. Social workers, on the other hand, find it 'very difficult to talk freely about their worries . . . if they feel the police are going to need to investigate further'. [105] As one senior social worker put it to the House of Commons Select Committee: '[t] he police . . . need to understand that we can protect children without necessarily thinking that the prosecution of adults is the only way in which we can achieve this'. [106] The Select Committee has recommended that a police officer, sufficiently senior to have discretion, should be invited to all case conferences. [107] Ultimately the best way to promote confidence and thus collaboration is for each profession to understand how the other works and this can best be achieved through training and experience. The DHSS letter of 1976 referred to the problem but avoided recommending any solution. A circular issued in November 1976 has attempted to promote understanding of the respective roles of the police and other services. It recognises that the police retain the capacity to take action independently of the case conference but believes they have a valuable contribution to make to the multidisciplinary management of non-accidental injury and should be involved 'as closely as possible in the case conference structure'. It is too early to estimate the impact of this circular. [108]

Two further comments should be noted. Castle discovered that on a number of occasions recommendations of case conference with regard to court proceedings have been frustrated by magistrates' refusal to consider care orders on 'technical grounds'. [109] Unfortunately the point is not amplified; nor are we told what is meant by 'technical'. If the suggestion is that the existing grounds are not wide enough then this is the sort of information that ought to be passed to area review committees and on from them to the DHSS. The grounds in the 1969 Act were not designed with battered children specifically in mind. If, on the other hand, the feeling is that cases are failing, for example, because relevant evidence is not admissible, then the agencies concerned should be turning their attention to wardship proceedings, for High Court judges in chambers are far more likely to admit such evidence. [110] This leads to the second comment. The House of Commons Select Committee Report makes the point that 'the decisions made . . . will not provide a justification for the treatment plan unless the reasons for choices are given'. [111] The reasons for a course of action may be absence of resources or inability to take care proceedings, but unless recorded it is difficult to monitor the operational problems which may distort the ideal of a blueprint such as the DHSS circular. [111a]

Registers

The keeping of registers is proving the most controversial feature of the management of child abuse. There is no system of mandatory reporting in England, as there is in the USA. [112] Registers of abused children and children at risk were nonetheless being kept by the NSPCC in the mid-1960s. Although the importance of registers was stressed by the Standing Medical Advisory Committee in 1970, [113] the origin of central registers is the recommendation of the DHSS circular of 1974. A new institution is fortunate if it escapes teething troubles, let alone rank criticism. Registers have escaped neither. Both BASW and the NCCL are concerned about how they operate and the Family Service Units have, in the course of the fullest survey of registers yet published, also made some general criticism of the ways in which they work.

The 1974 circular stated that '[a] central record of information in each area is essential to good communication between the many disciplines involved in the management of . . . cases' [114] of child abuse. It did not elaborate further. It did not say why it was essential, nor how it should be used. The 1976 letter offered some detailed advice but no guidance on these essential questions. It told us that the majority of registers were kept by social services departments, though the area health authority and NSPCC special units also undertook responsibility in some areas. Registers, we were informed, varied greatly, which is hardly surprising in view of the original open-ended recommendation. The letter made a number of recommendations on confidentiality and security and minimum requirements that should be satisfied by all register systems (the recording of certain essential details, the necessity for a built-in review procedure, the desirability of distinguishing children known to have been injured from those believed to be at risk). It also offered the following comment: '[t]he considerable problem of forming a reliable estimate of the incidence of non-accidental injury cannot be overcome by register systems alone . . . , but it is aggravated by the absence of any common core of information'. [115] This gives a clue as to one of the possible motives for setting up a system of registers.

The House of Commons Select Committee in its report noted that one important function of registers was that they provided 'a record for statistical purposes'. [116]   But this can hardly be a primary motivating factor. If it were, more attention would have been paid to the question of mandatory reporting, though even this in no way guarantees accuracy. This suggestion thus begs a number of questions. The other function noted by the Select Committee Report begs as many in asserting that registers provide 'a safeguard for the child by aiding detection of a sequence of injuries and facilitating discovery of "mobile families" '. [117]   The report also notes that 'registers are necessary in the interests of the child and . . . this should override all other considerations'. [118]   That the child's interests should be paramount is not contested. What is debatable is whether the keeping of registers is the best way of achieving this, and whether it is concern for the child which is the primary motivating force in the setting up and administration of registers. Solnit has argued that the child abuse reporting laws passed in the USA in record time in the 1960s 'were not intended and probably have contributed little to protecting children. They were intended mainly to safeguard the conscience and legal vulnerability of our adult society'. [119]   It can be argued that registers serve a similar function in England — that they are there to protect the agencies rather than the children. Indeed, one Director of Social Services was recently quoted as describing them in some areas as 'bureaucratic devices which act as an insurance policy for the local authority, instead of meeting the needs of clients'. [120]   It is all too easy for administrative procedures to assume an importance of their own. Is this what is happening with registers?

One of the main values of a system of registers is often said to be that they can assist in diagnosis. It is envisaged that whenever a professional of any discipline confronts a child who exhibits symptoms of having suffered abuse he would check with the register to see if the child was on it, whether any agency was currently involved, and whether another child in the same family had caused concern at any earlier period. But a survey conducted by BASW in 1976 found that professionals were not making inquiries of the register. [121]   Thirty-nine registers had received fewer than 50 inquiries, some had received under 10, and 3 reported that they had had no inquiries in a year. Indeed, over half the registers had received less than 100 queries. These figures may underestimate the extent of usage, for many queries may not be recorded, but they do not suggest the registers are being used as an aid to diagnosis. And, as BASW comments, '[i] f they are not being used for diagnosis one must ask what is the purpose of registers'. [122]

With this underlying ambivalence about their rationale the variable practice is hardly surprising. The criteria for inclusion and removal

92

of names vary. Martel commented that '[a] ll too often no thought has been given to criteria for inclusion on or removal from the register'. [123] Some area review committees direct inclusion of children with injuries proved or suspected to be non-accidental. Others include those deemed to be 'at risk'. In other areas, children suffering from actual serious neglect, general neglect, serious failure to thrive and emotional abuse are included. The problem is that physical abuse is one aspect of a wider question so that the separation of those who have been subjected to violence is artificial. But the 'at risk' category can become so large as to be inoperable with the result that fewer rather than more children are protected. BASW, in its memorandum to the House of Commons Select Committee, noted quite rightly that '[i] f children are placed on the register unnecessarily it falls into disrepute and becomes of little significance'. [124] The Select Committee itself favours the separate listing of injured children and those at risk. [125]

If a child is categorised as 'at risk' how long should his name remain on the register? The DHSS 1976 letter recommended a built-in procedure to ensure the regular review of cases but its concern was the inclusion of other siblings rather than the exclusion of a recorded name. [126] At root the problem is one of definition: if, for example, the cause of abuse is seen to lie in environmental stress, then children remain at risk for as long as stressful circumstances continue; if, on the other hand, the explanation of violence is to be sought in cultural factors, there is a case for including the whole child population on a register. Ultimately two considerations must be balanced: the civil liberties issue including the effects of labelling, and the question of the effectiveness of a register clogged up with out-of-date information including the possibility that absence of removal procedures may deter professionals from notifying names in the first place. Martel [127] found that in one area names were never to be removed: eight area review committees issued no guidelines and the remaining 10 areas which had registers required all-agency agreement before a name was deleted. The NSPCC procedure commends itself. In cases of suspected injury all agencies concerned complete a quarterly return and, after three clear quarters, removal of the name is automatically considered.

There is also significant variation on what information is kept. Some registers contain a detailed file; others list merely brief facts and the name of the key worker. Neither is there a uniform practice on who has access to the registers or when. The DHSS suggested that, wherever possible, an adult's agreement should be sought to the sharing of information about him with professionals from a different discipline. [128] It seems that care is taken to ensure that information on the registers is given only to legitimate inquirers. Many registers operate a phone-back system. Even so some alarm has been expressed as to the risk of unwarranted stigmatisation. Martel [129] found that in some areas only the name of the key worker was divulged, but in others anything was revealed. She was concerned that in some areas very full details of the child and its background were readily available to approved inquiriers. But six areas (i.e. a third of those surveyed) did not give the police access to information from the register and three denied information to 'teachers'. Some registers are more readily available than others. Both Martel and BASW found that half were available in office hours only. [130] Whilst this reflects resources and manpower problems, if a major function of registers is to facilitate speedy communication when there is the possibility of diagnosing non-accidental injury, 24-hour availability is essential. The House of Commons Select Committee has recommended 24-hour access to registers. [131]

The question as to whether parents should be told is controversial. The DHSS have given no advice. There is no doubt that in law the reports in the register are privileged. [132] But this does not get us very far. In evidence to the House of Commons Select Committee the NSPCC sat on the fence. [133] BASW thought parents should know unless there were very good reasons why they should not. The decision to inform them should, it thought, be taken by the case conference. [134] NCCL has recently come out strongly in favour of telling the parents. [135] The Select Committee's view was that parents should normally be informed and that responsibility for this should rest with the agency making the notification and not with a case conference. [136] The Select Committee was right to think that 'leaving it to the professional consensus is [not] sufficient recognition of the principle . . . enunciated'. [137] Martel found that the majority of the areas in the Family Service Unit survey had no policy at all on the question. Some informed families with all-agency agreement, some left it to the discretion of the key worker, and others informed families if they asked. [138]

Finally, once a child's name is notified to the register what action is taken? It seems obvious that in combination with notification to a register should go intensive preventive work, including, for example, the provision of day care facilities. Of course, registers are relatively cheap whilst preventive activity is expensive both in time and resources. The Family Service Units [139] are pledged to this kind of work and in their survey, reported by Martel, they asked whether constituent agencies on the area review committee had agreed that families on the register should receive priority in the allocation of resources. Three of the 22 committees had no register. Of the rest 6 replied affirmatively and an affirmative answer could be inferred from 6 other replies. But 7 committees, that is nearly a third, had made no decision on this crucial question. [140]

A register is 'not a panacea . . . It is a working tool, not an end in itself, and it can be counter productive if workers are lulled into a false sense of security when a child has been placed on a register'. [141] So wrote the British Association of Social Workers in its memorandum to the Select Committee. Registers are in their infancy and too many important questions have not been satisfactorily answered. Practice is too variable and guidance too indefinite. If the DHSS wants registers, and they have mushroomed under its stimulus, it must face up to the many problems they entail, not least those concerned with bureaucracy, civil liberties and issues of privacy.

Mandatory reporting of child abuse

Legislation requiring the mandatory reporting of child abuse was passed throughout the USA in the 1960s. [142] Eight of the Canadian provinces and the Yukon territory also have mandatory reporting laws, [143] as has South Australia. [144] In the USA the legislation followed swiftly on Kempe's revelations. [145] In Britain there have been calls for a similar system. [146] But the House of Commons Select Committee has not recommended such a system, the influential Tunbridge Wells Study Group reached no decision [147] and Jean Stark's oft-cited article is inconclusive. [148] Whilst conceding that the situation in Britain is not entirely comparable with that in the USA (the existence of the NSPCC, local authority social services departments and area review committees all making it more likely that cases of abuse will surface to attention), it is my view that legislation requiring the medical profession and possibly others to report cases of child abuse to a central register should be considered immediately. A mandatory reporting law is not a panacea. As Paulsen has written: '[r]eporting . . . is not enough. After the report is made, something has to happen . . . No law can be better than its implementation, and implementation can be no better than resources permit'. [149] In legislating for mandatory reporting we can learn much from the experience of other countries, notably the USA.

In the USA a number of legislative models was offered to the states. The most influential was undoubtedly that drawn up in 1963 by the Children's Bureau. It is reproduced as an appendix. [150] It placed on the medical profession a primary duty to report. It was recognised that doctors were failing to alert the community's resources for child protection to suspected cases of child abuse. Some feared civil or criminal liability. Others were 'reluctant to play the role of the "officious intermeddler", particularly when they might have to face angry parents. Some . . . regarded reporting as a breach of the special confidential relationship between physician and patient. Some [did not] report because they did not know to whom to report and had no reason to believe that it would benefit the child'. [151] The case for mandatory, as opposed to permissive, reporting 'rests upon the judgment that the decision to report is not properly a medical matter' but one of 'social policy'. [152]

It is sometimes argued that parents will not seek medical assistance for their injured child because of the fear that they will be reported. This obviously does occur, though with what frequency it is impossible to estimate. Some accidentally injured children will also suffer because of such parental fears. Second, the passing of legislation will not necessarily stimulate doctors into reporting. Silver et al. found that more than half the physicians they questioned did not know the correct procedure to follow in their community. [153] Gil's nationwide survey revealed a net increase of 10.41 per cent in the annual count of reported incidents of physical child abuse from 1967, for many states the first full year of reporting, to 1968, but there were decreases in more states than increases. [154] Third, the passage of mandatory reporting laws is not valuable if, either through absence of will or resources, the families concerned are not given the necessary assistance. But, as Paulsen has commented,

> [o]n balance, mandatory reporting provides a considerable social gain. It will spur some reporting. It protects physicians and reminds them of their professional obligation to assist children in trouble. The number of parents who are willing to risk the life of their child by not seeking medical help is likely to be small . . . Perhaps most important of all, the reporting laws have encouraged reporting by providing an easy, well publicized way of doing it and by encouraging educational projects among physicians in respect to the nature and extent of the problem. [155]

The drafting of reporting legislation raises a number of questions. First, should there be a mandatory duty or permissive power to report? It has been suggested [156] that, in relation to the medical profession, social policy dictates the need for a duty to be imposed. As far as others are concerned the decision must depend on how wide the net is cast. There is always the danger that everybody's duty can become nobody's. Yet in the USA a number of states make the duty to report universal. The case for confining mandatory reporting to doctors and other medical personnel is cogent if it is believed that only they have the knowledge and skill to detect abuse. On the other hand, many professionals are capable of reasonable suspicion and, as it is this state of mind rather than certain knowledge which should be expected of the reporter, a duty to alert the authorities could be imposed on this wider category.

In the USA the case for a permissive law is often put in terms of the immunities granted to the reporter. [157] In this country, whilst the medical profession has to grapple with the problems surrounding ethics of confidentiality, it is clear that the authorities to whom a report would currently be made would not have to disclose the source of their information. [158] A permissive law could not, therefore, be justified on this ground. It might, however, be considered that the imposition of a duty on more peripheral concerns is unnecessarily crude and ultimately a self-defeating strategy. The American Humane Association has, however, argued in favour of 'a universal obligation of all responsible citizens'. [159] On the other hand, it might be thought unnecessary to stipulate, as some American states do, that any person may provide information. Any person may, after all, currently inform social services departments or the NSPCC. But such a specific provision might have considerable symbolic impact and stimulate reporting (some of which would be unfounded or even malicious) by neighbours, relatives, shopkeepers and others connected with the family. There is no reason why, given a move away from punitive reactions, parents should not be encouraged to report themselves. In a number of American states there is provision for self-reporting and the American Bar Association Juvenile Justice Standards Division in its model Child Abuse and Neglect Reporting Law, promulgated in 1975, provides for anonymous self-reporting as a method of directing an abusing parent to a voluntary treatment programme or as a method of getting them in touch with a caseworker or someone to whom they may speak confidentially. [160] In the Netherlands self-referrals to the medical referees are not uncommon. Indeed, in that country abused children and their siblings have been known to make such references. [161]

This raises the question as to which resource to designate for receiving reports of child abuse. This is an important decision for on it hinges the course of action which is to be taken to intervene. In the USA absence in some communities of child protective agencies led to law enforcement officials being designated, as they constituted the only chain of services which was sure to exist and be accessible. This was by no means ideal. For, as Delaney has written, [162] reports should really be made to a 'non-threatening source' and mandatory reporting to the police 'connotes criminal or punitive response rather than a civil or therapeutic one'. He concedes that some abuse is serious enough to invoke the criminal law but argues that the social service agency should be trusted to pass on to the police those cases which merit a criminal prosecution. That reports should go to a child protective agency rather than to the police is undeniable, though a group decision taken by a case conference including a senior police officer as to whether criminal proceedings should be brought is preferable to unilateral action by any agency.

The natural receptacle for reports in England would be the local area review committees. They exist throughout the country, have gained experience in the problem of abuse and co-ordination of services to help the abused child and his family, and have under their aegis both registers and case conferences. There would certainly be no support, outside certain sections of the police force, for designating police authorities as the bodies to whom reports should be made. An alternative to area review committees would be local authority social services departments. As a specialised agency committed to the problem the NSPCC also cannot be ruled out. Another possibility might be to utilise medical personnel along the lines of the Dutch medical referee or confidential doctor. The ultimate choice depends on a consideration of a number of criteria. Which receptacle would maximise reporting? In which body is there greatest confidence? Which body is best geared to stimulate the necessary preventive and supportive steps upon receipt of a report? The answer to each of these questions need not coincide, in which case a choice amongst them would depend upon a balancing of the considerations.

The discovery of child abuse depends very largely on medical practitioners. Having heightened their awareness of the problem, the next step is to ensure the information they have is not suppressed. It is my belief that they would be more likely to report their suspicions to another doctor than to a bureaucratic organisation such as an area review committee or local authority social services department. There is no evidence for this but there is the success of the Dutch confidential doctor scheme to support it. There is also the fact that under the existing social services-oriented case conference the attendance of medical personnel is disappointingly low. [163]

The Dutch system has been described elsewhere. [164] Briefly it uses doctors, usually paediatricians, as go-betweens. There is no system of mandatory reporting in the Netherlands. There are, nevertheless, confidential doctors in 10 major centres of population to whom all are encouraged to report cases of suspected child abuse. Most reports do, in fact, emanate from general practitioners [165] but schools, social welfare departments, the police, as well as relatives, friends and neighbours figure in the statistics as purveyors of information. Once seised of a report the referee gives advice and assistance and, where the family is already known to agencies, co-ordinates. He is also the centre of a recording system and plays an important part in continuing surveillance and after-care. My concern here is not so much with the actual work tasks of the confidential doctors, though these are important, as with the question as to whether such an institution causes more abuse to surface to attention. Doctors, it is suggested, would be more willing to divulge their suspicions to fellow profession-als. The general public also has greater confidence in its doctors than in bureaucracies of local government, though the NSPCC ('the cruelty people') are, with it, an effective conduit. In the Netherlands there is close collaboration between the *Vereniging tegen Kindermishandeling* (the equivalent of our NSPCC) and the confidential doctors, and a similar scheme could doubtless be worked out here.

Of the three criteria set out two (maximisation and confidence) suggest a medical reference point as the source to be designated. The third (preventive and supportive services) requires both a combination of skills suitably co-ordinated and access to resources. No one agency possesses all the skills but there is no reason why the medical profession should not assume the role of 'key worker' guiding case conferences and maintaining registers. This happens in some places already. It is difficult to see the medical profession getting or wanting control over resources to meet the needs of abusing families but this hardly matters so long as a viable relationship is maintained with the social services department. The suggestion that reports should be made to designated medical personnel, probably senior paediatricians, does not mean that the existing structure of area review committee or case conference should be superseded. The reporting of child abuse should, however, make this work more effectively and efficiently.

What should be reported? How should child abuse be defined? The American statutes have been criticised as using language 'laced with ambiguity'. [165] Some have argued for 'no arbitrary limits' on the definition. Daly argued that 'society knows what abuse is, even with-out a specific definition, and may thus approach the problem with the individual characteristics and the best interests of the child as the primary considerations'. [166] Wald, [167] by contrast, has urged careful examination of any decision coercively to limit parental autonomy in raising children. He concedes that 'the clearest case for intervention arises where a child has been physically abused'. It is 'relatively easy to identify', and provides 'concrete standards for intervention to limit intervention based on subjective value judgments'. [168] But mental abuse, emotional neglect, inadequate parenting and sexual abuse all cause definitional problems particularly where there are cultural differences in a pluralistic society. In spite of these obvious difficulties the temptation to limit reporting to serious (a word itself not free from difficulty) physical abuse must be resisted. This book concentrates on abuse; neglect is often a completely different phenomenon. A child merits protection from both and a reporting law must encompass neglect as well as all forms of abuse. The dangers in this must be recognised and guarded against.

A number of other questions must be considered. What should the report contain? Should it be required, for example, to name the person believed to be responsible for the abuse? How should the report be made? The common American practice is to maintain a 'hot-line' to receive oral reports of abuse and to require those persons mandated to report to follow up the telephone report within 48 hours with a written report. What is the position of accidentally caused injuries? Should they be reported too? There is the danger that non-accidental injuries may be missed if accidental ones are not reported. Further, some accidental injuries are caused by parental negligence and, as Paulsen has commented, 'if caretakers are so inattentive that a child is regularly placed in a situation of great risk to his safety, there is an obvious case for public intervention to improve the situation'. [169] On the other hand families deserve protection from state intervention where there is no culpability at all. A further question is how certain the reporter should be before he is required (or encouraged by a permissive law) to report. Most American statutes couch the required state of mind in terms of 'reasonable cause to believe'. A person mandated to report would thus fail in his duty if a reasonable man in similar circumstances would have suspected abuse even though he did not form such a belief. This raises the question of penalties for failure to observe a duty to report. One American commentator thought these (which ranged from fines to short terms of imprisonment) 'unduly harsh' as well as unenforceable and useless. [170] Illinois actually abolished its penalties. [171] On the other hand it has been argued that the existence of penalties makes it easier to report in the presence of parental disfavour, [172] and removes psychological barriers to acting as an informer. [173]

It is regrettable that the House of Commons Select Committee did not consider the pros and cons of introducing reporting legislation in this country. Legislation in the USA has, on the whole, proved useful.

It has not overcome the problem of spiteful reports, or of the legislation itself being abused. The New York Civil Liberties Union recently reported that 45 per cent of complaints from non-professionals were groundless: 'A landlord who wants to get rid of a tenant, a husband who wants to antagonize his wife, a rejected boy friend, and a spiteful neighbour are some of the people who have used the law for their own ends'. [174] Nor have the dangers of undue labelling and stigmatisation been surmounted. Too often, as well, the report has been seen as an end in itself, leading to what Paulsen has called 'case-carrying' [175] rather than case work. But with American mistakes to learn from, and a better institutional structure to start with, given the resources, there is every reason to believe that a mandatory reporting law could work well in Britain.

Notes

[1]   O. Stevenson and P. Parsloe in *Social Work Today*, vol.9, no.4, 1977, p.11.
[2]   Idem, p.15.
[3]   Idem, p.1.
[4]   Idem.
[5]   *The Times*, 12 September 1974.
[6]   *Report of the Care of Children*, Cmd 6922. The events leading up to the establishment of the committee are found in P. Boss, *Exploration into Child Care*, RKP 1971.
[7]   Children Act 1948.
[8]   Curtis regarded this as the ideal substitute (see para. 447).
[9]   Op.cit., note 6, para. 7.
[10] *Post*, p.88, 94.
[11] Ingleby Committee, *Children and Young Persons*, Cmnd 1191, 1960.
[12] Figures quoted in J. Packman, *The Child's Generation*, Blackwell and Robertson, 1975, p.69. See also J. Heywood and M. Allen, *Financial Help in Social Work*, Manchester University Press, 1971; R. Lister and T. Emmett *Under the Safety Net*, CPAG, 1976; and M. Hill and P. Laing, *Money Payments, Social Work and Supplementary Benefits*, University of Bristol, 1978.
[13] J. Packman, op.cit., note 12, p.128.
[14] *Report of the Committee on Local Authority and Allied Personal Social Services*, Cmnd 3703.
[15] Local Authority Social Services Act 1970.

[16] See *Minutes of Select Committee on Violence in the Family*, q.353 *per* David Jones (BASW evidence).

[17] Idem, q.352 *per* Chris Andrews (BASW evidence).

[18] Idem, *per* Sally Beer (BASW evidence).

[19] Idem, q.1 *per* Mrs J. Ross. Derbyshire County Council decided to do so after being recommended so to do by their Inquiry into the Karen Spencer case (1978) (see paras 3.65-3.66).

[20] The result of local government reorganisation.

[21] See M.D.A. Freeman, *The Children Act 1975*, Sweet and Maxwell, 1976, p.v.

[22] *The Finer Report on One-Parent Families*, Cmnd 5629, 1974.

[23] *The Houghton Report*, Cmnd 5107, was the main source of the Children Act 1975.

[24] *Post,* p.87 ff.

[25] See op.cit., note 17, p.233, 234.

[26] Idem, q.1 *per* J.K.H. Anderson.

[27] A point stressed in the DHSS Colwell Report.

[28] See op.cit., note 17, p.227 (memorandum of BASW).

[29] An article in *The Sunday Times*, 8 September 1974 graphically described a day in the life of one social worker.

[30] See Somerset Area Review Committee, *Wayne Brewer Report,* 1977, para 4.19.

[31] *Social Work Today*, no.2, 15 April 1976, p.78.

[32] *First Report from Select Committee on Violence in the Family*, para. 155.

[33] DHSS, *Report of Committee of Inquiry into Provision and Co-ordination of Services to family of John Auckland*, 1975, chs 16-18.

[34] A. Skinner and R. Castle, *78 Battered Children*, NSPCC, 1969, p.20.

[35] *Cf* J. Young, *The Drugtakers*, Paladin, 1971, ch.5.

[36] B. Jordan, 'Is the Client a Fellow Citizen?', *Social Work Today*, vol.6, no.15, 1975.

[37] See note 34.

[38] J. Renvoize, *Children in Danger*, RKP, 1974, chs 4 and 5.

[39] J. Howells, *Remember Maria*, Butterworths, 1974, being the clearest indictment.

[40] DHSS, *Report of Committee of Inquiry into Care and Supervision provided in relation to Maria Colwell*, para. 255.

[41] See *post*, p.95.

[42] See E. Tauber et al., 'Child Ill-treatment as considered by the Italian Criminal and Civil Codes', Paper to International Congress on Child Abuse and Neglect, Geneva 1976.

[43] See M.D.A. Freeman in *Family Law*, vol.7, 1977, p.53.
[44] R.A. Pitcher in C.H. Kempe and R. Helfer, *Helping the Battered Child and his Family*, Lippincott, 1972, p.242.
[45] See M.D.A. Freeman, *The Legal Structure*, Longman, 1974, p.148.
[46] K. Bottomley, *Decisions in the Penal Process*, Robertson, 1973, pp 44-52.
[47] M. Punch and T. Naylor, 'The Police — A Social Service', *New Society*, 17 May 1973, p.358.
[48] *Minutes of Evidence,* q.97.
[49] See *post,* p.184.
[50] *Minutes of Evidence*, p.44.
[51] *Minutes of Evidence*, p.32.
[52] Idem, p.33.
[53] Op.cit., note 44, p.243.
[54] Op.cit., note 51, p.31.
[55] Idem, q.73.
[56] Idem, pp 23, 50.
[57] Idem, p.36.
[58] See R.A. Pitcher, op.cit., note 44, p.244.
[59] H. Davies, *Police Journal*, vol.44, 1971, p.193.
[60] J.H. Arthur et al. *British Medical Journal*, vol.1, 1976, p.1363.
[61] See NSPCC, *At Risk*, RKP, 1976.
[62] See Sheila Martel, *Non Accidental Injury*, FSU, 1977.
[63] See J. Renvoize, *Children in Danger*, RKP, 1974, ch.5.
[64] See H.K. Bevan, *Child Protection and the Law*, University of Hull, 1970.
[65] Select Committee on Violence in the Family, H.C.329, 1976-7, q.825 (Mr Roland Moyle)
[66] A. Forder, *Concepts in Social Administration*, RKP, 1974.
[67] Op.cit., note 65, para. 91.
[68] J. Howells, *Remember Maria*, Butterworths, 1974, p.103.
[69] M. Rein, *Social Policy*, Random House, 1970.
[70] Committee of Inquiry into the Care and Supervision provided in relation to Maria Colwell, HMSO, 1974.
[71] See *Report of Committee of Inquiry into the Provision and Co-ordination of Services to the Family of Auckland*, DHSS, 1975.
[72] Op.cit., note 70, para. 240.
[73] Essex Area Health Authority and Essex County Council, Inquiry into the case of Max Piazzani, 1974, para. 20(c).
[74] Somerset Area Review Committee, *Report of Review Panel in Wayne Brewer Case*, 1977, para. 5.20.

[75] P. Marris and M. Rein, *Dilemmas of Social Reform*, Penguin, 1974.

[76] J. Carter, 'Co-ordination and Child Abuse', *Social Work Service*, no.9, April 1976, p.22.

[77] W. Reid, 'Inter Agency Co-ordination in Delinquency and Control', *Social Service Review*, vol.38, 1964, p.418.

[78] Op.cit., note 76, p.22.

[79] LASSL (74) 13, 22 April 1974.

[80] Earlier guidance was Standing Medical Advisory Committee, *The Battered Baby*, HMSO, June 1970; *An Analysis of Reports*, May 1972; *Report of Tunbridge Wells Study Group*, October 1973.

[81] The expression was first used in LASSL (76) 2, para. 29.

[82] LASSL (76) 2.

[83] J. Pickett in M. Borland (ed.) *Violence in the Family*, Manchester University Press, 1976, ch.4.

[84] J.W. Freeman in DHSS, *Non-Accidental Injury to Children*, HMSO, 1975, ch.7.

[85] Op.cit., note 82, p.1.

[86] Idem, para. 16.

[87] *First Report from Select Committee on Violence in the Family*, HC 329, 1977, para. 107.

[88] Op.cit., note 87, para. 31. We are told that 'urgent consideration is being given by the DHSS and Home Office to ways in which the respective roles of the police and other professions who may participate in case conferences might be clarified'.

[89] Op.cit., note 82, para. 12.

[90] Idem, para. 5.

[91] Idem.

[92] Minutes, p.254.

[93] Op.cit., note 87, para. 100.

[94] S. Martel, *Non-Accidental Injury*, FSU, 1977, p.47 and see Chris Andrews, *Minutes*, q.364.

[95] Op.cit., note 76, p.24.

[96] See T. Tomlinson in M. Borland (ed.) *Violence in the Family*, Manchester University Press, 1976, ch.8.

[97] *The Lancet*, 31 May 1975.

[98] R. Castle, *Case Conferences: a cause for concern?* NSPCC, 1976.

[99] Op.cit., note 62.

[100] Idem, p.48.

[101] *Cf Minutes* , q.363.

[102] Op.cit., note 87, para. 94.

[103] Op.cit., note 98, p.11.

[104] *Minutes*, p.22.
[105] Idem, q.362.
[106] Idem, (Miss Sally Beer).
[107] Op.cit., note 87, para. 119.
[108] LASSL (76) 26; Home Office 179/76.
[109] Op.cit., note 99, p.11.
[110] *Ante*, p.62.
[111] Op.cit., note 88, para. 97.
[111a] There is now a useful discussion of case conferences in the
Portsmouth area in E. Reinach et al., *Non-Accidental Injury to
Children*, Social Services Research and Intelligence Unit, 1978. *Inter
alia*, the question is raised as to whether parents should be invited to
case conferences.
[112] *Post*, p.95.
[113] Standing Medical Advisory Committee, *The Battered Baby*,
HMSO, 1970.
[114] Op.cit., note 79, para. 17.
[115] Idem, para. 23.
[116] Op.cit., note 87, para. 101.
[117] Idem.
[118] Idem.
[119] A. Solnit, 'Child Abuse: the Problem', 2nd World Conference
of the International Society on Family Law, Montreal 1977, p.9.
[120] John Chant, quoted in *Social Work Today*, vol.9, no.4,
20 September 1977, p.2.
[121] BASW, *The Central Child Abuse Register*, BASW, 1978,
summarised in *Social Work Today*, vol.9, no.3, 1977, pp 2 and 5 and
no.4, 1977, p.2.
[122] BASW in *Social Work Today*, vol.9, no.3, 1977, p.5.
[123] Op.cit., note 62, p.53.
[124] *Minutes*, p.228.
[125] Op.cit., note 88, para. 103.
[126] Op.cit., note 82, para. 23 (iv)
[127] Op.cit., note 62, p.51.
[128] LASSL (76) 2, para. 25.
[129] Op.cit., note 62, p.50.
[130] Idem, p.49 and *Social Work Today*, vol.9, no.3, 1977, p.2.
[131] Op.cit., note 87, para. 108.
[132] *Re D.* [1970] 1 WLR 1109.
[133] *Minutes*, q.246.
[134] Idem, 1.356.
[135] P. Hewitt, *Privacy: The Information Gatherers*, NCCL, 1977.

[136] Op.cit., note 87, para. 112.
[137] Idem, para. 111.
[138] Op.cit., note 62, p.52.
[139] For examples see part I of idem.
[140] Idem, p.48.
[141] *Minutes*, p.228 (para. 11).
[142] See M. Paulsen, 'Child Abuse Reporting Laws: The Shape of the Legislation', *Columbia L. Review*, vol.67, 1967, p.1; M. Paulsen, G. Parker and L. Adelman, 'Child Abuse Reporting Laws — Some Legislative History', *Geo. Wash. L. Review*, vol.34, 1966, p.482; A. Sussman, 'Reporting Child Abuse; A Review of the Literature', *Family L.Q.*, vol.8, 1974, p.245.
[143] See Report to House of Commons (Robinson Report), *Child Abuse and Neglect*, Ottawa, 1976, pp 85-7.
[144] Since 1969 (now in Community Welfare Act 1972). According to the Murray Report (1976) very few reports are made. There were only 24 in 1974. New South Wales followed South Australia's example in 1977.
[145] See M. Paulsen, 'The Legal Framework for Child Protection', *Col. L. Review*, vol.66, 1966, pp 679 and 711.
[146] See, for example, NSPCC, *At Risk*, RKP, 1976, p.211; S. Maidment, *Current Legal Problems* (forthcoming 1978).
[147] A. Franklin, *Concerning Child Abuse*, Churchill Livingstone, 1975, p.134.
[148] J. Stark, 'The Battered Child — Does Britain Need a Reporting Law', *Public Law*, vol.48, 1969.
[149] *Per* M. Paulsen, 'Legal Protections against Child Abuse', *Children*, vol.13, 1966, p.48.
[150] *Post*, p.242. See also now Institute of Judicial Administration American Bar Association, Juvenile Justice Standards Project, *Standards Relating to Abuse and Neglect*, Ballinger, 1977.
[151] Op.cit., note 149, p.45.
[152] M. Paulsen, 'Law and Abused Children' in R. Helfer and C.H. Kempe, *The Battered Child* (2nd ed.), University of Chicago Press, 1974, p.162.
[153] L.B. Silver et al., 'Child Abuse Laws — Are They Enough? JAMA, 199, 1967, p.65, reprinted in J. Leavett, *The Battered Child*, General Learning Corporation, 1974, p.101.
[154] D. Gil, *Violence against Children*, Harvard University Press, 1970, p.96 ff.
[155] Op.cit., note 152, p.163.
[156] Idem, p.184.

[157] A. Sussman, 'Reporting Child Abuse', *Family L.Q.*, vol.8, 1974, pp 245, 292-5.

[158] See *D. v. NSPCC* [1978] A.C.171.

[159] American Humane Association, Children's Division, *Child Abuse Legislation*, 1966, p.17.

[160] American Bar Association Juvenile Justice Standards Division Child Abuse and Neglect Reporting Law, p.18. For a proposal that Missouri should provide for and facilitate voluntary self-reporting see K. Krause, *Missouri Law Review*, vol.42, 1977, pp 207 and 267.

[161] See M.D.A. Freeman in *Family Law,* vol.7, 1977, p.53.

[162] J. Delaney, 'New Concepts of a Family Court' in R. Helfer and C.H. Kempe, *Child Abuse and Neglect*, Ballinger, 1976, pp 335, 342.

[163] R. Castle, *Case Conferences: a Cause for Concern?* NSPCC, 1976. See also C. Desborough and O. Stevenson, *Case Conferences*, University of Keele, 1977, pp 18-21.

[164] Op.cit., note 161.

[165] A. Sussman, op.cit., note 142, p.250.

[166] B.L. Daly, 'Willful Child Abuse and State Reporting Statutes', *University of Miami L.R.*, vol.23, 1969, pp 283-4.

[167] M. Wald, 'State Intervention on Behalf of "Neglected" Children: A Search for Realistic Standards' in M. Rosenheim (ed.) *Pursuing Justice for the Child*, University of Chicago Press, 1976, ch.12 (also in *Stanford L. Review*, vol.27, 1975, p.985.)

[168] Idem, p.256.

[169] Op.cit., note 152, p.164.

[170] R.E. Shepherd, *Wash. and Lee L. Review*, vol.22, 1965, pp 182 and 192.

[171] See R. Spiwak, *De Paul L. Review*, vol.15, 1964, pp 453 and 459.

[172] M. Paulsen, op.cit., note 152, p.163.

[173] A.H. McCoid, 'The Battered Child and other Assaults upon the Family', *Minn. L. Review*, vol.50, 1965, pp 1 and 43.

[174] *Family Law Reporter*, vol.2, 1976, p.2203.

[175] M. Paulsen, 'Child Abuse Reporting Laws: The Shape of the Legislation', *Col. L. Review*, vol.67, 1967, pp 1 and 3.

5 Preventing child abuse

The problem of child abuse can be tackled on a number of different levels. Policies directed towards its prevention can be conceptualised as strategies of primary prevention or of intervention. They can be located within the existing structure or view its solution or alleviation within a reconstruction of society. They can be piecemeal or contain more radical blueprints for society. They can rely on professional and administrative measures or they can use political initiatives.

In tandem with the psychopathological model the dominant emphasis in the literature, the writings of Gil and Gelles and one or two others excepted, is on the abusers, on how potential abusers may be predicted and known abusers helped. Only recently has the question been explored as to whether some children are more susceptible to abuse. Even more rarely is it hypothesised that the roots of abuse are embedded within society itself.

It was Richard Light, in one of the best articles on child abuse, who wrote that 'few easy answers exist for reducing the maltreatment of children'. [1] Many programmes utilising a variety of techniques have sought an answer. This chapter considers and questions a few of these. The chapter concludes with some remarks which question whether child abuse is endemic to our society as presently organised and whether we can hope to eliminate the problem within the confines of existing structures.

Can abuse be predicted?

One of the keys to the problem of child abuse is early prediction. We are now only beginning to answer the question as to how to identify the problem early enough for preventive measures to be undertaken. Part of the problem consists in knowing what to identify. Thus Helfer [2] opens an essay with the statement '[u]nusual child rearing practices are manifested in a variety of ways'. This is echoed by Gray et al. who refer to 'abnormal parenting practices'. [3] But does the fact that something is 'unusual' or 'abnormal' necessarily make it pathological so that intervention can be justified? Do we yet know enough of the social profile of abusing families to be able to discriminate adequately between them and non-abusing families? [4]

In the USA predictive screening questionnaires are being developed to identify potential high-risk cases. It is recognised that abusers are not a 'totally homogeneous group' [5] and, therefore, the tendency has been to identify clusters of factors associated with abuse. Thus Schneider, Hoffmeister and Helfer identified six major clusters: 'problems with parents, problems with self-esteem, isolation, expectations of children and reactions to crises'. They assert that the 'single best predictive cluster is the one indicating problems with self-esteem'. [6] Further, 'the single best item for discriminating the known abuses from those high risk parents who are not known to have abused is "When I was a child my parents used severe physical punishment on me"'. [7] From this they draw the conclusion that 'prevention of child abuse in the present is likely to contribute to prevention in the future'. [8]

Predictive studies are also being undertaken at the Park Hospital in Oxford by Margaret Lynch and her colleagues. A three-year study has shown that in the case of abused children there were likely to have been medical problems surrounding their birth (59 per cent of cases as compared with 24 per cent in a control sample); it was likely that concern over the mother's relationship with her baby was written into maternity hospital records (72 per cent against 15 per cent); and the abused child's parents were found to have a series of interlocking and long-term social problems at the time of the child's birth from which there was no likely escape route (90 per cent against 27 per cent). Lynch notes that the medical and social information which can be used for the prevention of child abuse is in many cases already available. But, she adds, 'it cannot be of any use until the professional workers of all the disciplines involved in the care of mother and child feel that they share in the responsibility of identifying and helping families at risk'. [9] A later article by Lynch and Roberts identified signs of bonding failure and warned that '[n] o one isolated factor can be used to predict abuse'. [10] Five factors, however, were significantly more common in the abused group than among their controls: mother aged under 20 at birth of first child; evidence of emotional disturbance including depression, suicide attempts and drug addiction; referral of the family to the hospital social worker; baby's admission to special care unit; and recorded concern by maternity hospital staff over mother's ability to care for her child. Adverse social conditions are also noted though the comment is offered that 'it is the severity of the relationship problems that is most striking'. [11]

Screening has a number of problems. Use of any predictive instrument requires the establishment of careful policies, procedures and safeguards. There are complicated methodological problems

analysed in Light's article. [12] Most significant, however, are a
number of ethical considerations. Is it right to delve into family and
personal life to determine how parents are going to behave towards
their children? In answer to this Helfer states that '[F]ew question
our "right" and responsibility to screen a pregnant woman for tuber-
culosis, high blood pressure or syphilis'. [13] The analogy is
misleading. The medical conditions referred to are relatively value-
free; not so poor child-rearing potential. A causative link between
conditions in the mother and damage to the child can be sustained but
no such link is possible with child abuse; there are too many intervening factors ranging from stress induced by subsequent
unemployment to difficulties encountered in bringing up a child who
is particularly 'hard to love'.

Second, identification through screening may induce a self-
fulfilling prophecy. As Eisenberg has put it: '[t]he behavior of man is
not independent of the theories of human behavior that men adopt'.
[14] The identification of potential behavioural problems may result
in the creation of that very same problem. This, a point made by
Jordan and others, was discussed earlier in the book. [15]

Third, identification is a highly stigmatising act. Once identified as
a potential abuser the removal of this most adhesive of labels is
difficult to accomplish. And there will be false positive test results as
well, though how many one cannot estimate as without the identification it cannot be certain how much abuse there would have been.
Brody and Gaiss [16] are concerned to minimise the emotional
impact of such labelling but every effort must be made to extend
such protection to all acts of identification.

Fourth, a prediction having been made, what happens then? 'The
idea', say Justice and Justice, 'would be not to label parents who fall
into a high-risk category, but to offer them support and guide them
to helpful services'. [17] The forms of support they have in mind
include counselling, the services of a parent aide or homemaker and
courses in parent training and in human needs. Treatment projects in
different settings have shown that prevention is possible. The problem
is that no matter how they are described, and the programmes which
follow a prediction are conceptualised as voluntary assistance, it is
difficult to stop them becoming mandatory and punitive. The
medicalisation of deviance and the growth of the therapeutic state
are familiar phenomena. [18] From this, it is not far to a situation
where a licence is required before one can become a parent. Thus,
Alvin Toffler in *Future Shock* can point to the irony of allowing
parenthood to remain 'the greatest single preserve of the amateur'
[19] and Kempe is convinced that if a licensing law for parenthood

existed, there would be a dramatic reduction in the number of abused and unwanted children. [20] Lord and Weisfeld have argued that for the good of society 'potential parents [should] have at least some rudimentary knowledge and skill in the field of effective parenthood'. [21] They see the licensing of parenthood as a very real possibility — in the 21st or 22nd century. A person who ill-treats a dog may be prohibited from keeping dogs [22] but, apart from the obvious differences, the sanction follows an adjudication upon his conduct. Here, there is merely a prediction based upon supposed character traits, attitudes and background circumstances.

Finally, there is the question as to whether screening programmes are to be voluntary or mandatory and hence routine. Brody and Gaiss point out that 'those who are most at risk may be the last to admit the need for assistance' so that a voluntary programme might have a 'low yield'. [23] They admit that a mandatory programme might be justified if 'concern over the rights of parents is overridden by the need to protect the more essential rights of the child'. [24] It is easier to justify such preventive intervention when actual physical harm or gross neglect can be predicted. But Helfer's concern, and it is not untypical of advocates of screening, is with 'unusual child rearing practices' and he warns of the apparent impossibility of developing a test which predicts specifically physical abuse. [25] 'Psychological harm' is, however, too nebulous and value-laden a concept to serve as a basis for mandatory intervention. Is the increased yield of positive test results worth the infringement of individual liberties involved? Nor should the effect which such supposed violation of civil liberties would have upon confidence in the medical profession be ignored for, if fewer cases of actual abuse were thus brought to its attention, the net result might be worse than it was before screening was conceived. The ultimate yield of a voluntary programme might then exceed that of a mandatory one. Additionally, forcing conscripts to learn parenting skills may prove self-defeating; those who have voluntarily sought screening will be more highly motivated to learn. On balance, at present, voluntary rather than mandatory screening is more readily justifiable. The House of Commons Select Committee which favoured screening [26] gave little attention to the concept or the implications of its proposal.

Working with abusive families

Where once the response to child abuse was to punish the parents and remove and rehabilitate the children, the emphasis is now on comprehensive family-oriented therapy. As Beezley, Martin and Alexander write '[a] consistent and coherent look at the total family must be a part of the therapeutic efforts for both parents and children'. [27] Child abuse, they insist, is 'not a simplistic problem that can be appreciated as a simple illness'. [28] It is 'but the indicator of a dysfunctioning family that brings the child and the entire family' [29] to attention. So, they argue, it is impossible to deal with the dysfunction by only 'preventing the occurrence of one of the symptoms, that is the abuse of a child. [30] What is required is treatment of the underlying causes of the syndrome. 'We must', they claim, 'tend to and offer treatment for *all* the consequences of this situation, not just the medical consequences of the physical trauma'. [31] They emphasise that 'the family must always be considered as a unit'. [32] A number of programmes try to implement these ideals.

One of those is centred on the Park Hospital in Oxford. [33] This contains an in-patient unit which provides residential assessment and treatment for the abused child and his family. The programme incorporates medical, psychiatric, social work and legal expertise. According to Lynch and Ounsted, '[i]n treatable cases medical treatment, practical help and the initiation of ongoing psychotherapy make it possible for . . . troubled families to be rehabilitated without prolonged separations'. [34] Not all families are regarded as treatable: excluded are families where the mother is grossly psychotic or the abuse particularly sadistic — about one in five of families referred come into this category. Between 1972 and 1977, 81 families were admitted to the Unit for actual or threatened abuse. The majority of families admitted stay for between three and six weeks. Before discharge weekends are spent at home and after discharge follow-up and continuing therapy is shared between the hospital and workers in the community. The treatment programme is adapted to meet the needs of each individual family. Much of the treatment is informal psychotherapy. Legal proceedings, usually for a care order, are taken where necessary. According to Lynch and Ounsted, 'an appearance in a juvenile court can act as a useful catharsis. Parents can purge themselves of their guilt openly and feel that they have begun to act as responsible people'. [35]

How effective has the Park's residential therapy been? Eighty per cent of the families between 1973-75 returned home with their children. Several of the rest, after prolonged therapy, had their children returned. In 40 families returning home with their children there has been one serious injury and one death in a brain-damaged child. [36] If this seems a high percentage it should not be forgotten that 132 children died in care in 1976. [37] Many families continued to need support and help in times of crises. But instead of denying this need, which is common, 'it is being asked for and accepted'. [38] The House of Commons Select Committee was most impressed by the work done at the Park Hospital and recommended that it should set an example to other regions. [39]

Similar ideas and ideals are to be found in the sociotherapeutic institute known as De Triangel in Amsterdam. [40] The centre is a 'hostel' for problem families. Whilst its admissions are not restricted to families where there has been ill-treatment of children, such families figure prominently in the centre. Child abuse is seen as a crisis point in a disturbed family life rather than as a phenomenon in itself. De Triangel is large and can take up to 20 families at a time. There is a large staff which works with each family member as an individual and as a member of their total family unit. Close links have been forged with the medical referee [41] of Amsterdam. Families may stay in residence for up to six months. The therapy provided emphasises family living. The goal is restoration of a normal family life. 'The principal implicit purpose of the group process is', according to Rob van Rees, one of the organisers of the Institute, 'the creation of a climate, in which possibilities may arise for an unprejudiced acceptance of the "self" and "the other"'. [42] The scheme is a highly-praised one though no information as to its success is available. [43]

Both these projects utilise therapeutic techniques in efforts to reconstruct the family. Specific therapeutic attention is given to children as well as parents. A psychopathological model [44] is assumed and professional skills used.

Relieving families of pressure

A major cause of child abuse is environmental stress. [45] The House of Commons Select Committee saw 'the reduction of stress' [46] as the theme running through all its proposals on preventive work. It is argued in the last section of this chapter that their proposals do not get to the real roots of the stresses they identify.

The Committee stressed the importance of education for parenthood. [47] Light, however, has shown that, whilst this is an excellent idea in its own right, it has not been demonstrated that it influences decisively the effects of abuse. Widespread family planning education, however, might be more effective in preventing child maltreatment. [48] No proposals were made in this direction.

The House of Commons Committee also recommends that every

effort be made to ensure adequate facilities for care of the under-fives. It emphasises the importance of mother and toddler clubs, pre-school playgroups, day care centres and day nurseries and child-minding facilities. Current provision of all these is inadequate and the Committee's recommendation must be strongly endorsed. [49] It stressed also how '[p]eriods in temporary care [are] often extremely important, providing as they do an escape hatch for a parent to use to leave the child for a period of hours for shared care when tension gets too high'. [50] The NSPCC Denver House nursery was praised for doing just this. [51] Again, the importance of crisis nurseries cannot be underestimated.

The Committee also endorsed the concept of Parents Anonymous. [52] This originated in the USA, where it now has over 150 chapters and 1,500 members, and is spreading to this country. They are self-help groups stimulated by the recognition that many abusive parents have a basic distrust of authority figures and feel more comfortable telling their problems to people who are or have been in the same predicament. 'Parents change their behavior by modeling themselves after others in the group who have proved that it is possible to stop inflicting violence on children'. [53] What the Select Committee called 'substitute grannies' [54] also received its support. In the USA the terms 'parent aide' or 'mothering aide' are commonly used. He or she goes into the home of an abusing family and establishes a caring relationship.

A final but all-important producer of stress, referred to by the House of Commons Select Committee, is inadequate housing. It can, the Committee noted, 'turn difficult but normal circumstances of child upbringing into almost impossible ones'. [55] The Committee saw social isolation caused by the break-up of the extended family as the key factor. It recommended that local authorities be encouraged to make provision for housing young people in the areas in which they had grown up. [56] Like the Finer Report on One-Parent Families, [57] it urged that discrimination against lone parents in the allocation of council houses on the grounds that they are 'less deserving' than others should cease. [58] Both these proposals are to be supported. Anything which improves housing conditions or relieves unemployment is likely to alleviate the problem of child abuse.

Receiving children into care

An earlier chapter discussed the provisions which exist for taking children in care. Children may also be voluntarily received into care under an administrative procedure laid down in the Children Act 1948. [59] There are 100,000 children in care in England and Wales. Of the 51,590 who came into care during the 12 months ending on 31 March 1975, 12,660 were received because of the short-term illness of a parent or guardian and another 4,930 because of unsatisfactory home conditions; homelessness accounted for another 1,664 and unmarried mothers unable to provide accounted for a further 1,814. [60]

The Children Act 1948 s.1 imposes a duty on a local authority to receive a child into care where it appears to it that (a) the child has neither parent nor guardian or has been and remains abandoned by his parents or guardians or is lost or (b) his parents or guardian are, for the time being or permanently, prevented by reason of mental or bodily disease or infirmity or other incapacity or any other circumstance from providing for his proper accommodation, maintenance and upbringing and in either case, that its intervention is necessary in the interests of the welfare of the child. Children once received into care may be boarded out with foster parents or placed in children's homes. [61] Most children received into care remain for a short time though many stay for long or indefinite periods.

The existence of the institution of voluntary reception into care is important. It enables the parent living in stressful circumstances to be relieved of the additional responsibility of coping with children who, given their parents' circumstances, may be in real danger of being abused. The voluntary nature of the reception must be emphasised. Section 1(3) states that '[n]othing in this section shall authorise a local authority to keep a child in their care . . . if any parent or guardian desires to take over the care of the child . . . '. [62] However, where a child has been in care for six months a minimum of 28 days' notice of intention to remove must be given to the local authority. This provision, in s.56 of the Children Act 1975, followed the Houghton Report argument that 'a sudden move, without preparation, can be damaging to the child and may have long-term repercussions'. [63] The provision itself may prove harmful if, to avoid it, the return of children is requested by parents who are not in a fit state to resume care. The 1975 Act also increases the powers of a local authority to assume parental rights in respect of a child in its care [64] and strengthens the hands of foster parents both against the parents and the local authority. [65] This may lead to parents' reluctance to part with their children for fear of losing parental rights over them in circumstances where it would be beneficial for the children to be admitted to care. It is probable that private fostering, over which the community has much less control, will increase. [66]

Local authorities are authorised by s.1 of the Children and Young Persons Act 1963 to try to prevent family breakdown and the reception of children into care by means of casework and, if necessary, assistance in kind, for example, food, clothing, furniture, or, in exceptional circumstances, in cash in the form of grants, loans, rent guarantees etc. Social services departments have been given 'enormous power over clients . . . [Their] brokering activities . . . give them the power to do things that clients want'. [67] Seebohm was 'impressed by the amount of preventive work amongst families accomplished since the CYPA 1963'. [68] Others see 'absence of precise eligibility rules, the apparent arbitrariness of decisions . . . the stigma imposed', the uneven distribution of expenditure by local authorities, and the uneasy relationship with the Supplementary Benefits Commission as having deleterious effects. [69] There is no doubt, though, that helping parents to manage their children is preferable to receiving them or admitting them into care under a court order.

Are some children more liable to abuse?

Until recently the assumption in the literature appeared to be that the child played a passive role in abuse. [70] The evidence now suggests that certain children may be most at risk. [71] No one characteristic can be isolated as a predisposing factor but certain features do recur with a frequency which suggests that children who possess them are more likely to be subjected to abuse.

There is some evidence of an association between prematurity and low birth-weight on the one hand and abuse on the other. There are two ways of trying to explain this relationship as causal. One suggestion is that their frailty requires more sensitive mothering and that this may not be forthcoming where the baby is less attractive physically and less responsive. A further consideration is that such children may spend a long time in special care units and this may interfere with 'imprinting'. [72] Margaret Lynch has compared the early life histories of 25 abused children with those of their non-abused siblings. She found disproportionately high rates in the abused group of abnormal pregnancy, abnormal labour, neonatal separation as well as other separation in the first six months, and illness during the child's first year of life either of the child or the mother. Thus, in 21 of the 25 cases of abuse either the mother or child had been ill during that first year and in 6 cases both had suffered from ill-health. Lynch accordingly emphasises 'bonding failure'. [73]

116

Several researchers have reported a high incidence of mental retardation among abused and neglected children. [74] But, as Friedrich and Boriskin write, 'the complexity of the phenomenon and the large number of interacting variables make any position as to cause and effect most tenuous'. [75] Brain damage resulting from battering may well be a primary factor in the finding of increased frequency of mental retardation among abused children. Again, there is some evidence of an association between physical handicap and abuse. [76] Birrell and Birrell found congenital physical abnormalities in 11 cases out of 42 they studied. [77] The finding is an isolated one; other research results, whilst pointing to physical handicap, cannot substantiate that the abnormalities in question were congenital or occurred before the abuse. [78] References in research findings are also made to 'difficult' children; children who are 'slow-to-warm up' or moody or hyperactive may, it seems, be more prone to abuse than more 'normal' children. [79] Korner's conclusion seems apposite: 'there is more than one way of providing good child care; . . . the only way to do so is to respond flexibly to . . . each and every child'. [80]

The part which the child himself plays in his abuse is not yet understood. [81] It is clear, however, that a two-way process is involved, and an understanding of this and further research into factors which make it more likely that some children will be abused rather than others are necessary preconditions for any effective strategy of prevention.

Can child abuse ever be eliminated?

There are strong taboos and legal sanctions against adults assaulting their neighbours. Physical force against children is not only not prohibited but is even encouraged in specified circumstances. Gil suggests four reasons for this marked difference. [82] First, adults are stronger than children so that in terms of the survival needs of adults there has never existed a compelling necessity for the development of sanctions against the use of physical force by adults against children. Second, children were long regarded as the property of their parents (more properly their fathers). This concept has not entirely vanished. Third, the fact that parents are allocated primary socialisation functions cannot be discounted, for the socialisation function is 'invariably structured in a manner that bestows dominant status, rights and power upon the adult, and subordinate status and minimal rights and power upon the child'. [83] Fourth, force is seen as a legitimate means for attaining ends, particularly in 'imbalanced, interpersonal relationships, such as master-slave, male-female, guard-prisoner, and adult-child'. [84]   This goes some way towards explaining wife abuse as well.   Can abuse ever be eliminated so long as adults may assault children?

English law at present permits reasonable physical chastisement by parents, teachers and others having 'lawful control or charge of a child'. [85]   In the USA Stark and McEvoy found that at least 93 per cent of all parents spanked their children [86] and Straus and Steinmetz show that, as late as the last year in high school, about half of the students experienced physical punishment or threats of it. [87] The Newsons' Nottingham studies show that 62 per cent of Nottingham babies had been smacked by the time they were one year old: [88] by the time they were four [89] 97 per cent had been spanked, some with canes, straps, slippers or wooden spoons but mostly with parental hands on their legs and backsides.   Seven per cent of mothers smacked more than once a day and 68 per cent between once per week and once per day.   They quote a packer's wife as saying: 'on average, he gets the stick about three times a week' and in answer to a prompt as to whether she also used her hand: '[Y]es oh very often; every time he passes me, I'm helping him on his way!' [90]   Class I and II mothers were on the whole less prepared to smack and Class V mothers were inclined to do so.   This difference was most marked when the 'offence' was genital play: 5 per cent in the professional and managerial group would punish this, whereas 48 per cent in the unskilled group would. [91]

The House of Commons Select Committee did not question the use of corporal punishment.   Its Canadian counterpart [92] looked into the problem but refused to recommend the abolition of physical punishment.   The American Supreme Court has recently upheld its constitutionality. [93]   In Nottinghamshire children's homes the cane has just been reintroduced: physically handicapped and psychologic-ally disturbed children are not to be exempted; nor are girls. [94]   In Newcastle the education committee has just taken the decision to increase the weight of the leather strap used to punish children in its schools. [95]   Gil's view that 'educational philosophies tend to reflect a social order and are not its primary shapers' is persuasive.   He continues:

> [E]ducation tends to recreate a society in its existing image, or to maintain its relative status quo, but it rarely if ever creates new social structures.   Violence against children in rearing them may thus be a functional aspect of socialization

into a highly competitive and often violent society, one that puts a premium on the uninhibited pursuit of self-interest and that does not put into practice the philosophy of human cooperativeness which it preaches on ceremonial occasions and which is upheld in its ideological expressions and symbols. [96]

Much abuse of children is the result of corporal punishment gone wrong; either the consequence of deliberate action causing more harm than was intended or the product of loss of self-control. But in reality it is the action and not its consequences which should be regarded as abusive. It would not be easy to abolish corporal punishment of children nor can we assume that enactment of legislation would affect parenting practices. And there are punishments more harmful and humiliating than a spanking. But it is difficult to see how the evil of physical abuse of children can be rooted out so long as certain physical attacks on children are regarded as proper. Parliament must take a lead and abolish corporal punishment in schools, community homes and other institutions where it still exists. This would symbolise society's rejection of violence against children. A programme of public education could at the same time make parents aware of the dangers of hitting children and of alternative educational measures. It may take several generations before corporal punishment begins to disappear but at least a start would have been made to direct society away from using violence as a means of socialising children.

Our cultural definitions of childhood and acceptable uses of force are in part the explanation of child abuse. Another of the causes is, as we have seen, environmental stress. The two often go hand in glove. It is in stressful circumstances that adults, who have learned that violence against children is legitimate, abuse their children or those in their care. It is not surprising that child abuse has come to be associated with poverty for it is the 'multi-faceted deprivations of poverty and its correlates, high density in ever-crowded, dilapidated, inadequately served neighborhoods, large numbers of children, especially in one-parent, mainly female-headed households; and the absence of child care alternatives' [97] which are major causes of stress in our society. To this Gil adds 'the alienating circumstances in most work places' [98] caused by 'competitive and exploitative human relations . . . and its hierarchical and authoritarian structures'. Violence against children or against a spouse becomes a way of discharging the pressure built up, as does alcoholism, drug addiction and various other forms of deviance. Work alienation is a serious problem; it must not, however, be assumed to exist only in capitalistic societies, any more than child abuse itself. Further steps towards the elimination of child abuse lie then in the removal of the culture associated with poverty and in improving work conditions and finding an economic system where work alienation is minimised.

Gil's thesis does not ignore the fact that some abusers may be psychologically disturbed. 'To the extent', he argues, 'that psychopathology is not rooted in genetic and biochemical processes, it derives from the totality of life experiences of the individual, which are shaped by continuous interactions between the person and his social setting'. [99] Further, the symptoms of disturbance are but 'exaggerated or negated forms' [100] of normal behaviour. Were physical force not sanctioned, he argues, 'intrapsychic conflicts and psychopathology would less often be expressed through violence against children'. [101] So the root of the problem is once again a culture which regards physical attacks on children as legitimate.

Gil's programme is one for the reconstruction of society. There is no doubt that in a more just, egalitarian humane social order the amount of child abuse would be minimised but there is even less doubt that such a society will not be achieved in the foreseeable future. Child abuse will be with us for a long time yet.

Notes

[1]   R. Light, 'Abused and Neglected Children in America: A Study of Alternative Policies' in *Harvard Educational Review* reprint, *The Rights of Children*, 1974, pp 198, 237.
[2]   R. Helfer in R. Helfer and C.H. Kempe (eds), *Child Abuse and Neglect*, Ballinger, 1976, p.363.
[3]   J.L. Gray et al., 'Perinatal Assessment of Mother-Baby Interaction' in idem, pp 377, 387.
[4]   *Cf* R. Light, op.cit., note 1.
[5]   *Per* C. Schneider et al., 'The Predictive Questionnaire: A Preliminary Report' in C.H. Kempe and R. Helfer (eds), *Helping the Battered Child and his Family*, Lippincott, 1972, p.271.
[6]   'A Predictive Screening Questionnaire for Potential Problems in Mother-Child Interaction' in op.cit., note 2, pp 393, 405.
[7]   Idem.
[8]   Idem.
[9]   M. Lynch, 'Child Abuse — The Critical Path', *Journal of Maternal and Child Health*, July 1976, p.25.
[10] M. Lynch and J. Roberts, 'Predicting Child Abuse: Signs of Bonding Failure in the Maternity Hospital', *British Medical Journal*,

vol.1, 1977, pp 624-5.

[11] Idem.

[12] Op.cit., note 1.

[13] Op.cit., note 2, p.366.

[14] L. Eisenberg, 'On Humanizing of Human Nature', *Impact of Science on Society*, vol.23, 1973, p.213.

[15] *Ante*, pp 80-1.

[16] H.L. Brody and B. Gaiss, 'Ethical Issues in Early Identification and Prevention of Unusual Child Practices' in op.cit., note 2, p.372.

[17] B. Justice and R. Justice, *The Abusing Family*, Human Sciences Press, 1976, p.244.

[18] *Cf ante* p.13.

[19] Alvin Toffler, *Future Shock*, Bodley Head, 1970, p.216.

[20] C.H. Kempe, 'A Practical Approach to the Protection of the Abused Child', *Paediatrics*, vol.51, 1973, p.805.

[21] E. Lord and D. Weisfeld, 'The Abused Child' in A.R. Roberts (ed.) *Childhood Deprivation*, Thomas, 1974, p.80.

[22] Protection of Animals Act 1911 s.3.

[23] Op.cit., note 16, p.373.

[24] Idem, p.374.

[25] Op.cit., note 2.

[26] *First Report from Select Committee on Violence in the Family*, 1977, p.329-i.

[27] P. Beezley et al., 'Comprehensive Family Oriented Therapy' in op.cit., note 2, p.169.

[28] Idem, p.182.

[29] Idem.

[30] Idem.

[31] Idem.

[32] Idem, p.194.

[33] On which see M. Lynch, et al., 'Family Unit in a Children's Psychiatric Hospital', *British Medical Journal*, 1975, vol.2, p.127.

[34] M. Lynch and C. Ounsted, 'Residential Therapy — A Place of Safety' in R. Helfer and C.H. Kempe (eds), *Child Abuse and Neglect*, Ballinger, 1976, p.206.

[35] Idem, p.205.

[36] Idem.

[37] HC, *Written Answers*, January 1978.

[38] Op.cit., note 34, p.206.

[39] *Report on Violence in the Family 1976-77*, para. 140.

[40] On which see Rob van Rees, 'Five Years of Experience with Child Abuse as a Symptom of Family Problems', 1977.

[41] *Cf ante*, p.98-9.
[42] Op.cit., note 40.
[43] A third example is the Parents' Centre Project for the Study and Prevention of Child Abuse in Brighton, Massachusetts. On which see R. Galdston, 'Preventing the Abuse of Little Children', *American Journal of Orthopsychiatry*, vol.45, 1975, p.372.
[44] *Cf ante*, p.21.
[45] *Cf ante*, p.27.
[46] Op.cit., note 39, para. 55.
[47] Idem, para. 60.
[48] R. Light, 'Abused and Neglected Children in America: A Study of Alternative Policies' in Harvard Educational Reprint, *The Rights of Children*, 1974, pp 214-7.
[49] Op.cit., note 39, paras 69-79.
[50] Idem.
[51] Idem, para. 50.
[52] See C.H. Kempe and R. Helfer, *Helping the Battered Child and his Family*, Lippincott, 1972, pp 48-53 and B. and R. Justice, *The Abusing Family*, Human Sciences Press, 1976, pp 204-9.
[53] *Per* B. Justice and R. Justice, op.cit., note 52, p.204.
[54] Op.cit., note 39, para. 74.
[55] Idem, para. 80.
[56] Idem, para. 81.
[57] *Finer Report on One-Parent Families*, Cmnd 5629, 6. 70.
[58] Op.cit., note 39, para. 82.
[59] Children Act 1948 s.1.
[60] *Children in Care in England and Wales*, HMSO, 1976.
[61] The local authority's duty is to give 'first consideration' to the welfare of the child (Children Act 1975 s.59).
[62] This is clear despite judicial dicta to the contrary. See *Bawden* v. *Bawden* (1976) 6 Fam Law 79, *Johns* v. *Jones* (1978) 8 Fam Law 139.
[63] *Houghton Report*, Cmnd 5107, para. 152.
[64] Children Act 1975 s.57.
[65] ss 29, 33, 41.
[66] See M.D.A. Freeman, *The Children Act 1975*, Sweet and Maxwell, 1976, Introduction.
[67] *Per* J. Handler, 'The Coercive Social Worker', *New Society*, 3 October 1968, pp 485, 487.
[68] *Report of Committee on Local Authority and Allied Personal Social Services*, Cmnd 3703, 1968, para. 430.
[69] *Per* J. Heywood and M. Allen, *Financial Help in Social Work*, Manchester University Press, 1971, p.71. See also B. Jordan, *Poor Parents*, RKP, 1974, pp 86-7.

[70] Probably as much as anything due to the emphasis on parental psychopathology and refusal to take cognisance of interactional patterns involved. See R. Gelles, 'The Social Construction of Child Abuse', *American Journal of Orthopsychiatry*, vol.45, 1975, p.363.

[71] See, for example, A. Sangrund et al., in *American Journal of Mental Deficiency*, vol.79, 1974, p.327; R. Helfer, *The Diagnostic Process and Treatment Programs*, Office of Child Development, 1975.

[72] M. Jobling, *The Abused Child*, NCB, 1976, p.6.

[73] M. Lynch, 'Ill-Health and Child Abuse', *The Lancet*, no.7929, pp 317-9.

[74] E.g. C. Morse et al., 'A Three Year Follow-Up of Abused and Neglected Children', *American Journal Dis. Childhood*, vol.120, p.439.

[75] W.N. Friedrich and J.A. Boriskin, 'The Role of the Child in Abuse', *American Journal of Orthopsychiatry*, vol.46, 1976, pp 580, 583.

[76] B. Johnson and H. Morse, 'Injured Children and their Parents', *Children*, vol.15, 1968, p.147.

[77] R.G. Birrell and J.H.W. Birrell, 'The Maltreatment Syndrome in Children', *Medical Journal of Australia*, vol.2, 1968, p.1023.

[78] See M. Baron et al., 'Neurologic Manifestations of the Battered Child Syndrome', *Paediatrics*, vol.45, 1970, p.1003.

[79] See M. Herbert and D. Iwaniec in *New Society*, 21 April 1977, p.111; I.D. Milowe and R.S. Lourie in *Journal of Paediatrics*, vol.65, 1964, p.1079; H. Schaffer and P. Emerson in *Journal of Child Psychology and Psychiatry*, vol.5, 1964, p.1.

[80] A. Korner, 'Individual Differences at Birth', *American Journal of Orthopsychiatry*, vol.41, 1971, pp 608, 617.

[81] A good review of current knowledge is op.cit., note 75.

[82] *Per* D. Gil, *Violence Against Children*, Harvard University Press, 1970, pp 10-11.

[83] Idem, p.11.

[84] D. Gil, 'Unraveling Child Abuse', *American Journal of Orthopsychiatry*, vol.45, 1975, pp 346, 351.

[85] *Ante*, p.45. See CYPA 1933 s.1(7).

[86] R. Stark and J. McEvoy 'Middle Class Violence', *Psychology Today*, vol.4, 1970, p.52.

[87] See S. Steinmetz and M. Straus, *Violence in the Family*, Dodd, Mead, 1974, pp 159, 166.

[88] J. and E. Newson, *Infant Care in an Urban Community*, Allen and Unwin, 1963.

[89] J. and E. Newson, *Four Years Old in an Urban Community*, Allen and Unwin, 1968 (Penguin 1970).

[90] Idem, p.442 (Penguin edition).

[91] Idem, pp 375-83. By the time they are seven 22 per cent have received corporal punishment via some implement and a further 53 per cent have been threatened with this. Classes I and II are less likely to threaten but just as likely as other groups to use an implement. Middle-class parents favour a cane; working-class a strap or belt. See J. and E. Newson, *Seven Years Old in the Home Environment*, Allen and Unwin, 1976 (Penguin edition 1978, pp 352-3).

[92] The Robinson Committee, *Child Abuse and Neglect*, House of Commons, Ottawa, 1976, p.18.

[93] *Ingraham* v. *Wright*, 430 U.S.651 (1977). A case challenging the use of a tawse in Scotland is being taken to the European Court on Human Rights.

[94] *Social Work Today*, vol.9, no.12. It is arguable that the use of a cane in a community home is contrary to s.59 of the Children Act 1975. (*Cf* C. Andrews in *Social Work Today*, vol.9, no.15, 1977, p.1). The Secretary of State for Social Services has now let all directors of social services know that he believes the use of corporal punishment in community homes to be undesirable and improper in a professional caring relationship. (*Social Work Today*, vol.9, no.44, 1978, p.2).

[95] *The Times*, August 1977.

[96] Op.cit., note 87, p.142.

[97] Idem, p.352.

[98] Idem.

[99] Idem, p.353.

[100] Idem.

[101] Idem.

PART II

WIFE ABUSE

6 Battered wives

The second part of this book is about the problem of women
physically ill-treated by the men with whom they live. Man's pro-
verbial inhumanity to man is matched only by his inhumanity to
wife. Nor is the problem confined to wives; the absence of a wedding
ring is no safeguard against brutal assault, and women are battered
by men with whom they cohabit as well as by their former husbands.
Further, the violence is not all one way for, as is now becoming clear
from recent American research, [1] husbands are battered as well.
This phenomenon is discussed in a later chapter. It cannot be underestimated, though the real problem is the violence perpetrated against
women in the domestic setting.

In discussing this problem reference is made to 'wives'. Unless
otherwise stated this must be taken to refer to cohabitees as well.
The law may distinguish their situation (though increasingly it
assimilates it to that of wives [2]); the problem is basically the same.
If anything the plight of cohabitees is worse than wives.

What is a battered wife?

A definition of what constitutes a battered wife is not easy. The
term lacks a precise meaning and much depends on individual interpretations. A useful starting place is Jack Ashley's speech in moving
the Battered Wives (Rights to Possession of Matrimonial Home) Bill
in 1975. He distinguished 'normal domestic disputes' from 'real
domestic brutality'. He gave examples of 'real brutality': 'pregnant
women being kicked, or women being beaten and even burned; the
breaking of bones and the crushing of spirits'. [3] The problem is
graphically portrayed in Erin Pizzey's *Scream Quietly or the
Neighbours will Hear* [4] and is documented in great detail in the
Minutes of Evidence of the House of Commons Select Committee on
Violence in Marriage. [5] Tales are told of 'a level of violence parallel
only to that of torture'. [6] The violence perpetrated on women in
the domestic situation is said to be 'severe and sustained'. [7]
According to Gayford, it may involve 'punching with the closed fist'
or 'at the worst attacks with broken bottles, knives and shootings'.
[8] Abuse may, of course, involve emotional assault as well as
physical attack. Though important, this is not the central concern of

this book. For my purposes a battered wife is a wife or cohabitee who has suffered persistent or serious physical assault at the hands of her partner.

Discoveries of the problem

If child abuse was 'discovered' in the 1960s, then wife battering seems to have emerged as a problem a decade later. Violence against women has however always been with us. Only rarely is the objective condition interpreted as a problem worthy of attention.

One of the earliest reported cases concerns Margaret Neffeld of York who, in 1395, produced witnesses before an ecclesiastical court to show that her husband had once attacked her with a knife, forcing her to flee into the street 'wailing and in tears'. On another occasion he had set upon her with a dagger, wounding her in the arm and breaking one of her bones. He claimed that whatever he had done was solely for the purpose of 'reducing her from errors'. The court held that no cause for divorce *a mensa et thoro* (what we should call judicial separation) had been made out; the couple were compelled to continue to live together. [9] Though many centuries old many of the features of this case have recurred through history.

Violence against women is largely to be explained in terms of the subordinate position they occupy in society. For this reason it is hardly surprising that the problem of violence against women tend to be perceived as a problem in periods when there is an active feminist movement.

Striking parallels to current interest are to be found in the latter half of the 19th century. This was the period of John Stuart Mill, Caroline Norton, Frances Power Cobbe and the beginning of the Suffragette movement. The position of women was far worse than it is today. The early reformers saw the problem as the product of the degradation of working-class life (husbands wanted to return home to 'a comfortable arm chair, a singing kettle, a tidied room' [10]) and the unequal legal status of wives. So social reform to improve the material conditions of existence, legal reform to remove inequalities and legal remedies to deal with men who, for pathological reasons, persisted in brutal attacks on their wives would, so they thought, eliminate the problem. What they failed to understand is that violence is endemic in any society which treats women as unequal. The removal of formal legal inequalities is a step in the right direction but it is only a step. The improvement of material conditions ignores the undoubted fact that violence against wives exists in all strata of society. This was not understood by 19th century reformers whose efforts were concerned with finding a way of protecting working-class wives.

In the 1870s there was considerable anxiety about the prevalence of violence, especially in the case of men against their wives, in such areas as Liverpool's 'Kicking District'. [11] How was the problem to be tackled? Stiffer penalties had been introduced in 1853 (Henry Fitzroy on that occasion had asked for defenceless women to be given the same protection as 'poodle dogs and donkeys' [12]). The judges now favoured flogging. [13] This was used in Maryland [14] (indeed, it was only finally abolished in 1953). But Frances Power Cobbe rejected this expedient. 'After they had undergone such chastisement, however well merited, the ruffians would inevitably return more brutalised and infuriated than ever; and again have their wives at their mercy.' [15] Instead, in her pamphlet *Wife Torture in England*, published in April 1878, she argued for the concept of the separation order and for jurisdiction to be granted to magistrates' courts. [16]

The pamphlet had immediate effect and the Matrimonial Causes Act 1878 gave magistrates' courts the power to grant a separation order with maintenace to a wife whose husband had been convicted of aggravated assault upon her 'if satisfied that the future safety of the wife [was] in peril'. The proviso was removed in 1895. [17]

Little more is heard of violence against wives until the problem re-emerged recently. Certainly the facilities of the magistrates' courts were used extensively. But the problem had not been solved and violence against wives has continued from that day until this.

As ever solutions depend on how a problem is perceived. Today there are a number of interpretations. The dominant explanation is well represented in the writings of Erin Pizzey, [18] whose pioneering work at Chiswick has done more than anything to publicise the plight of the battered woman and sensitise public conscience to it. But, seeing the problem in terms of the pathology of the men concerned (and sometimes the women as well), she individualises a problem which is embedded in the social structure. [19] Her emphasis on refuges is important, and they undoubtedly alleviate the problem, but they are no more likely to solve it than were separation orders a hundred years ago. Pizzey has been extremely influential but she was speaking to an audience already softened up by the Women's Movement. [20]

The existence of a strong Women's Movement, its involvement in the National Women's Aid Federation and its insistence on redefining the position of women in society and removing those factors which make women powerless against male violence, offers greater hope that the problem can eventually be conquered.

The extent of the problem

How much violence is perpetrated by men on the women with whom they live? We do not know. Our knowledge is so scanty that there is no way of determining whether it occurs more now than it did in past ages or whether it is more common in England than in societies with different economic or cultural bases. Jalna Hanmer has written that 'the use of force and its threat . . . is of sufficient importance in our own western industrialised society to be recognised as a major component in the social control of women by men'. [21] And so it is. But does it occur less frequently in non-industrialised societies or outside the West? We have no evidence one way or the other, but it may be doubted.

We do have some statistics but these tell us what the police and courts do, [22] not the incidence of violent behaviour. It is certain that only a small percentage of incidents reaches the attention of the police anyway. Much domestic violence does not come to attention as various disavowal techniques are employed to keep it 'in the family'. [23] It may be normalised or denied or its seriousness may be attenuated. [24] The victim-wife may protect her battering husband from societal intervention in much the same way as alcoholism and mental illness and other phenomena of deviance are screened off. [25] This is not surprising given known police attitudes which favour non-intervention [26] and given the serious potential consequences should intervention take place. So cases reported to the police represent only the tip of the iceberg and the great majority of assaults on wives do not appear in any official records.

The Criminal Statistics [27] themselves are deficient in that they do not provide data on the sex of the victim except for homicide. The victim's sex is not distinguished in the category 'violence against persons'. We know that a woman is more likely to be killed by someone she knows than a total stranger. [28] This applies to rape as well [29] and probably to other crimes of violence. There is some evidence that, as the degree of violence decreases, the percentage of strangers committing the offence goes up. [30] McClintock, in a study in London, accounted for 30 per cent of homicides as domestic disputes. [31] Similar evidence is available from Detroit [32] and Chicago [33] and from the USA as a whole, [34] as well as from Portugal, [35] Denmark [36] and Eire. [37]

Patterns of assault are similar to those of homicide. This is shown in Pittman and Handy's study of aggravated assault in St Louis, where a husband or wife was the victim in 11 per cent of such assaults, [38] in Pokorny's research [39] and most notably in the findings of Dobash and Dobash. [40] They examined the offences reported to police departments in Edinburgh and one district in Glasgow in 1974 which were prepared for and/or dealt with by the courts. Less than 10 per cent of such reports concerned violence of any sort but of the reports about violence 34.5 per cent involved family members and of these cases (a total of 1,044) wife assault and alleged wife assault accounted for 75.77 per cent (759 cases of wife assault and 32 of alleged wife assault). There were 12 reports of husband assault and 6 of mutual assault. Of non-family violence only 13 per cent was directed by men against women thus lending substance to the view that to marry or cohabit is to court the risk of physical abuse.

A study conducted at ten Metropolitan Police stations over a three-month period in 1974 revealed 89 cases of wife battering reported to the police. If the same pattern was reported throughout the Metropolitan Police District this would mean a total of 6,336 cases a year, if these stations were representative. [41] We have also been informed that about 65-70 per cent of all homicides known to the police occur in the domestic situation. [42] Further, 'a recent survey carried out in a city centre division of one of our larger cities showed than 22 per cent of all weekend emergency calls for police concerned domestic disturbances'. [43]

We also know that violence is often cited as a cause for marital unhappiness and divorce. Chester and Streather's analysis of English divorce petitions bears this out. [44] So does O'Brien's study: he found spontaneous mentions of overt violence occurred in 25 of 150 interviews he conducted of 'divorce-prone' families. Eighty-four per cent of these reports of violence came from women. [45] Levinger, in another divorce study, found that physical abuse was an important factor in 23 per cent of the middle-class couples and 40 per cent of the working-class sample. Wives complained eleven times more frequently than husbands about physical abuse (36.8 per cent of wives and 3.3 per cent of husbands said that their partner hurt them physically). [46] It is probable that these figures underestimate the amount of physical violence because there were probably violent incidents not mentioned spontaneously or which were not listed as a major cause of the divorce. There is a discrepancy between O'Brien and Levinger's figures. How is this to be accounted for? Is physical violence less for couples who have not applied for divorce? To answer questions like these and uncover the dark figure of domestic violence better measurement techniques are required.

Gelles undertook informal depth interviews of 80 families in two small New Hampshire towns. [47] Half the families were known to social agencies or the police as violent; the other half were neighbours of these known violent families. He found that of 44 families using violence 21 (that is 26 per cent of the entire sample) were participants in husband-wife assaults on 'a regular basis', [48] ranging from half a dozen times a year to every day. 'In the neighbour families, 15 (37 per cent) had at least one incident of violence between husband and wife, while violence was a regular occurrence in five families (12 per cent). [49] Gelles's was a non-random sample and its representativeness is unknown. He himself believes its conclusions should be treated with caution. If anything, he suggests, the figures may underestimate the true incidence.

Straus [50] asked students at the University of New Hampshire about conflicts that had occurred in their families during their last year at school, and how these conflicts were tackled. The answers showed that 16 per cent of their parents had used physical force on each other during that year. The percentage who had ever used violence is likely to be much greater. But how much greater it is impossible to estimate.

The Gelles and Straus studies were pilots for a much more ambitious research project which Straus and his colleagues have recently completed. [51] They used the Response Analysis National Probability sample and conducted interviews with 960 men and 1,183 women. The sample was representative of major demographic attributes of American families. The interviews took place in the early months of 1976. They defined violence as 'an act carried out with the intention of, a perceived intention of, physically injuring another person'. [52] They found that in 1975 16 per cent of spouses had engaged in violent acts against the other and that 27.8 per cent had done so at some time during the marriage. If the types of violent act were limited to serious items (kicking, biting, hitting with fist, hitting or trying to hit with something, beating up or threatening or using a knife or gun) the percentages were reduced to 6.1 per cent and 12.6 per cent respectively. When husbands and wives are compared it was found that 12.1 per cent of husbands and 11.6 per cent of wives had committed acts of violence on the other spouse during 1975. What will surprise many is how many husbands are battered by their wives. Furthermore, where wives were violent they tended to engage in such acts more frequently than did husbands (10.3 times in the year compared to 8.8 times for the husbands). It is hoped that the finding that wives are also violent will not divert attention from the problem of wife battering.

First, some, or even much, violence by wives may be in response to violence initiated by husbands. Straus's data unfortunately do not tell us. Second, husbands have higher rates for the most dangerous forms of violence. Third, when violent acts are committed by a husband they tend to be repeated more often than is the case for wives. Fourth, it is supposed that there is greater under-reporting of violence by husbands than by wives. [53] Straus argues 'to be violent is not unmasculine. But to be physically violent *is* unfeminine'. [54] But one would have thought that for this very reason men are less likely to report acts of violence committed by their wives upon them. [55] Fifth, a disproportionately large number of attacks by husbands are on pregnant wives so that unborn children are affected as well. [56] Sixth, men are stronger and, therefore, potentially more dangerous. Finally, it is more difficult for a wife to leave her husband. [57]

From Straus's figures one can conclude that approximately 1.8 million wives are beaten by their husbands in any one year in the USA. The extent of wife beating is greater than had been supposed hitherto. Similar surveys are lacking in this country. Marsden and Owens, extrapolating from a small study of one small (72,000 population) town, estimate that serious violence may occur in as many as 1 in a 100 marriages in the United Kingdom. [58] On the basis of this the Welsh Office in its evidence to the House of Commons Select Committee on Violence in Marriage thought that there might be 5,000 battered wives in Wales each year. [59] Jack Ashley estimated, on the basis of Citizens Advice Bureaux statistics of women who sought help, that numbers of battered women varied from 25,000 per 50 million population in Prestwich (a middle-class suburb) to 75,000 in Ashton-under-Lyne (a predominantly working-class town). [60] On a later occasion he suggested that 25,000 women at least suffered from habitual serious brutality. [61]

The House of Commons Select Committee concluded that 'despite our efforts we are unable to give any estimates of what the likely numbers are'. [62] Much, of course, depends upon definition and the victims themselves may define wife battering more widely than do the professionals. If that is so we would do well to heed their perceptions of the phenomenon.

There is no reason to believe that wife battering is any less prevalent in this country than in the USA. If that is right and 3.8 per cent of married women in the USA are battered each year, as Straus suggests, then on the basis of there being approximately 13 million married women in England and Wales, one may predict that in any one year as many as half a million of them may be beaten by their husbands. This figure is far in excess of earlier suggested statistics. It must, of course, be speculative but it can be stated with sufficient confidence that suggested figures for this country are considerable under-estimates.

Some myths about wife battering

When we inquire into the aetiology of wife battering we are confronted with a number of myths [63] that have grown up as putative explanations of the phenomenon. The myths are a form of defence mechanism; the family is an important social institution and the myths have grown up as shields to protect it. [64]

Thus, it is frequently asserted that violence in the home is a working-class phenomenon, and this is attributed to a lower-class sub-culture of violence [65] which, it is said, encourages violent acts. However, violence in the home certainly occurs at all levels of society. Examples of professional men battering their wives are to be found, *inter alia*, in Pizzey's *Scream Quietly*. [66] There is no doubt that there is more intra-familial violence the lower one goes down the socio-economic status continuum. This is borne out in Straus's latest research. He found a consistent tendency for more violence to have occurred in marriages of blue-collar husbands as compared to the white-collar occupation group. He notes that 'although about as many white collar husband families have experienced at least some violence during the course of the marriage as blue collar families, the frequency and seriousness of family violence is considerably greater in the blue collar sector of the society'. However, when Straus examined attitudes there was no difference between the two groups on the proportion viewing violence as 'good' and almost no difference in the extent to which violence is regarded as 'normal', but the blue collar rate of viewing violence as 'necessary' is considerably higher than the white collar group's rate. This suggests, Straus argues, 'that the basis for the wide belief in social class differences in attitudes towards violence . . . is the fact that lower class people live in a situation where violence is present and often necessary for self-preservation. They do not favor violence any more than middle class people. But the blue collar group seems to differ in regarding violence as an inevitable — even though disliked and disapproved — aspect of life'. [67]

Those who attribute wife battering to a subculture of violence do not account for the existence of those cultural norms. They can best be explained in terms of adaptation to basic structural conditions.

Some of these, such as lack of adequate resources and frustrating life experiences, though present throughout the social continuum, affect the working classes more. The so-called subculture of violence simply reflects then the realities of working-class existence and is not the cause of the violence in question. It is, of course, working-class wife abuse which is most likely to come to the attention of the police or welfare agencies or refuges and official statistics, in reflecting this, distort reality.

A second myth argues that violence is sexual relations is directly related to violence against wives because marriage is the main way in which sexual intercourse is made legitimate. Sexual drives are seen as violence-producing mechanisms. There is evidence that sex and violence accompany each other. The sex act is typically accompanied by mild violence. [68] Rape in war is endemic. Despite this, there is little biological linkage between sex and violence though the two are linked in our society and many similar societies. Anthropological evidence suggests that the strength of the sex drive depends on the demands of individual cultures. The Arapesh of New Guinea [69] and the Gusii of the Kenyan highlands [70] may be profitably compared. The Arapesh are a small, tightly knit community who survive in a frugal environment by mutual co-operation. There is no trace amongst them of aggression and competitiveness. They apparently know nothing of rape 'nor do [they] have any conception of male nature that might make rape understandable to them'. [71] The Gusii, on the other hand, have virtually institutionalised rape. They are frag- mented into hostile clans but, as they believe in exogamy, wives have to be imported. Marriage is a union between a man and a woman from hostile groups and the Gusii attitude towards sexuality reflects this. Sexual intercourse is regarded as an act of subjugation. This comparison shows that sex and violence can be linked. The important question concerns the social conditions which produce the association.

A further myth (the catharsis myth) 'asserts that the expression of "normal" aggression between family members should not be bottled up'. [72] It suggests that 'if normal aggression is allowed to be expressed, tension is released and the likelihood of severe violence is . . . thought to be reduced'. [73] The roots of this theory are in Aristotle. [74] Modern psychoanalysis has given it rebirth. Thus, Freud can refer to 'the liberation of affect' [75] through the re- experiencing of blocked or inhibited emotions and Dollard, applying this to aggressive behaviour, can state: 'the occurrence of any act of aggression is assumed to reduce the instigation to aggression'. [76] Although instinct theory assumptions have long been discarded in the social sciences, they persist in this context. [77] Berkowitz has written of Freud's views that of all his 'speculation, his interpretation of aggressive behaviour is the one most removed from facts'. [78] The principal objection to this thesis is that it confuses immediate with long-term effects for, whilst the short-term effect may well be cathartic, the long-term result of violent acts is to act as a stimulus towards the use of violence as a standard mode of social interaction.

Like many myths each of these contains a scintilla of truth. But none of them adequately explains the phenomenon. The complete answer to the question as to why violence occurs in marriage is not known. The House of Commons Select Committee on Violence in Marriage noted that 'hardly any worthwhile research into . . . causes . . . ha[d] been financed by the Government'. And, one may add, 'or any other government'. [79] Research has now begun in Bristol, [80] Canterbury [81] and Keele [82] in this country and in New Hampshire [83] in the USA. Our knowledge of the causes of wife battering is increasing all the time. The rest of this chapter discusses various theories which have been put forward and stresses that violence against women must be seen as a necessary concomitant of woman's generally oppressed position.

The causes of wife battering

As with child abuse there is no one cause of wife battering and a multidimensional explanation must be sought. As with child abuse also the dominant explanation localises the source of wife battering within the pathology of the individual batterer. Such an explanation is convenient for it gives social control agencies something to treat. The social origins of individual problems are thus conveniently ignored. In this section four explanations why wives are battered are set out; none can be entirely overlooked though it is believed that the last, which emphasises an ideology of superiority, is the most meaningful.

Pathological interpretations

It is most frequently hypothesised that wives are battered by husbands who have sick or inadequate personalities. The tendency is to isolate particular characteristics and assert their existence in statistically significant numbers of husbands who have battered their wives. The behaviour is then attributed to possession of the particular pathological characteristic in question. This view individualises the problem. It treats it, in William Ryan's language, as 'exceptionalistic'. [84] It

136

concentrates attention on behavioural characteristics of 'official' deviants. [85] Thus, it is commonly asserted that battering husbands are alcoholics or drug addicts or have 'personality disorders' or that they are psychopaths. Their violent behaviour is said to be 'irrational' rather as other deviance is categorised as 'mindless' or 'meaningless' or 'stupid'. [86]

Erin Pizzey, the most influential of publicists on the plight of the battered wife, subscribes to this view. Thus, in a forthright article in *The Spectator* in 1974 she wrote: 'no one likes the word "psychopath", everyone is afraid of it, but that is exactly what he is — aggressive, dangerous, plausible and deeply immature'. [87] Similarly, in her evidence to the House of Commons Select Committee she wrote:

> in a democratic society laws are made for reasonable men . . .
> These men are outside the law, they have been imprinted
> with violence from childhood, so that violence is part of
> their normal behaviour. All the legislating and punishment
> in the world will not change their methods of expressing
> their frustration. I believe that many of the children born
> into violence grow up to be aggressive psychopaths, and it
> is the wives of such men we see at Chiswick. I feel that the
> remedies lie in the hands of the medical profession and not
> in the court of law, because the men act instinctively, not
> rationally. [88]

Dr John Gayford, whose *British Medical Journal* article, published in 1975, was one of the first pieces of research into the problem, [89] is largely in agreement with Pizzey. When questioned by the Select Committee he spoke of the husbands' 'pathological jealousy' produced by alcohol and not susceptible of being removed by 'logical reasoning'. He describes the men as 'badly brought up': they had been spoiled or indulged as children. They were often incapable of looking after themselves. Both drink and gambling were problems. Gayford also emphasised what may be regarded as pathological features in the women who suffer abuse: for example, the fact that their marriages were often 'undertaken precipitately by a desire to leave home', short courtships and early and unplanned pregnancies. [90] Gayford's sample consisted of 100 women who had sought refuge in Chiswick's Women's Aid.

Some battering husbands are undoubtedly psychopaths and many do have drink problems. Many also have been battered as children. These factors are important. Where the pathological interpretation goes wrong is in seeking to explain the phenomenon of wife battering in these terms. In doing so it seeks an exceptionalistic explanation of a universalistic problem. [91]   Like positivistic interpretations of crime it sees the problem as the problem of the batterer. He is different from the rest of us and carries within himself certain stigmata which cause his behaviour. [92]   Positivistic interpretations lead inevitably to suggestions of treatment-orientated solutions: more refuges, better medical provision, more social workers, an attack on alcoholism etc. [93]   Where this form of positivistic criminology differs from the conventional is that it rarely examines the deviant himself. Nearly all the research has concentrated on the wife-victims and has not examined the husband-batterers. Gayford did just this. So did Snell and his associates. [94]   Conclusions about the batterer's 'pathology' are thus usually drawn from what his wife says about his personality and disposition. Nor are the wives a representative sample of those who have been subjected to violent attacks by their partners. The samples questioned are drawn from women who seek refuge or report the attack to the police or a social welfare agency.

It may be valuable to examine the evidence put forward to support one of the biophysical variables which is alleged to 'cause' the deviance in question, i.e. alcoholism. Certainly, many of the women who are beaten by their husbands attribute the violence to drink. One wife told Gelles: 'he wouldn't ever slap me when he was sober, no matter how mad he got'. [95]   But Bard and Zacker, [96] American specialists in police crisis intervention programmes, [97] have shown that the emphasis on alcohol as a trigger of family violence is highly exaggerated. They studied the West Harlem police crisis intervention programme for 22 months. Specially trained officers visited 962 families on 1,388 separate calls during this period. The complainant was observed by the officers to have used alcohol in 26 per cent of the cases and the accused in only 30 per cent of the cases. In only 10 per cent of the cases did the complainant allege that the accused was drunk and the officers agreed with only 43 per cent of these allegations. They perceived alcohol to be primary in the origins of only 14 per cent of the total number of cases, though it was used by the accused in 21 per cent of the complaints. Of course, if the police are taught to expect the participants to be drunk they may well so perceive them and this goes for any agency intervening in a violent domestic disturbance. The effect this has on theory building hardly needs to be spelt out.

It is far more likely that men drink to get 'dutch courage'. Gelles puts it this way: 'individuals who wish to carry out a violent act become intoxicated *in order to carry out the violent act.* Having become drunk and then violent the individual either may deny what occurred ("I don't remember, I was drunk"), or plead for forgiveness

138

("I didn't know what I was doing"). In both cases he can shift the blame for violence from himself to the effect of alcohol'. [98] Del Martin puts her finger on the essential point when she writes: '[v]iolent actions often seem to be more acceptable — or at least more comprehensible — in our society when they are performed by a person who is intoxicated'. [99] The attribution of marital violence to drink, convenient though it might be, will not do. It may release the trigger of violence but it is not a direct cause.

The criticisms made earlier in the book [100] of the psychopathological model as applied to child abuse apply to the problem of wife battering as well. What was said there is equally true here for, if anything, the model has reached a lower level of sophistication when applied to marital violence than child abuse. Again, as the dominant paradigm, it has done much to influence the direction of social policy. But, finding out what is wrong with known batterers and treating them will not solve the problem.

Structural factors

A second view attributes marital violence to frustration, stress and blocked goals. [101] It locates the sources of wife battering in social structural factors. The British Association of Social Workers puts it like this:

> economic conditions, low wages, bad housing, over-crowding and isolation; unfavourable and frustrating work conditions for the man; lack of job opportunities for adolescents/school leavers, and lack of facilities such as day care (e.g. nurseries), adequate transport, pleasant environment and play space and recreational facilities, for mother and children were considered to cause personal desperation that might precipitate violence in the home. [102]

To the Dobashs 'numerous factors of a structural and interactional nature . . . might be considered as amplifying the potential for violence between spouses'. They believe that important structural elements are 'socialisation into a sub-culture of violence; limited access to and achievement of status within the larger social system; lack of effective sanctions on the part of the immediate social audiences and of relevant social agencies, and the general status of women'. [103] The last element is, it is believed, the most important and is considered in detail later in the chapter. [104]

Gelles's researches led him to conclude that 'violence is an adaptation or response to structural stress'. He argues that structural stress 'produces frustration, which is often followed by violence (expressive violence). Structural stress also produces role expectations (particularly for the husband) which, because of lack of resources, only can be carried out by means of violence (instrumental violence)'. To this he adds, as a second major precondition, the socialisation experience: 'if an individual learns that violence is an appropriate behaviour when one is frustrated or angry . . . then this will be the adaptation to stress employed'. [105] Another factor noted by Gelles was the comparative social isolation of violent families. [106] This was not confirmed by Jobling [107] in her review of reports of wife battering collected from Citizens' Advice Bureaux; many of the abused wives were in regular contact with their families though ashamed to talk of their experiences. But were the husbands in contact with, or cut off from, their families? It may, of course, be that violent families are socially isolated because of their violence, and not violent because they are isolated.

The lower socio-economic classes are most likely to suffer from the stressful conditions depicted here. [108] This may have contributed to the assumption that marital violence is a part of a subculture of violence. Violence may be an adaptation to stressful structural conditions but the theory does not explain why. What is the precise causal relationship, if any, between economic conditions or over-crowding and violence, particularly wife beating? It does not take much imagination to realise that in a situation of overcrowding there is little privacy, with the result that temporary escape from the other's clutches is more difficult. But even so it is only in a culture which legitimates violence against wives that such a response would seem appropriate. An emphasis on structural factors does not provide the ultimate explanation.

Goode's resources theory

It is Goode's thesis that 'most people do not willingly choose overt force when they command other resources because the costs of using force are high'. [109] He, therefore, hypothesises that the greater the other resources an individual can command, the less he will use force in an 'overt manner'. He continues his line of argument in this way:

> [t]he husband in the middle or upper class family commands more force, in spite of his lesser willingness to use his own physical strength, because he possesses far more other social resources. His greater social prestige in the larger society and

140

the family, his larger economic possessions, and his stronger emphasis on the human relations techniques of counter-deference, affection and communication give him greater influence generally, so that he does not have to call upon the force or its threat that he can in fact muster if he chooses . . . [110]

Some of Goode's ideas have been developed in the research of O'Brien, to which reference has already been made. [111] O'Brien's assumption is that the family is a social system in which dominance patterns are based on social categories of age and sex. He argues that violence is to be found where the male/adult/husband fails to possess the superior skills, talents and resources on which his superior status is supposed to be legitimately grounded. Accordingly, he expected violence to be prevalent in families in which the husband/father was deficient in relation to the wife/mother on achieved status character-istics. He found that the husbands in his violent subgroup showed evidence of under-achievement in work roles as well as being deficient in achievement potential. They were, for example, dissatisfied with their jobs or education drop-outs. In as many as 84 per cent of his sample the husband's income was the source of serious and constant conflict. Komarovsky's finding that wives who have had higher education are at greater risk of violence than those who have had none would appear to be consistent with this. [112]

O'Brien's interpretation of his research is in terms of status inconsistency where superior ascribed status category fails to live up to achieved status characteristics. Violence, he hypothesises, results from a reassertion of male dominance. O'Brien can see a case 'for social intervention of a type intended to strengthen the earning and achievement potential of husbands'. [113] This is quite contrary to current social policies which are moving, albeit slowly, towards egalitarianism. Whitehurst has argued that the current move towards greater equality in marital roles may, in the short term, lead to an increase in marital violence. 'Men simply have no culturally approved ways of coping with "uppity" women who want to be really free'. [114]

The ideology of superiority

Whitehurst's remarks lead conveniently to the final and most persuasive explanation as to why women are beaten by the men with whom they live. As the development of the Women's Movement has been a primary factor in sensitising our consciences to the plight of the battered woman, it is hardly surprising that theories as to the aetiology of male violence towards woman should have developed within the ideology of its liberation politics. [115] Nor is it surprising that the views of militant feminists should have created so little interest amongst government departments, the media or the general public. To them Erin Pizzey and Chiswick epitomise the problem and her definitions and solutions have become public property. The National Women's Aid Federation with a definition of the problem which indicts society is accorded little or no attention; its views, its solutions are too unpalatable for society to stomach.

The Women's Movement sees violence as a necessary concomitant of woman's generally oppressed position in the social structure. 'The challenge of Women's Aid', Weir writes, 'is that it demands a fundamental change in the way in which women are defined'. [116] The patriarchal bias endemic in culture and history and reflected in literature has been excellently documented by Millett [117] and Bullough. [118] The view is thus propagated that the purpose of male violence is to control women. Male violence results from a Macho ideology which supports the male's use of violence to maintain his dominance over his mate. [119]

Erin Pizzey quotes one battering husband who taunts his wife by saying to her: '[W] here can you go? What can you do?' [120] This encapsulates the state of powerlessness and dependence in which many women find themselves. [121] How is this to be explained? What part does socialisation into stereotypical sex roles play in this? Where does the State come in? And if, as most think, the ideological hegemony of men is socially established, how is it that it appears to be almost universal? These questions have long been neglected. Until very recently a sociology of sexual stratification did not exist. Sociologists like Goode saw the 'family' as the 'keystone of the stratification system'; [122] individuals, particularly women, were not the object of its study. This is beginning to change as the writings of Firestone, [123] Mitchell,[124] Zaretsky [125] and Delphy [126] show. How then is patriarchal exploitation to be explained?

Eva Figes believes the 'motivation' for male domination over women is connected with the idea of paternity. She writes:

> [O] nce a man knows that there is a physical link between
> himself and the child in his woman's womb, that, provided
> no other man has been allowed to impregnate his woman, the
> child will be definitely his, a continuation of himself, all kinds
> of things become possible. The idea of personal continuity
> is born, if man can only control his woman he becomes, in a

sense, immortal . . . Since no man can control all other men it is primarily the woman he must control, mentally or physically. [127]

Whilst there is some truth in this, Figes, in a rather different way from Pizzey or Gayford, is individualising the problem, putting the blame on the male psyche and neglecting the social dimensions of the problem. She also makes the mistake of believing that in our society there has been a shift from direct physical control to a system of complex and subtle taboos. But she does state rightly that in a 'patriarchal society male dominance must be maintained at all costs, because the person who dominates cannot conceive of any alternative but to be dominated in turn'. [128] The sex act ('the missionary position' [128]) she argues, symbolises this situation.

To what extent is this ideology sustained by women? According to Bell and Newby 'the belief on the part of many wives that not only do their husbands possess greater power but that, in the last analysis, they *ought* to do so, is the kind of belief that occurs in other highly stratified social situations'. [129] Wives believe in the authority of their husbands and believe it is right to defer to them. Bell and Newby argue persuasively that '[t]he origins of deference lie in the processes of legitimation by tradition of the power of those in super-ordinate positions'. [130] Deference derives from power but becomes in time a moral position. Sex-role socialisation both within the family and schools is a vital social mechanism for the creation and maintenance of ideological control. [131] So are ideologies of the home and home-centredness: a woman's place is in the home partly because to seek fulfilment outside could threaten the control which confinement within it promotes.

Ann Oakley's study *Housewife* [132] is useful here. She shows how in pre-capitalist societies and in the early stages of capitalism work and family life overlapped. The household was a basic unit of production — the home a place of work. There was no clear distinction between the role of worker and of family member. Women were undoubtedly oppressed but the form of their oppression was different. With industrialisation and capitalist production the nature of work and family life changed radically. Productive work now took place not in the home but in the factory. At first women (and children) were used by the factory system but increasing industrialisation brought unemployment and women were driven out into dependency upon husbands. Work done in the home was increasingly restricted to looking after husband-workers and producing children. Nor was it seen as 'real' work, for it was not sold

143

for a wage. Zaretsky [133] has described how at the same time the family became idealised, as did the familial role of woman, and the home became a refuge from demands of capitalist society, a private place to which people withdrew. Man was now the breadwinner; woman the dependent homemaker. The ideology encapsulated by this was adopted by the middle classes first and only later by the working classes. Women today are seen as being non-productive (a myth effectively demolished by Delphy [134]), economically dependent and as occupying a position outside society. That a high percentage of married women now work [135] is not relevant; their identification with home-centred, non-productive familial roles is firmly entrenched in the consciousness of society.

Sex-role socialisation and the ideologies associated with the home are sufficiently effective strategies to have turned might into right in most marriages. But as Bell and Newby point out,

> 'might' remains very close to the surface. Deference stabilizes the hierarchical nature of the husband-wife relationship, but . . . the relationship is embedded in a system of power — and the naked use of this power can be, and is, resorted to if the relationship threatens to break down. Two sorts of power . . . form the constant background to the deferential dialectic between husbands and wives. These are the power of the hand and the power of the purse. [136]

Nothing needs to be said here about the former; the potency of the latter is undeniable. We know from Marsden's *Mothers Alone* [137] and from the Finer Report [138] that women, whose earning power is less and who may have additional child-care responsibilities, have great difficulty in surviving without husbands to support them.

At this point it is pertinent to ask what role the State plays in creating dependence. In 1974 the Women's Movement demanded legal and financial independence. [139] It challenged the legal definition of women as dependents of men as this manifests itself in the tax and social security system, home ownership, tenancies and countless other areas. They saw it as indicative of 'the way the State upholds the family in its present form and, thereby, forces women into a position of dependence on men'. [140] This prompts the question as to why the State should uphold female dependence. Elizabeth Wilson's thesis [141] that women's unpaid work in the home is the cheapest way of reproducing the labour force for capital is not convincing. More persuasive is Hilary Land's argument [142] that it is in the interests of the State for men to be kept at work by having dependent wives and children to support. She shows how arguments deployed against family allowances and tax credits have reflected these interests.

The social security system reflects at every turn the supposed economic dependency of women. Men and women are not treated equally by it. Assumptions about the place of married women derive from economic and demographic concerns of the 1930s. The laws relating to national insurance pensions, supplementary benefit, sickness and unemployment benefit, family income supplement and tax are all based on stereotypical sex classifications. The cohabitation rule ('living together as man and wife') makes the assumption that if a man lives with a woman he supports her. The married woman's role as a worker is underestimated by the system, despite the fact that some one-sixth of households are dependent on a woman's earnings; [143] the Beveridge report, still the foundation of the principles of the system, did state, after all, that 'maternity is the principal object of marriage'. [144] Not surprisingly, therefore, women are entitled to larger benefits when pregnant than when sick or unemployed. Further, the situation in which a father stays at home while mother works is not countenanced by the social security system. For example, for a couple to qualify for family income supplement the man must be in full-time work. [145] This supplement is paid to low wage earners and women (a secondary work force) earn lower wages than men; yet despite this a woman living with a man is not eligible for the supplement in her own right. Examples like this can be multiplied. The conclusion they point to is that the social security system, 'by perpetuating inegalitarian family relationships, is a means of reinforcing, rather than compensating for, economic inequalities'. [146]

This inequality is reflected too in the law regulating marriage. [147] A husband has a duty to maintain his wife. [148] She gets upkeep for various services. [149] What she gets varies with her husband's financial status. So long as they are living together the law refuses to intervene in their financial relationship; the husband sets their standard of living. [150] If he refuses to maintain her she can leave and require maintenance from him. Until 1978 if she committed adultery she forfeited her right to any maintenance. [151] The assumption once more appears to be that the man with whom she has fornicated is (or ought to be?) supporting her. On divorce she may get one-third of their joint incomes; that her former husband gets twice this was explained by Lord Denning on the ground that the husband was likely to have greater expenses than the wife (he might have to employ a housekeeper, whilst she would look after herself and on remarriage he would incur additional liabilities and she would become dependent on another man). [152] The law intervenes to share housekeeping savings between husband and wife but only where the husband gives the wife an allowance. [153]

In Britain today there is but one type of marriage; its nature is not negotiable, rights and duties being fixed by law, not agreement between the parties. [154] A husband cannot in law rape his wife: [155] the marriage licence is seen as giving him a virtually irrevocable licence for having sexual intercourse with her. There was a time, as recently as the 1960s, when the courts were willing to construe refusal by a wife as cruelty but to explain away a man's refusal on psychological grounds. [156] A marriage must be consummated: consummation is defined as full and complete intercourse [157] — for the man. In one case the court held that the fact that the wife could obtain no pleasure from intercourse with her artificially extended plastic vagina was irrelevant to the question whether the marriage had been consummated. [158] Although much of the more explicit discrimination against wives has been removed in recent years, sexist justice is still with us.

This is the setting in which violence against wives take place. The husband-wife relationship is an asymmetrical one and this is recognised by the State and found in statutory provisions, the operational activities of institutions like the police, [159] business practices, such as those concerned with credit and housing policies. It has been taken for granted that refuges should receive wives and children fleeing from battering husbands, but, as the House of Commons Select Committee asked, surely rhetorically, 'why should we not create hostels to receive the battering husband?' [160]

In this perspective it becomes possible to see that the State represents the interests of the dominant group, i.e. men. Jalna Hanmer writes:

> Thus it is consistent that in domestic disputes the status of the victim determines the response of that section of the state given the task of controlling violence. That men unknown to the woman (the policemen) would back up the man known to her (the husband) in pursuit of their joint state-defined interest is to impartially enforce the law for the state defines women as less equal. This knowledge, however, comes as a shock to most women when they seek protection from the police for the first time. [161]

Violence then is used to control women both within and outside the home. A survey by Whitehurst showed that 'threats of violence

146

are frequent among husbands as a means of controlling wives'.[162] He describes a case where a husband catching his wife *in flagrante delicto* 'set upon the two of them in a jealous rage'. He interprets this reaction in terms of 'the husband's own need to control his wife and feel superior', and explains that this was 'too much of an emotional burden for him to handle without recourse to violence'. [163] The major content of teasing in the pubs of rural Herefordshire is, according to Ann Whitehead, the degree of control a married man exerted over his wife's behaviour. 'The men acted as if a married man should be able to do just what he liked after marriage. He should be able to come to the pub every day . . . He could and must row with his wife, hit her or lay down the law. Rows and quarrels in which he had the upper hand brought a man esteem, but if his wife rowed with him, locked him out of the house or refused to cook for him, he lost esteem'. [164]

Women are also controlled by the threat of violence outside the home. They learn to avoid certain areas. As Hanmer puts it: '[u]rban space for women is compartmentalised, to deviate from women's alloted space is to run the risk of attack by men'. [165] The fear of violence, particularly rape, has the effect of driving women to seek protection from men, of making them dependent. [166] Ironically, women feel safer in the company of husbands and boy friends though they are more likely to be attacked or raped by them than by the dangerous strangers they are taught to fear. [167]

If male violence to women is to be seen in this way then there are no straightforward solutions, for what is being demanded is nothing less than a complete social revolution. This is explicitly recognised by many who interpret the problem in this way. Whitehurst, for example, has put the case for 'alternative family structures', [168] families which contain more people than the traditional nuclear family, such as communes and group marriages. He rejects the hierarchical structure of the traditional family and looks to greater interpersonal openness. But, as Steinmetz and Straus recognise, there is no evidence that such families would be free of violence. [169] There are anthropological findings that male violence to woman antedates monogamy, [170] and Hanmer recognises that it is 'not an unfortunate vagary of human nature called forth by class oppression'. [171] Further, Abrams and McCulloch have not found communes to be immune from the societal hegemony of male-female relations. [172]

Hanmer herself is less ambitious. She calls for women to challenge the use of force by males. She demands that the 'problem of men be raised theoretically and with it the question of the extent to which men can be re-educated'. [173] A redirection of current socialisation processes would be a useful place to begin. Tackling the problem of women's false consciousness would be another useful starting point. Given this interpretation what is surprising is not that women are beaten by men with whom they live, but that more women are not battered. A redefinition of male-female relationships would go some way towards cutting down the prevalence of male violence. The odd psychopath, alcoholic, drug addict would still terrorise and beat up the woman with whom he lived. But the present tendency to assume that there is something inherently wrong with men who do is to mistake the problem. [174]

Notes

[1] See M. Straus, R. Gelles and S. Steinmetz, *Violence in the American Family* (forthcoming, 1978).

[2] See D. Oliver, 'The Mistress in Law', *Current Legal Problems* (forthcoming, 1978).

[3] HC, vol.884, col.214, 14 January 1975.

[4] E. Pizzey, *Scream Quietly or the Neighbours will Hear*, Penguin, 1974. See also D. Martin, *Battered Wives*, Glide, 1976 and R. Langley and R. Levy, *Wife Beating — The Silent Crisis*, Dutton, 1977.

[5] HC, 248, 1974-75.

[6] *Per* Miss J. Richardson, HC, vol.905, col.861.

[7] *Per* Mrs H. Hayman, HC, vol.905, col.873.

[8] J. Gayford in *British Medical Journal*, 1975, p.194.

[9] R.M. Helmholz, *Marriage Litigation in Medieval England*, Cambridge University Press, 1974, p.105.

[10] *Per* J.W. Kaye in *North British Review*, 25 May 1856, pp 249-50.

[11] O. McGregor, *Divorce in England*, Heinemann, 1957, p.22. See also A.H. Manchester, '*The Legal History of Marital Violence in England and Wales 1750-1976* (forthcoming).

[12] HC, vol.124, col.1414. *Cf* J. Ashley in 1975 saying 'it is the kind of cruelty which would cause a mass outcry throughout the country and marches on Parliament if it were inflicted on a dog or a cat' (HC, vol.884, col.215).

[13] Reports to the Secretary of State for the Home Department on the State of law relating to Brutal Assaults (1875) C.1138. A.H. Manchester, op.cit., note 11, discusses the report.

[14] On this see further S. Steinmetz and M. Straus, *Violence in the Family*, Dodd, Mead, 1974.

[15] F. Power Cobbe, *Autobiography*, Bentley, 1894, vol.2, pp 220-1.

[16] Interestingly, her Bill would have provided for injunctions to restrain husbands visiting wives without their consent. Magistrates even today do not have such powers.

[17] By the Summary Jurisdiction (Married Women) Act 1895.

[18] See *post*, p.137.

[19] C. Wright Mills, *The Sociological Imagination*, Oxford University Press, 1959.

[20] See A. Weir, 'Battered Women: Some Perspectives and Problems' in M. Mayo (ed.) *Women in the Community*, RKP, 1977, pp 109, 113.

[21] J. Hanmer, 'Violence and the Social Control of Women', in G. Littlejohn et al., (ed.), *Power and the State*, Croom Helm, 1978, pp 217, 219.

[22] J. Kitsuse and A. Cicourel in *Social Problems*, vol.ll, 1963, p.131.

[23] See, generally, A. Biderman, 'When Does Interpersonal Violence Become Crime', International Sociological Association Conference, Cambridge, 1973 and R. Block in *Criminology*, vol.11, 1974, p.555.

[24] See E. Rubington and M. Weinberg, *Deviance — The Interactionist Perspective*, Macmillan, 1973, p.31.

[25] See M.R. Yarrow et al., in *Journal of Social Issues*, vol.11, 1955, p.12; J.K. Jackson, *Q.J. of Studies on Alcohol*, vol.15, 1954, p.564; R. Gelles, *The Violent Home*, Sage, 1972, p.58 ff.

[26] R. Parnas, Wisconsin L.R. 914 (1967); M. Dow 'Police Involvement' in M. Borland (ed.), *Violence in the Family*, Manchester University Press, 1976, p.129.

[27] An annual Home Office publication, published by HMSO.

[28] E. Gibson and S. Klein, *Murder 1957-68*, HMSO, 1969; Bedford College Legal Research Unit, *Criminal Homicide in England and Wales 1957-68*, 1969. 'Both estimates suggest that over the period of the study about forty women a year were killed by their husbands.' (*per* M. Gregory 'Battered Wives' in M. Borland, op.cit., note p.110.) Homicides have increased since 1968.

[29] M. Amir, *Patterns in Forcible Rape*, University of Chicago Press, 1971.

[30] D. Mulvihill et al., *Crimes of Violence* (Staff Report to National Commission on Causes and Prevention of Violence, vol.11), 1969.

[31] F. McClintock, *Crimes of Violence*, Macmillan, 1963.

[32] J. Boudouris in *Journal of Marriage and the Family*, vol.33, 1971, p.667.

[33] H. Voss and J. Hepburn in *Journal of Criminal Law, Criminology, Police Science*, vol.59, 1968, p.499.

[34] M.E. Wolfgang, *Patterns in Criminal Homicide*, Wiley, 1958 and in *Psychology Today*, vol.3, 1969, pp 54, 72.

[35] M. Maldonado in *Boletim da Administracao Penitenciaria e dos Institutos de Criminologia*, vol.23, 1968, p.5.

[36] S. Siciliano, *Annals Internationales de Criminologie*, vol.7, 1968, p.403.

[37] P. McCarthy in J. De Wit and W. Hartup (eds), *Determinants and Origins of Aggressive Behaviour*, De Mouton, 1974.

[38] D.J. Pittman and W. Handy, 'Patterns in Criminal Aggravated Assault', *Journal of Criminal Law, Criminology, Police Science*, vol.55, 1964, p.462.

[39] A.D. Pokorny, 'Human Violence', *Journal of Criminal Law, Criminology, Police Science*, vol.56, 1965, p.488.

[40] R. Dobash and R. Dobash, *The Nature and Extent of Violence in Marriage in Scotland*, Scottish Council for Social Service, 1976 and 'Wife Beating — Still a Common Form of Violence', *Social Work Today*, vol.9, no.12, 15 November 1977, p.14. See also *Violence Against Wives: A Case against the Patriarchy*, Free Press (forthcoming, 1978).

[41] *Minutes of Evidence to Select Committee on Violence in Marriage*, p.375 (Metropolitan Police evidence).

[42] Idem, p.362 (Police Superintendents' Association evidence).

[43] Idem.

[44] R. Chester and J. Streather, 'Cruelty in English Divorce: Some Empirical Findings', *Journal of Marriage and the Family*, vol.34, 1972, p.706.

[45] J. O'Brien, 'Violence in Divorce Prone Families', *Journal of Marriage and the Family*, vol.33, 1971, p.692.

[46] G. Levinger, 'Sources of Marital Dissatisfaction among Applicants for Divorce', *American Journal of Orthopsychiatry*, vol.36, 1966, p.803.

[47] R. Gelles, *The Violent Home*, Sage, 1972.

[48] Idem, p.48.

[49] Idem, p.50.

[50] M. Straus, 'Leveling, Civility and Violence in the Family', *Journal of Marriage and the Family*, vol.36, 1974, p.13.

[51] M. Straus, R. Gelles, S. Steinmetz, *Violence in the American Family* (forthcoming, 1978). The results are summarised in two papers ('Normative and Behavioral Aspects of Violence between Spouses', March 1977, and 'Wife-Beating — How Common and Why?' June 1977).

[52] In 'Normative and Behavioral Aspects', op.cit., p.7.

[53] See *post.* p.228.

[54] 'Wife-Beating' op.cit., note 51, p.7.

[55] See *post,* p.228.
[56] See R. Gelles, 'Violence and Pregnancy', *Family Co-ordinator,* vol.24, 1975, p.81.
[57] See *post,* p.157.
[58] D. Marsden and D. Owens, 'Jekyll and Hyde Marriages', *New Society,* 8 May 1975, p.333.
[59] *Minutes of Select Committee on Violence in Marriage,* q.1529 (*per* Mr B. Jones). 600 cases a year come to the notice of social services departments in Wales each year (Idem, p.349 — Memorandum of Welsh Office).
[60] HC, vol.859, col.218.
[61] HC, vol.895, col.982.
[62] *Report on Violence in Marriage,* p.vii.
[63] A good discussion of these myths is S. Steinmetz and M. Straus, *Violence in the Family,* Dodd, Mead, 1974, pp 6-17.
[64] A. Ferreira, 'Family Myth and Homeostasis' in N. Bell and E. Vogel (eds), *A Modern Introduction to the Family,* Free Press, 1968.
[65] M.E. Wolfgang and F. Ferracuti, *The Subculture of Violence,* Tavistock, 1967.
[66] E. Pizzey, op.cit., note 4.
[67] M. Straus, 'Normative and Behavioral Aspects of Violence between Spouses', pp 14-16.
[68] C. Ford and F. Beach, *Patterns of Sexual Behavior,* Harper, 1951.
[69] M. Mead, *The Mountain Arapesh,* Muller, 1972.
[70] See R.A. LeVine, 'Gusii Sex Offences: a Study in Social Control', *American Anthropologist,* vol.61, 1959, p.965. See also D. Chappell 'Cross-Cultural Research on Forcible Rape', *International Journal of Criminology and Penology,* vol.4, 1976, p.295.
[71] Quoted in B. Toner, *The Facts of Rape,* Arrow, 1977, p.41.
[72] Op.cit., note 63, p.14.
[73] Idem.
[74] For whom it referred to the purging of passions or suffering of spectators through vicarious participation in the suffering of a tragic hero as this is portrayed in tragedy.
[75] S. Freud, 'On the History of the Psychoanalytic Movement' in *Collected Papers,* vol.1, Hogarth, 1924, pp 284-389.
[76] J. Dollard, *Frustration and Aggression,* Yale University Press, 1939, p.50.
[77] S. Steinmetz and M. Straus, op.cit., note 63, give five reasons for the persistence of the catharsis myth (pp 14-16). They quote an extract from Bruno Bettelheim urging that children should learn about violence to learn how to handle it (pp 299-303). Another good

example of this thesis in operation is G.R. Bach and P. Wyden, *The Intimate Enemy*, Morrow, 1968. *Cf* Straus's research in op.cit., note 50.

[78] L. Berkowitz, *Aggression: A Social Psychological Explanation*, McGraw Hill, 1962, p.10, and see also A. Bandura and R. Walters, *Social Learning and Personality Development*, Holt, Rinehart and Winston, 1963.

[79] *Report of Select Committee on Violence in Marriage*, 1974-75, HC 553-i, para. 5.

[80] Under M. Murch (personal communication).

[81] Under J. Pahl (personal communication).

[82] Under T. and B. Faragher (personal communication).

[83] See *ante*, note 1.

[84] W. Ryan, *Blaming the Victim* (revised ed. 1976), Vintage Books, p.17.

[85] *Cf* S. Box, *Deviance, Reality and Society*, Holt, Rinehart and Winston, 1971, ch.1.

[86] Good illustrations of this are to be found in S. Cohen, *Images of Deviance*, Penguin, 1971.

[87] E. Pizzey, 'Violence begins at Home', *The Spectator*, 23 November 1974.

[88] *Minutes of Evidence*, p.2.

[89] J. Gayford in *British Medical Journal*, 25 January 1975, p.194.

[90] *Minutes of Evidence*, p.43, and in *British Medical Journal* article, op.cit., note 89.

[91] *Cf* W. Ryan, op.cit., note 84.

[92] On positivism in criminology see I. Taylor, P. Walton and J. Young, *The New Criminology*, RKP, 1973, ch.2.

[93] *Cf* House of Commons *Select Committee Report on Violence in Marriage*, HC 553, 1974-75, para. 17.

[94] J. Snell, 'The Wifebeater's Wife', *Archives of General Psychiatry*, vol.11, 1964, p.107; Del Martin, *Battered Wives*, Glide, 1976, p.45 ff also makes this point.

[95] R. Gelles, *The Violent Home*, Sage, 1972, p.78.

[96] M. Bard and J. Zacker, 'Assaultiveness and Alcohol Use in Family Disputes', *Criminology*, vol.12, 1974, p.283.

[97] On which see *post*, p.188.

[98] Op.cit., note 95, p.117. Another similar example is C. McCaghy, 'Drinking and Deviance Disavowal: the Case of Child Molesters', *Social Problems*, vol.16, 1968, p.43.

[99] D. Martin, *Battered Wives*, Glide, 1976, p.57.

[100] *Ante*, p.25,

[101]   *Cf* R. Merton, 'Social Structure and Anomie', *American Sociological Review*, vol.3, 1938, p.672.
[102]   Discussion Document of BASW Working Party on Home Violence, *Social Work Today*, vol.6, 1975, p.409.
[103]   R. Dobash and R. Dobash, 'Violence Between Men and Women within the Family Setting', VIII World Congress of Sociology, Toronto, 1974.
[104]   *Post*, p.141.
[105]   Op.cit., note 95, p.185. See also M. Tidmarsh, 'Violence in Marriage', *Social Work Today*, vol.7, no.2, 15 April 1976, p.36.
[106]   R. Selles, idem, pp 132-5.
[107]   M. Jobling, 'Battered Wives — A Survey', *Social Services Quarterly*, vol.47, 1974, p.142.
[108]   And Gelles found that violence was more likely to occur in lower socio-economic families.
[109]   W. Goode, 'Force and Violence in the Family', *Journal of Marriage and the Family*, vol.33, 1971, pp 624, 628.
[110]   Idem.
[111]   *Ante*, p.131.
[112]   M. Komarovsky, *Blue Collar Marriage*, Vintage Books, 1967.
[113]   J. O'Brien in *Journal of Marriage and the Family*, vol.33, 1971, pp 692, 697.
[114]   R. Whitehurst, 'Violence in Husband-Wife Interaction' in S. Steinmetz and M. Straus (eds), *Violence in the Family*, Dodd, Mead, 1974, p.77.
[115]   A useful pamphlet is E. Wilson, *The Existing Research into Battered Women*, NWAF, 1976.
[116]   In M. Mayo (ed.), *Women in the Community*, RKP, 1977, p.119.
[117]   K. Millett, *Sexual Politics*, Hart Davis, 1969, partic. pp 43-7; her critique of Henry Miller (ch.6); and her comparison of Mill and Ruskin (pp 99 ff).
[118]   V. Bullough, *The Subordinate Sex*, Penguin, 1974.
[119]   On the social control of women see B. Smart and C. Smart, *Women, Sexuality and Social Control*, RKP, 1978.
[120]   E. Pizzey, *Scream Quietly or the Neighbours will Hear*, Penguin, 1974, p.43.
[121]   A useful recent discussion is R. Dobash and R. Dobash, 'Love, Honour and Obey', *Contemporary Crises*, vol.1, 1977, p.403.
[122]   W. Goode, *The Family*, Prentice Hall, 1964, p.80.
[123]   S. Firestone, *The Dialectic of Sex*, J. Cape, 1971.
[124]   J. Mitchell, *Women's Estate*, Penguin, 1971.

[125] E. Zaretsky, *Capitalism, the Family and Personal Life*, Harper and Row, 1976.

[126] C. Delphy, *The Main Enemy*, Women's Research and Resources Centre Publications, 1977.

[127] E. Figes, *Patriarchal Attitudes*, Panther, 1972, p.39.

[128] Idem, p.52.

[129] C. Bell and H. Newby, 'Husbands and Wives: the Dynamics of the Deferential Dialectic' in D.L. Barker and S. Allen (eds), *Dependence and Exploitation in Work and Marriage*, Longman, 1976, p.154.

[130] Idem, p.155.

[131] See S. Sharpe,*'Just Like a Girl' : How Girls learn to be Women*, Penguin, 1976, and A.M. Wolpe, *Some Processes in Sexist Education*, WRRCP, 1977.

[132] A. Oakley, *Housewife*, Penguin, 1974.

[133] Op.cit., note 125, pp 51 ff.

[134] Op.cit., note 126, pp 3-13.

[135] That is outside the home. They are a secondary work-force. See R.D. Barron and G.M. Norris in D.L. Barker and S. Allen (eds), op.cit., note 129, p.47. See also Conference of Socialist Economists Pamphlet No.2, *On the Political Economy of Women*, 1977.

[136] Op.cit., note 129, p.164.

[137] D. Marsden, *Mothers Alone*, Penguin, 1973.

[138] *Finer Report*, Cmnd 5629, pt.5.

[139] *The Women's Liberation Campaign for Independence* (the Fifth Demand Campaign).

[140] Idem, p.1.

[141] E. Wilson, 'Women in the Community' in M. Mayo (ed.), *Women in the Community*, 1977, pp 1-2.

[142] H. Land, 'Women: Supporters or Supported?' in D.L. Barker and S. Allen (eds), *Sexual Divisions and Society, Process and Change*, Tavistock, 1976, p.108. See also in J. Chetwynd and O. Harnett (eds), *The Sex Role System*, RKP, 1978, ch.10.

[143] See H. Land, 'The Myth of the Male Breadwinner', *New Society*, vol.29, 1975, p.71.

[144] *Social Insurance and Allied Services*, Cmnd 6406, p.50.

[145] Family Income Supplements Act 1970 s.1.

[146] *Per* H. Land, op.cit., note 142, p.129.

[147] See D.L. Barker 'The Regulation of Marriage: Repressive Benevolence' in G. Littlejohn et al., (ed.) *Power and the State*, Croom Helm, 1978, p.239.

[148] P. Bromley, *Family Law* (5th ed.), Butterworths, 1976, p.496.

[149] *McGuire* v. *McGuire* (1953) 59 N.W. 2d. 336.

[150] *Cf Caras* v. *Caras* [1955] 1 All E.R.624.

[151] *Chilton* v. *Chilton* [1952] P.196,202. See now Domestic Proceedings and Magistrates' Courts Act 1978.

[152] *Wachtel* v. *Wachtel* [1973] Fam 72,94, criticised in M.D.A. Freeman, 'When Marriage Fails', *Current Legal Problems* (forthcoming 1978).

[153] Married Women's Property Act 1964 s.1. Money saved or property derived from an allowance given by a wife to a husband belongs to her on the principle of the resulting trust.

[154] See L. Weitzman, 'Legal Regulation of Marriage', *California L.R.* vol.62, 1974, p.1169. She describes the conception of a single structure for all marriages as 'tyrannical' (p.1170).

[155] *Post*, p.178.

[156] See *Sheldon* v. *Sheldon* [1966] P.62 and N. Michaels, *M.L.R.*, vol.29, 1966, p.196.

[157] A marriage is consummated as soon as the husband achieves full penetration. The leading definition is Dr Lushington's in *D-E* v. *A-G* (1845) 1 Rob. Eccl. 279, 298.

[158] *S.* v. *S. (orse W.) (no.2)* [1963] P.37.

[159] In their attitudes to rape as well as wife battering. On the former see S. Brownmiller, *Against our Will*, Secker and Warburg, 1975.

[160] *Minutes*, pp 190, 216. Men's Aid began in 1976.

[161] J. Hanmer, 'Violence and the Social Control of Women', op. cit., note 21, p.227.

[162] R. Whitehurst, 'Violence in Husband-Wife Interaction' in S. Steinmetz and M. Straus, *Violence in the Family*, Dodd, Mead, 1974, p.80.

[163] Idem, p.81.

[164] A. Whitehead, 'Sexual Antagonism in Herefordshire' in D.L. Barker and S. Allen (eds), *Dependence and Exploitation in Work and Marriage*, Longman, 1976, p.193.

[165] J. Hanmer, op.cit., note 21, p.228.

[166] S. Griffin suggests that rape is a form of social control in that it constrains women's behaviour. ('Rape: All American Crime', *Ramparts*, September 1971, p.35). On the role of press reports in this see B. Smart and C. Smart, *Women, Sexuality and Social Control*, RKP, 1978, pp 100-2.

[167] According to M. Amir (*Patterns in Forcible Rape*, University of Chicago, p.1971), 48.9 per cent of victims and offenders in rape cases were known to each other, 55.7 per cent of rapes took place in the home, where 26.5 per cent of rapists made initial contact with

their victims. Furthermore, some 70 per cent of rapes were planned rather than spontaneous responses to sexual arousal or opportunity. It is difficult to know how far Amir's study, based on Philadelphia, can be generalised but it certainly suggests that the image of rape to be found in the press is a distorted one.

[168] R. Whitehurst, 'Alternative Family Structures and Violence Reducation' in op.cit., note 162, p.315.

[169] S. Steinmetz and M. Straus, idem, in their introduction to Whitehurst.

[170] R. Delmar, 'Looking Again at Engels's Origins of the Family' in J. Mitchell and A. Oakley (eds), *The Rights and Wrongs of Women*, Penguin, 1976, p.271.

[171] Op.cit., note 21, p.232. On discrimination against women in the USSR (violence is not mentioned, though it doubtless exists) see M. Yanowitch, *Social and Economic Inequalities in the Soviet Union*, Robertson, 1977, ch.6.

[172] P. Abrams and A. McCulloch, *Communes, Sociology and Society*, Cambridge University Press, 1976, ch.5. *Cf* A. Rigby, *Alternative Realities*, RKP, 1974.

[173] Op.cit., note 21, p.24.

[174] The House of Commons Select Committee in its *Report on Violence in Marriage* is a good example of this. Note, for example, the questioning of witnesses that took place in Newcastle (qs 986, 996, 1052): the attribution of drink as the reason for wife battering by members of the committee. This is reflected in the emphasis placed upon reducing alcoholism in the report itself (para. 17).

7 The battered wife — her responses and her needs

The responses of battered wives to the violence perpetrated upon them are by no means uniform. Some put up with their lot. Quite how many no one knows — they are the missing persons of the official statistics. There is no doubt, however, that they constitute the majority of women who have been subjected to violent abuse in the domestic setting.

That amongst so many there should be no positive response is hardly to be wondered at. Women in our society are subjected to all sorts of pressure — cultural, emotional and economic — to marry. They are entrapped within nuclear familialism; forced into dependency. They are taught that 'the love of a good woman can save any man'. [1] Further, if she draws her plight to the attention of control or caring agencies, the police, the courts, the social work profession, she will find their policies supportive of the family and geared towards re-integrating her within it. [2] She may even believe that husbands are supposed to use force against their wives. [3]

Her response may also be conditioned by her physical and psychological state. Erin Pizzey describes this as follows:

> [a]nyone who has been badly knocked about loses all sense
> of reality and ability to cope. Battered women are almost
> permanently in a shocked state. The constant fear of
> another beating leaves them very tense and nervous. Some
> can't eat, others sleep little. Even the toughest find it
> hard to fight off . . . depressions . . . [4]

Who stays and who leaves?

The considerations already referred to apply to women generally. But, are some women more likely to stay than others, as Gelles's findings indicate? [5] He found that three factors in particular influenced the actions of abused women.

First, the less severe and less frequent the violence, the more likely it is that a woman will remain with her husband and not seek outside

157

help. He also found that frequency of violence was related to the type of intervention that the wife sought. Women assaulted most frequently tended to call the police, whilst those beaten less often were inclined to seek a divorce or legal separation. Gelles posits a number of possible explanations for this and, though all of them are plausible, the difference may reflect nothing more than a difference in the socio-economic class of the women affected, working-class women relying on police intervention, where middle-class women sought the advice of the legal profession to solve their marital problems.

Second, it appears that the more the wife was struck by her parents when a child, the more inclined she is to stay with the violent husband. 'Victimization as a child raises the wife's tolerance for violence as an adult'. [6] This is consistent with the social learning hypothesis put forward in the opening chapter. [7]

Third, the more resources a wife has the lower is her threshold of violence. In other words, the less dependent she is on her husband the more willing she is likely to be to seek outside intervention. Gelles found that the wives who stayed were the most poorly educated and the unemployed. Having a job not only gives the wife a certain independence but gives her the opportunity to see what the outside world is like. Gelles quotes one wife as saying: 'when I started being a waitress I used to love to sit there . . . and watch the people — the mother and the father with their children — and see how they acted. And I started to feel like I was cheated . . . and it started to trouble me . . . ' [8] Gelles also found, as Snell and his associates had done in an earlier piece of research, [9] that the presence of an older, particularly teenage, child motivated women to take their husbands to court. The motive, Gelles points out, was to protect their children rather than themselves. One difficulty with this resources hypothesis is that it is middle-class women who may well have most to lose by leaving their husbands. Their standard of living will decline to a greater extent than that of working-class women who may well be on state assistance anyway.

A further factor to which Gelles draws attention is what he calls 'external constraint in the form of police, agency, and court lack of understanding about marital violence'. [10] A woman does not seek outside assistance when she lacks confidence in the support she thinks she is going to receive. She may also fear the courts, and believe she is going to be victimised by, for example, having her children taken away from her.

Finally, there is 'the wife's fear that the myth of her peaceful family life will be exploded'. [11] Privacy is highly cherished; the washing of dirty linen in public is frowned upon. What the neighbours will think is an important constraint on wives seeking help. Scream quietly or the neighbours will hear [12] encapsulates this philosophy. The last thing that most of us want is for details of our personal lives to be exposed in the newspapers.

Gelles puts these factors forward as a partial explanation. They go a considerable way towards explicating why so many wives put up with so much marital violence. A factor which does not figure prominently in Gelles's reasoning but which, it is suggested, is of considerable importance is the existence or otherwise of young children. Many women put up with violent husbands because of the fear of losing their children; the only alternatives open to them may be to leave the children with the father or put them into care. It is also particularly difficult for women with young children to obtain employment: the lack of day care, nursery and other pre-school facilities can cause grave problems. Part-time employment is difficult to obtain and often badly paid. Thus, it is a perception of the children as being economically dependent on the husband/father which may induce many women to stay with a violent partner.

Another important consideration may be the existence or otherwise of sufficient confidence to take the initiative. Women entrapped in marriage may not be used to taking decisions and may lack the confidence to work out something constructive for themselves. It is here that women's centres and refuges play such a vital part, for support, understanding and empathy from fellow sufferers may give the battered wife the strength and confidence which she has not known before, and with this may come the ability to take positive steps about her marriage and her future. [13]

The battered wife's needs

The main needs [14] of a battered wife are, first, medical attention and treatment; second, the need for physical protection; third, access to advice, support, aid and assistance; fourth, alternative sources of accommodation should she not wish to stay with her husband; and fifth, the need for money to support herself and her children.

The question of physical protection as it is dealt with by legal machinery is covered in the next chapter. The more immediate protection afforded by refuges is considered here.

The need for medical assistance is self-evident. It may involve attention to physical injury as well as treatment of psychological disturbance, the result of mental stress caused by the husband's behaviour. The medical profession's response to the battered wife has not been satisfactory. [15] General practitioners have been unwilling to become involved and reluctant to provide forensic evidence. The prescription of anti-depressant drugs as a convenient palliative is common. Hospitals have been accused of being totally insensitive, patching up a battered wife and discharging her without ensuring that she has somewhere safe to go. Mental hospitals' over-willingness to perform leucotomies and administer E.C.T. has been censured, notably by Pizzey. [16]

The rest of this chapter concentrates on the battered wife's other three primary needs: advice, accommodation and economic assistance. It includes a discussion of refuges and the contribution they make towards alleviating the battered wife's plight.

The provision of advice

One battered wife, quoted by Pizzey, must have spoken for many when she said: '[i] t's one vicious circle of very large perimeter, with the woman in the middle and the husband and bureaucracy hitting out from all points'. [17]

In addition, many of the women, in common with the majority of the population, will have at best only a hazy knowledge of what to do, and how to go about doing it, in a crisis. Friends and relatives are a potential source of succour but some will have no friends or relatives to help them solve their problems. Glastonbury et al. found that 'the knowledge, understanding and image that the public holds of the social services is complex, confused and in many important ways inaccurate'. [18] McKay et al. report that less than one-third of consumers knew what to expect of a social services department and that there is a link between lack of expectations and lack of knowledge about the department. [19] Confusion between the role of local authority social services departments and social security particularly appears to be rife. The public's knowledge of the law and the availability of legal services is also poor. [20] A survey in 1969 reported that of people who had been in road accidents only 67 per cent of those interviewed had received advice from a solicitor as to the possibility of making a claim for damages, and that 46 per cent of the respondents professed no knowledge at all of the state Legal Aid and Advice scheme. [21] Nor is there much attempt to publicise its existence.

The battered wife is unlikely to have a solicitor. Even in middle-class property-owning business families the solicitor is likely to be the husband's. Much of the profession is not interested in the casual client in off the streets, particularly where he or she brings a problem, the financial rewards for dealing with which may not be commensurate with the time and effort involved. Many solicitors are not geared towards obtaining emergency legal aid, treating an application for an injunction as a priority and most will have little knowledge of, or experience in dealing with, problems of homelessness or council house tenancies. The local legal centres, which have grown up in the 1970s as a response to unmet legal need, have also tended not to concern themselves with matrimonial problems. [22] Only Lambeth, [23] of the centres in London, has put much effort into helping battered women. There are signs that this is changing but at present, even if a battered wife takes the initiative of seeking legal assistance, she cannot be assured of a ready response.

The battered wife, however, may not even know what help she needs. Her problems are complex and interacting. She may, for example, be faced with sudden homelessness in the middle of the night or at a weekend. What she needs above all else is advice to enable her to sort out and cope with her problems. This was recognised by the Select Committee of the House of Commons in its report on Violence in Marriage. It recommended the setting up of 'well-publicised family crisis centres open continuously to which wives, husbands and children can turn'. [24] The centres would, it argued, have three primary roles:

> Firstly, they should provide an emergency service, hence the 24-hour requirement. This means that they will need to develop very close liaison with the local medical, social, legal and police services. A very important link will be with the refuges . . . Secondly, they should be specially responsible for the co-ordination of the local arrangements already available to women and children in distress. We have been impressed by the fact that one of the prime problems for the family in stress is the need to consult with several different agencies, very often not relating together very effectively . . . The third and non-emergency role we see for the family crisis centres is the development of specialist advisory services, education and publicity programmes, group support and meetings for women with similar problems. [25]

There is currently a multiplicity of organisations which give advice, support and assistance to battered women. They range from the police, social services departments and lawyers on the one hand to housing aid centres, community centres, the Samaritans and the National Council for the One-Parent Family on the other, not to mention women's organisations, the centres, refuges as well as groups like Gingerbread. But, one is struck, as the Select Committee was, by the lack of co-ordination, and by the fact that most advice is given when it is too late. Too few battered women take advice as a preventive measure. That they do not do so stems partly from their own lack of competence. [26] but as much from the lack of provision of such advice. The Select Committee's proposal is, therefore, to be supported. Little has, however, come of it. The government's observations on the Select Committee's report defend the failure to implement this proposal on the ground of cost in a period of severe economic constraints on local and central government. [27] This excuse was not unexpected but is no less disappointing for that. It is a question of priorities, as always, and if we really care about marital violence then 24-hour crisis centres should figure prominently amongst these.

A few 24-hour crisis centres have been established as a result of local initiative. The longest established is in Andover. [28] It is a general crisis and support centre set up in July 1975 by the Hampshire association for the care and resettlement of offenders. It was the brainchild of two local magistrates and was originally conceived as a preventive measure for people in danger of offending while under stress. It is funded in part by the Home Office which estimates that 20 per cent of its work relates to crime and pays that percentage of its costs. The centre works on self-help principles: according to its first report, its approach is a 'non-professional, non-directive one hopefully offering warmth, accurate empathy, non-judgmental listening and encouragement towards mobilisation of one's own resources'. [29] It does not see itself as offering help as such but rather as providing information and helping the 'client' to achieve a state of mind in which he or she can use the information to make decisions. In the first year the largest number of problems (241) concerned accommodation (27.5 per cent) with marital (170) and family (100) the next most significant problems. Men brought most accommodation problems (130), and women most marital problems (118). Over a third of all initial contacts were made by people known to have committed indictable offences; the largest number of these cases concerned battered women. There is provision for women to stay overnight. Some women reported that by having access to immediate refuge at the centre if necessary, they had been able to use the threat of leaving home and/or taking action against their partner as a restraining influence.

The Ormskirk centre was set up, shortly after the Select Committee report, by three energetic ladies, two of whom had themselves been battered wives. [30] It is now sponsored by the West Lancashire District Council. The centre is designated a 'family aid centre', its organisers believing that the word 'crisis' would put people off. Although the centre itself is only open on three days of the week between 10 and 4, advice is available throughout the week on a 24-hour basis. It gives advice to men as well as women. Its underlying philosophy is one of crisis intervention and it uses therapeutic skills towards solution of marital problems. It liaises effectively with many local organisations. [31]

Neither Andover nor Ormskirk can be described as a women's centre. Leicester can. Set up on the initiative of a local women's group it provides information on a 24-hour basis, as well as a drop-in centre for women and children, and support meetings for women who have set up as one-parent families having left violent homes. The centre is seen as offering a parallel and complementary service to the local refuge. In Canterbury, the Women's Centre was planned to provide 'not just a refuge and a meeting place, but advice and support, and such services as pregnancy testing and abortion counselling'. [32] But in its first year 'the "refuge" aspect of the enterprise became more and more dominant and the other activities either never got off the ground or ceased to be important'. [33] It remains a 'Women's Centre', 'something more than just accommodation', [34] but it is not a crisis centre as envisaged by the House of Commons Select Committee.

There have been other plans for crisis centres. One was mooted in Sunderland but did not get off the ground. Another was planned for in Stoke but proved impossible. [35] Nor is it likely that many more will get beyond the drawing-board stage. So it seems that a nationwide network of 24-hour crisis centres must remain merely a dream. The question, therefore, arises as to whether improved advisory services can be worked into existing structures. To that end the proposal of SHAC deserves serious consideration. [36]

It has recommended, amongst other proposals, the establishment of what it calls a 'Primary Advisory Service' for battered wives. Unlike a crisis centre, this would not necessarily require a fixed centre but could be based in a particular local authority department, a housing aid centre or in a citizens' advice bureau. This would cut down on the cost of establishing centres in separate premises. SHAC recognises the need to publicise such a service widely. To be successful there would have to be duty officers available on a round-the-clock basis similar to that which operates in social services departments.

The actual location of the service could prove troublesome. Neither housing aid centres nor citizens advice bureaux are to be found everywhere. However independent, they would tend to be associated in the public's mind with their 'parent' body. If experiences of this are bad, as they are of local authority social services departments, its deterrent image might be transferred to the service. Choice of a 'parent' body would depend on what the primary problem was perceived to be. If it was homelessness, housing aid centres might be seen as the most satisfactory location. The most obvious place, nevertheless, remains the women's refuge. This is the place where the battered wife is most likely to seek help. Above all else, one is struck by the importance of the advice being dispensed by women who have experienced the problem or who have experience in, and understanding of, the battered wife's plight. It is there that she is most likely to be treated as a 'person' and given the confidence (and information) so that she can take decisions herself. There are insufficient refuges as yet but the attachment of 24-hour crisis centres to the 130 or so that exist might prove more than a stop-gap measure. [37] It might demonstrate that these are the most sensible locations for crisis centres. At the same time the experiment should not prove unduly costly.

Wherever it comes from, there is no doubt that co-ordinated, expert and sympathetic advice is crucial if many of the women who suffer violence at the hands of their partner are to be relieved of their fears and feelings of impotence.

The problem of accommodation

The battered wife's major problem is often where to go. The country suffers from an accommodation crisis and homelessness has reached almost epidemic proportions. [38] The woman who is violently ill-treated by her partner is likely to be living in 'his' house. Most likely it will be rented property in the public or private sector; each way the husband is likely to be the tenant. It is possible that they will be joint tenants, very rare that she alone will be the tenant. If the house is being purchased there is an increasing chance that the legal estate will be vested in them jointly [39] and, in default of this, the wife is at the very least likely to have a beneficial interest. [40]

The battered wife's best strategy is to have her husband excluded from the property by an injunction or under the Matrimonial Homes Act 1967. [41] These remedies are considered in the next chapter. They lie within the discretion of the court, they are not final and take some time, however short, to obtain. Since the courts are now reluctant to turn a husband out of the matrimonial home on an *ex parte* application, [42] between 7 and 14 days are likely to elapse before any such application is heard. What is the battered wife to do in the interim period?

She may have relatives or friends with whom she can stay. There may be a refuge close at hand to which she can turn or she may find her way to Chiswick or one of the better known refuges. Squatting is another possibility. But the courts have already held that 'necessity' is no defence, [43] and that reasonable force may be used to eject squatters. [44] And the Criminal Law Act 1977, whilst not making squatting as such specifically criminal, has given the police powers to effect instant evictions. [45] It has frequently been argued that she is not technically homeless for she can always return to the matrimonial home. Many local authorities hitherto have operated such a ruling. Aylesbury, for example, claimed that battered women were voluntarily homeless; [46] it has refused to accept that she was homeless if her husband would have her back, regardless of her own choice or any danger she might face in returning. The National Women's Aid Federation found that only 20 of the 70 authorities where it had a group accepted battered women as homeless. [47]

How much of this will change as a result of the Housing (Homeless Persons) Act 1977 is difficult to predict. Certainly, on the face of it homeless persons generally and particularly battered women who find themselves homeless are accorded greater protection than hitherto. Thus, a person is defined as 'homeless' if it is probable that occupation of accommodation 'will lead to violence from some other person residing in it or to threats of violence from some other person residing in it and likely to carry out the threats'. [48] The *Code of Guidance*, issued by the Department of Environment, Department of Health and Social Security and Welsh Office asks housing authorities 'to respond sympathetically to applications from women who are in fear of violence'. [49] Certain groups are singled out by the statute as having a priority need for accommodation. [50] The Act does not specify battered women, though an amendment urged that it should do so. But a person with dependent children residing with him or who might reasonably be expected to reside with him is mentioned, and the Code adds '[o]ne-parent families, including battered women with their children, are included'. [51] Pregnant women are specifically included. [52] Non-pregnant battered women without children are not but the Code considers it appropriate to include 'battered women without children who are at risk of violent pursuit, or if they return home, at risk of further violence' under the umbrella 'any other special reason' which is found in the Act. [53]

A person, however, is not entitled to rehousing if he became homeless or threatened with homelessness intentionally. [54] This exclusion clause will certainly catch many and may well work injustice. The *Code of Guidance*, however, states that 'a battered woman who has fled the marital home should never be regarded as having become homeless intentionally because it would not be reasonable for her to remain'. [55] If housing authorities adopt this reasoning, and the Act says that they 'shall have regard' [56] to such guidance, this should lead to a complete reversal of the policies referred to earlier. We can only wait to see what happens.

Once a housing authority has satisfied itself as a result of inquiries that an applicant is homeless or threatened with homelessness, has a priority need and is not homeless or threatened with homelessness intentionally, its duty is 'to secure that accommodation becomes available for his occupation' [57] (or to take reasonable steps to secure that accommodation does not cease to be available for his occupation in the case of persons threatened with homelessness). The housing authority has a further out-clause: the applicant must have a 'local connection with their area'. [58] However, despite this, the duty remains where the applicant or any person who might reasonably be expected to reside with him or her 'will run the risk of domestic violence' [59] in the area of the housing authority with which he or she has local connection. The *Code of Guidance* advises that 'in considering this it will be relevant to take account of the fears of those concerned'. [60] This is of considerable advantage to the battered woman who may only feel safe when some distance from her husband but who hitherto has fallen foul of residency rules under which, for example, responsibility towards rehousing ceases when a person has been out of the area for 24 hours. Both Cardiff and York were known to apply this stringent rule. [61] In London, however, an agreement operates between boroughs (the London Boroughs Association Agreement) under which it is recommended that 'the authority in whose area the applicants were in residence the preceding night is the authority primarily responsible for the reception'. [62] SHAC found that most boroughs fulfilled at least some part of this agreement but some do not. [63] In Redbridge, for example, the woman is referred to the 'responsible Borough'. [64] Similar agreements operate outside: the National Women's Aid Federation found that 28 out of the 70 authorities in its study operated this type of scheme. [65] At least in some parts of the country the new statutory exception for battered women should prove beneficial.

Hitherto, local authorities have adopted variable attitudes towards the rehousing of battered women. Some have required her to have taken out legal proceedings against her husband before they will re-house her. Some have been satisfied when proceedings have been initiated; others have insisted that the divorce is completed. A number did not require a battered wife to start proceedings at all before granting temporary accommodation. A common and seemingly reasonable requirement has been that the children are in the woman's care. But this can lead to a Catch-22 situation when a woman is refused custody of her children because she is homeless and the local authority refuses to rehouse her as she does not have children in her care. The House of Commons Select Committee report recommended that local authorities have 'speedy and flexible policies' [66] for transferring tenancies from husband to wife in cases of marital break-down where the wife is caring for the children. These decisions are rarely taken with urgency; many housing committees meet only once in six weeks and not at all during the summer months. The husband's rent arrears commonly operate as a barrier to rehousing the wife. This practice was rightly deprecated by the House of Commons Select Committee. [67]

On a divorce the courts have power to transfer council tenancies to the wife, though they are reluctant to exercise their powers unless the local authority is co-operative. [68] The attitude of most London boroughs [69] (and it is typical of the country as a whole [70]) is to transfer tenancies to the wife's name where she has obtained custody of the children. Most of them require also that the wife has obtained a separation order or divorce before the tenancy transfer is effected, so that an interim custody order pending the divorce hearing will not of itself be sufficient. Final orders of custody can, however, only be obtained at the stage of a decree nisi and then only in cases where the custody application is not contested. Where it is, or where the divorce itself is contested, the entire case can take up to six months, or occasionally even longer. Even an uncontested case may take three months.

With all these problems many women not surprisingly fall back on the refuges or shelters established by Women's Aid or the National Women's Aid Federation. There were refuges before Erin Pizzey established one in Chiswick. As long ago as 1965 Al-Anon, a self-help group for families of alcoholics, set up a hostel in Pasadena, California. [71] But the establishment of Chiswick Women's Aid in 1971 was the starting-point for the current trend to create refuges specifically for battered women. Today there are well over 100 [72] in Great Britain and shelters also exist in many other countries.

Although the Department of Environment in its memorandum to

the House of Commons Select Committee argued that '[n]ot enough [was] yet known about violence to women to make it possible to conclude that special "refuge" or "shelter" accommodation, of a shared nature, such is at present being provided, is necessarily in the best — and particularly the longer-term interests of the wives and children', [73] the Committee itself was in no doubt that 'the Department must ensure that refuges are provided by local authorities and/or voluntary organisations'. [74] It recommended that there should be 'one family place per 10,000 of the population'. [75] This is almost certainly an underestimate of the need based, the Committee admits, on 'scant information'. [76] If one is right to think that the number of women violently treated by husbands and those with whom they cohabit is of the order of half a million, many more refuges than the Committee has envisaged are needed.

The National Women's Aid Federation thinks that 15,500 family places, or over 1,000 refuges will be needed to meet the Select Committee's 'initial target'. [77] In its report *And Still You've Done Nothing*, published in 1976, it stated that there were only 504 family places in 73 refuges and that often the provision was inadequate. [78] By December 1976 the government was estimating that there were over 100. [79] There are now (January 1978) about 140 refuges, some 130 of which are affiliated to the National Women's Aid Federation. [80] But even so, by the House of Commons Select Committee's standards, Great Britain is at least 860 refuges short of the recommended 'initial' provision, and this, be it noted, based on an almost certain underestimate of the problem.

The Select Committee also recommended that local authorities make available to voluntary groups some of the larger houses they own or may acquire, and stipulated that this should be regarded as a 'priority category for local authority expenditure and acquisition and improvement'. [81] Many local authorities have disregarded these recommendations and some have positively obstructed attempts to set up refuges. In Great Yarmouth, the Women's Aid group has been told to find a detached house with a large amount of land surrounding it, though no such properties exist there. [82] In Leeds an application for urban aid was turned down on the grounds of absence of need. [83] In Hastings battered women, after an 18-month campaign for a refuge, squatted in a derelict hotel and were evicted; the same day the social services department asked the refuge to take a woman and her four children! [84] The Canterbury Women's Centre, as indeed many others, also started as a squat. [85] Groups in Bradford, York and Hull are others to have encountered severe resistance from local authorities. Bradford, for example, has recently had its urban aid grant withdrawn, Leeds having earlier been refused a similar grant because Bradford had one. The government, which has helped the spread of refuges by making urban aid available, can no longer provide money for new projects concerning battered wives. [86]

Refuges provide accommodation but they provide much else besides. They give the battered woman protection, advice, comfort and confidence. Anne Marcovitch has written that 'support from other like-sufferers is perhaps the greatest strength of a refuge, and gives many confidence they have not known before'. [87] Some women stay a few days only; others may stay for more than six months. [88] Some refuges have half-way houses for women who have been accepted on local authority housing lists but not yet been found accommodation. Some women come to a refuge more than once, having returned home in the hope that their marriage will improve. Marcovitch noted that half the women in Acton returned to their husbands within a few weeks. [89] She says as a result 'coming to a refuge is not necessarily divisive of family life'. And Jan Pahl comments that 'the availability of a refuge can enable some marriages to continue'. [90] It may be that for some marriage to a violent husband is preferable to life in an overcrowded refuge. Others may realise that the alternatives to married life, given housing, employment, child care and other social policies, are limited and limiting. Too much should not be read into the fact that many women return home.

Some women prefer to seek refuge in a hostel away from their home locality. This is understandable. In a nearby refuge a woman may run the risk of her husband finding her and assaulting her again. Local authorities, of course, are more willing to support a refuge where the women to be housed are local. That some have fled from another town is a convenient excuse or rationalisation for failure to help in establishing or continuing a refuge. It is also more difficult for the woman who may find she loses housing rights in her own area and has difficulty getting on to the housing list in the place where she has sought refuge. Another difficulty may be that local housing authorities will not view a battered woman living in a refuge as homeless for the purpose of the Housing (Homeless Persons) Act 1977. It is understood that in Sheffield the Act has already been so interpreted. [91]

Under the Housing Act 1961 a local authority can fix the maximum number of individuals permitted to occupy, *inter alia*, a refuge at any one time. With a paucity of refuges the temptation to exceed the stipulated figure must be great. Better known refuges, like Chiswick, are invariably overcrowded. The London Borough of Hounslow, having fixed 36 as the maximum number of individuals permitted to occupy the Chiswick refuge, proceeded in 1976 to prosecute Erin Pizzey for exceeding that figure. On the relevant date the number of residents was 75. Pizzey's policy is never to turn away any woman who comes for shelter and protection and the number of residents often exceeds 100. The prosecution went right up to the House of Lords which held, with considerable regret, that, as the law stands, the occupier of a house of refuge for battered mothers and their children was not a single household, so that when the residents at any time exceeded 36, the occupier of the house could be prosecuted. [92] Lord Hailsham clearly indicated that the magistrates should exercise restraint and mercy in sentencing Pizzey and she was in fact conditionally discharged. [93] Unrepentant, she announced she had no intention of complying with the local authority demand and invited a further prosecution. It has not come though it cannot be ruled out.

The prosecution raises a number of important questions. When Parliament passed the Housing Act the problem of battered women had not been recognised, so that their plight was not in mind. It would be difficult to argue that women and children from many different families constitute a single household, and this is certainly not what a commonsense interpretation of this expression embraces. But what were the alternatives to Pizzey taking in nearly 40 additional persons? Was the London Borough of Hounslow in a position to provide alternative accommodation? Could other authorities, from some of which the women would anyway have come, assist and, if so, were they willing to? Would alternative accommo-dation, if it were available, have involved splitting mothers from their children, with the children going into care? If so, this must be seen, as the Housing (Homeless Persons) Act 1977 sees it, as an unacceptable solution.

The need for economic support

A battered wife who leaves her husband has two main sources of economic support: her husband and the Supplementary Benefits Commission. A third possibility is remunerative employment. If she has children, and the assumption in this section will be that she has, employment prospects will not be good. But whether she has children or not, even after the Equal Pay Act and Sex Discrimination Act, her chances of obtaining a good wage are not bright. [94] If she works full-time then Family Income Supplement may make good

170

some of the deficiency of her low wages but, as with all means-tested benefits, the take-up rate is low, [95] and without advice she may not know to apply for it.

The husband's duty to maintain is hardly worth considering. Until recently where she had committed adultery it did not operate. [96] Even if she can obtain a maintenance order she still has to enforce it. [97] Most orders, even if adequately enforced, cannot contribute much to the finances of the woman and her children, since the husbands will often be low wage earners. The problems of squeezing money out of deserting husbands are well enough known from the Finer Report [98] and Marsden's *Mothers Alone*. [99] Securing money from a battering husband cannot be any easier and is likely to prove more difficult. The woman who lives on maintenance payments and part-time earnings will probably be living below the supplementary benefit level. [100]

So she is likely to have to rely on supplementary benefit. Finer found that the main source of income of half the fatherless families other than widows' families was supplementary benefit. [101] It demonstrated that the numbers of fatherless families dependent upon supplementary benefit had increased fourfold since 1955 because 'it progressively became less worthwhile for a lone woman with children to take up full-time employment and cease to claim supplementary benefit unless she could earn well above the average wage for woman in full-time work'. [102] There are no separate statistics of the numbers of battered women on supplementary benefit. But their problems will be broadly the same as those of other fatherless families. Perhaps the stigma which attaches to being a battered wife is less than being divorced or separated, but so long as people believe 'she deserved it', this may not be so. [103]

Supplementary benefit is not an adequate way of bringing up a family. Although exceptional needs payments are available, usually to meet very ordinary needs like clothes, and a rent allowance is payable (to a refuge if the battered woman lives there), the basic level of resources provided by the supplementary benefit scheme is not calculated to ensure more than the merest existence. [104] According to the Finer Report nearly half of fatherless families (excluding widows with insurance benefit) had been on supplementary benefit for over two years. [105] Church showed recently that 'the allowance for all children 5-10 years old on supplementary benefit . . . is totally inadequate to provide enough food, even if as much as 75 per cent of the benefit is spent on food in the most efficient fashion'. [106]

Being on supplementary benefit has other disadvantages too. Primary amongst these is being subject to the cohabitation rule. [107]

If two persons who are not married live together as man and wife, only the man can normally become entitled to supplementary benefit. The woman, in such a case, cannot claim benefit in her own right any more than if she were married, unless the Supplementary Benefits Commission finds that there are exceptional circumstances to justify non-aggregation. The cohabitation rule makes it difficult for a woman on supplementary benefit to strike up any kind of relationship with a man, the fear being that should her activity be construed as cohabitation she would lose her entitlement to benefit. A woman on benefit is susceptible to constant surveillance and prying by special investigators whose job is to determine whether she, as a claimant, is accurately portraying her circumstances. The Supplementary Benefits Commission admits this is 'distasteful work'. The cohabitation rule and its administration ensure that many women who leave their husbands do not remarry. This fact, in its turn, condemns many of them to survive on supplementary benefit for a considerable period.

Conclusion

This brief survey of some of the main problems of the battered wife should go some way towards explaining the question posed at the beginning of the chapter. The alternatives to marriage in our society ensure that many women stay with their husbands however brutal their behaviour.

Notes

[1]   Per E. Pizzey, *Scream Quietly or the Neighbours Will Hear*, Penguin, 1974, p.41.
[2]   Idem, p.93 (on social services). On the police see HC *Minutes*, pp 366, 369. See also R. Holman et al., *Socially Deprived Families in Britain*, National Council of Social Service, 1970.
[3]   See R. Gelles, *The Violent Home*, Sage, 1972, pp 59-60. See also K. Millett's comment that females are 'rendered innocuous by [their] socialisation. Before assault [they are] universally defenceless both by physical and emotional training'. See *Sexual Politics*, Hart Davis, 1971, p.44.
[4]   Op.cit., note 1, p.41.
[5]   R. Gelles, 'Abused Wives: Why Do They Stay? *Journal of Marriage and the Family*, vol.38, 1976, p.659.

[6]   Idem, p.667.

[7]   *Ante*, p.

[8]   Op.cit., note 5, p.664.

[9]   J. Snell, 'The Wifebeater's Wife', *Archives of General Psychiatry*, vol.11, 1964, p.107.

[10] Op.cit., note 5, p.667.

[11] Idem, p.666. See also E. Truninger, *Hastings L. Journal*, vol.23, 1971, pp 259, 264.

[12] The title of Pizzey's book, note [1] .

[13] A point also made by A. Marcovitch, *Social Work Today*, vol.7, no.2, 1976, p.34.

[14] There is a good discussion of these in N. Miller, *Battered Spouses*, Bell, 1975, ch.2.

[15] Op.cit., note 1, pp 101-6.

[16] Idem, p.104.

[17] Idem, p.28.

[18] B. Glastonbury, et al., 'Community Perceptions and the Personal Social Services', *Policy and Politics*, vol.1, 1973, p.3. See also A. Glampson et al., 'Knowledge and Perceptions of the Social Services', *Journal of Social Policy,* no.6, 1977, p.1.

[19] A. McKay et al., 'Consumers and a Social Services Department', *Social Work Today*, vol.4, no.16, 1973, p.486.

[20] B. Abel-Smith, M. Zander and R. Brooke, *Legal Problems and the Citizen*, Heinemann, 1973.

[21] S. Harz, *New Law Journal*, vol.118, 1969, p.492.

[22] This is clear from their annual reports. Their rationale is that the private profession deals adequately with matrimonial problems. Certainly, until the withdrawal of legal aid from undefended divorces it appeared to do so.

[23] See its *Annual Report* 1975-76, p.24.

[24] Select Committee of the House of Commons, *Report on Violence in Marriage*, para. 20.

[25] Idem.

[26] *Cf* J. Carlin and J. Howard, *UCLA Law Review*, vol.12, 1965, p.381.

[27] *Observations on the Select Committee Report*, Cmnd 6690, paras 29-32.

[28] It is the only one known to the government (Cmnd 6690, para. 32).

[29] Andover Crisis Centre, 1st *Annual Report*, 1976.

[30] *The Times*, 8 December 1975.

[31] Though apparently not with social services departments.

[32] See J. Pahl, *The Canterbury Women's Centre 1975-76*, University of Kent, 1977, para. 2.15, (now published by HMSO, 1978)

[33] Idem.

[34] Idem.

[35] See T. and B. Faragher, University of Keele, Battered Womens' Project, 1977 (unpublished material).

[36] SHAC Report, *Violence in Marriage*, 1976.

[37] The exact number changes all the time and is not known for certain. This figure was computed on information supplied by the National Women's Aid Federation and takes account of the 10 or so centres not under their aegis.

[38] Despite a large number of empty houses, including empty local authority property. In 1976 there were 17.6 million households and 18.1 million dwellings (*Housing Policy — A Consultative Document*, Cmnd 6851, para. 3.04).

[39] See J.E. Todd and L.M. Jones, *Matrimonial Property*, HMSO, 1972, pp 9-12.

[40] If, for example, she has contributed towards the deposit or made a substantial contribution towards the improvement of the property. See *Gissing* v. *Gissing* [1971] A.C.886 and s.37 of the Matrimonial Proceedings and Property Act 1970.

[41] As amended by s.3 of the Domestic Violence and Matrimonial Proceedings Act 1976.

[42] See *Ansah* v. *Ansah* [1977] 2 All E.R.638 and *post*, p.200.

[43] *L.B. of Southwark* v. *Williams* [1971] Ch.734.

[44] *McPhail* v. *Persons Unknown* [1973] 3 All E.R.393.

[45] Criminal Law Act 1977 ss 6-8. There is a useful note by S. Tarlin, *LAG Bulletin*, December 1977, p.285.

[46] NWAF, *And Still You've Done Nothing*, 1976, p.2.

[47] Idem.

[48] Housing (Homeless Persons) Act 1977, s.1(2)(b). On this see HL, vol.386, col.660 *per* Lord Gifford.

[49] *Code of Guidance*, issued by Department of Environment and DHSS and Welsh Office, 1977, para. 2.10(b).

[50] Housing (Homeless Persons) Act 1977, s.2.

[51] *Code of Guidance*, op.cit., note 50, para. 2.12(a).

[52] s.2(2).

[53] *Code of Guidance*, op.cit., note 50, para. 2.12(c)(iii). A local authority housing committee decision that such a group should never be regarded as vulnerable could be challenged in court on the grounds of unreasonable fettering of discretion.

[54] s.17.

[55] *Code of Guidance*, op.cit., note 49, para. 2.16.
[56] Housing (Homeless Persons) Act 1977, s.12.
[57] Idem, s.4(3).
[58] Idem, s.5(1)(a)(i).
[59] Idem, s.5(1)(a)(iii), (11).
[60] *Code of Guidance* , op.cit., note 49, para. 2.20.
[61] NWAF, *And Still You've Done Nothing*, 1976, p.4.
[62] Quoted in SHAC Report, *Violence in Marriage*, 1976.
[63] Idem.
[64] Idem.
[65] Op.cit., note 61, p.9.
[66] Report of Select Committee, *Violence in Marriage*, HC 553 1974-75, para. 50.
[67] Idem.
[68] *Thompson* v. *Thompson* [1975] 2 All E.R.208; *Regan* v. *Regan* [1977] 1 All E.R.428. And see M.D.A. Freeman and C.M. Lyon, 'When the Matrimonial Home is a Council House', *Family Law*, vol.8, p.187 (1978).
[69] See SHAC Report, *Violence in Marriage*, 1976.
[70] On Hampshire see M. Grant, *Local Authority Housing: Law, Policy and Practice in Hampshire*, Hants LAG, 1976, p.31.
[71] D. Martin, *Battered Wives*, Glide, 1976, p.197.
[72] The exact number is not known but is about 140.
[73] *Minutes*, p.179, para. 14.
[74] *Minutes*, para. 29.
[75] Idem.
[76] Idem.
[77] Op.cit., note 62, pp 13-4.
[78] Idem, p.14.
[79] *Observations on the Select Committee Report*, Cmnd 6690, para. 35. It gives a list in Appendix 4.
[80] See note 37.
[81] Op.cit., note 66, para. 30.
[82] See op.cit., note 61, p.15.
[83] *Minutes of Select Committee,* pp 67-8.
[84] J. Melville 'In Search of Refuge', *New Society*, 25 August 1977, p.389.
[85] See J. Pahl, op.cit., note 32, para. 2.1.
[86] So stated in *Observations on the Select Committee Report*, Cmnd 6690, 1976.
[87] A. Marcovitch, 'Refuges for Battered Women', *Social Work Today*, vol.7, no.2, 1976, p.34.

[88] See J. Pahl, op.cit., note 32, para. 4.3 and table 2.
[89] Op.cit., note 87, pp 34-5.
[90] Op.cit., note 32, para 5.17.
[91] Information provided by NWAF.
[92] *Simmons* v. *Pizzey* [1977] 2 All E.R.432.
[93] *The Times*, 7 October 1977.
[94] Women earn on average two-thirds of the average male wages.
[95] See R. Lister, *Take-up of Means-Tested Benefits*, Child Poverty Action Group, 1974. The level of take-up has never exceeded 75 per cent.
[96] Matrimonial Proceedings (Magistrates' Courts) Act 1960, s.2(3)(b), now repealed by the Domestic Proceedings and Magistrates' Courts Act 1978.
[97] A problem considered by O. McGregor et al., *Separated Spouses*, Duckworth, 1970, ch.7.
[98] *Finer Report on One Parent Families*, Cmnd 5629, pt IV.
[99] D. Marsden, *Mothers Alone*, Penguin, 1973, ch.10.
[100] See Finer Report, op.cit., note 98, para 5.24 and Appendix 10.
[101] Idem, table 5.1 (p.244).
[102] Idem, para 5.11. See also figure 5.1 (p.245).
[103] The real question may be whether battered women are seen to pose a threat to marriage. *Cf* D. Marsden in *British Journal of Law and Society*, vol.1, 1974, p.175.
[104] R. Lister, *Patching Up the Safety Net?* CPAG, 1977.
[105] Op.cit., note 98, para 5.20.
[106] M. Church, 'Can Mothers Manage on Supplementary Benefit?' *Poverty*, no.33, pp 10, 13. See, further, E. Ferri, *Growing Up in a One-Parent Family* and E. Ferri and H. Robinson, *Coping Alone*, both National Foundation for Educational Research, 1976.
[107] It is doubtful if the reforms currently taking place in this (see SBC, *Living Together as Husband and Wife*, 1976) will have a significant impact on the problems created by its administration. On these see J. Streather and S. Weir, *Social Insecurity*, CPAG, 1974. The DHSS Report, *Social Assistance* (July 1978) supports the retention of the cohabitation rule (see para. 4.22).

8 Legal responses to the problem of the battered wife

The law cannot solve the problem of the battered wife. But it remains a weapon at her disposal. This chapter considers each of the remedies open to a battered wife. An understanding of these remedies requires first cognition of how women (particularly married women) are seen in English law.

Married women — in English law

The Christian conception of man and wife as one flesh is the foundation of much of the common law on husband and wife. [1] And, as has been said, [2] to this Pauline conclusion English law added the rider: 'and I am he'. The very being of the married woman was 'suspended' [3] during coverture. Most of the disabilities [4] have now been removed though significant vestiges remain; the cohabitation rule, already referred to, is an outstanding example. [5] The strength of the *Volksgeist* [6] in expressive relationships [7] has often been commented upon; law reform in family law does not guarantee a change in the *mores*. [8] As was shown in chapter 6 [9] the mores still reflect an inegalitarian relationship.

For centuries husbands had the right to chastise their wives. Hawkins would allow a man to exercise 'moderate correction' upon his wife as he would 'correct his apprentices or children'. [10] In Bacon's Abridgement of 1736 a husband is said to have the right to 'beat' his wife. [11] Blackstone, in words reminiscent of contemporaries who believe that wife batterers are confined to a working-class subculture, believed that the right was obsolete, having been doubted in the politer reign of Charles II, but that 'the lower rank of people who were always fond of the old common law still claim and exert their ancient privilege and courts of law still permit a husband to restrain a wife of her liberty in case of any gross misbehaviour'. [12] The right was 'finally abolished' [13] in 1891 in *R. v. Jackson*: the Master of the Rolls doubted whether 'it ever was the law' and the Lord Chancellor referred to 'quaint and absurd dicta'. [14] There are, however, dicta as late as 1840 [15] supporting a general right.

More recently, judges have defended the right of a husband to correct his wife. In 1946 Henn Collins J. in *Meacher* v. *Meacher* [16] held that a husband was within his rights in assaulting his wife when she refused to obey his orders not to visit her relations. The Court of Appeal did, however, reverse his ruling. In 1959 a judge held that it was cruelty when a husband gave his adulterous wife the 'hardest smacked bottom she had ever had' but added that if he had punished her as one punishes a naughty child it would not have been cruel. [17] Only three years ago a sheriff in Scotland, on fining a husband for hitting his wife in the face, remarked: 'it is a well known fact that you can strike your wife's bottom if you wish, but you must not strike her on the face'. He also expressed his support for the ancient principle that 'reasonable chastisement should be the duty of every husband if his wife misbehaves'. [18]

Do these judicial pronouncements, isolated as they are, reflect the common consciousness of a society ruled by the ethos of male domination? Do they go some way towards explaining the oft-quoted rationalisation of wife battering that 'they deserve it'. [19] Gelles found women who subscribed to this view. One said: 'he hit me once. It wasn't very long ago. The baby was about two months old . . . we were fighting about something. I have a habit of not keeping my mouth shut. I kept at him and at him. He finally turned round and belted me. It was my fault, I asked for it'. [20] Parnas also observed occasions where wives believed that a husband should beat his wife 'every once in a while'. [21] The deviance has, in other words, become normalised. Dunn J. though, got 'a wigging from wives' when he suggested that wives in the North of England didn't mind their husbands beating them but drew the line at adultery (he thought wives in the South were more tolerant of adultery than a hiding!). [22] And Faulks J. confessed to having made 'an ass' of himself when he insinuated that the wives of Welsh miners accepted their husbands' right to spank them. [23]

The problem of rape

This ideology is reflected in the attitude of English law towards rape. By definition it cannot exist within marriage, though the behaviour itself, forced sexual intercourse, may be functionally equivalent to comparable behaviour committed outside the bounds of marriage and given the official label of rape. [24] The cohabitee is thus theoretically in a better position, though it is doubtful if a jury would be willing to convict in such circumstances. In the past a husband could be convicted of raping his wife if magistrates had made a non-cohabitation order in her favour. [25]   Now a conviction could follow where a decree nisi of divorce has been pronounced, [26] and possibly also where a husband and wife have agreed to separate, particularly if they have entered into a separation agreement which contains a non-molestation clause. [27]

In 1972 Cairns L.J. expressed the opinion that 'the notion that a husband can, without incurring punishment, treat his wife . . . with any kind of hostile force is obsolete'. [28]   He held that the crime of kidnapping could thus be committed by a husband against his wife. Kidnapping and rape are not on all fours, but Cairns L.J.'s dictum is wide enough to cast doubt on the propriety of exempting husbands from prosecution for rapes upon their wives. Despite the existence of the immunity it is clear that a husband, though at liberty to have sexual intercourse with his wife, may not use force or violence to exercise that liberty. If he does so he may be charged with assault or some other criminal offence. The law rests on a fiction and is clearly inconsistent with civil law principles. A wife, for example, is not bound to submit to inordinate or unreasonable sexual demands by her husband [29] and she may refuse sexual intercourse if he is suffering from a venereal disease. [30]

The privilege of a husband to rape his wife has been repudiated in the criminal codes of Sweden and Denmark and in the USSR and a number of other countries in the Communist bloc. [31]   It was recently abolished in Delaware [32] and South Dakota. [33]   An attempt was made to abolish the exemption in England in 1976 but it failed. [34]

The act of rape may be seen as a cameo of male-female relationships; forcible penetration being at one end of a spectrum of male sexual dominance. [35]   Susan Griffin refers to it as 'a form of mass terrorism'. [36]   Davis believes that 'a primary goal of the sexual aggressor . . . is the conquest and degradation of his victim'. [37]   The Schwendingers see rape as 'a power trip . . . an act of aggression and an act of contempt'. [38]   Too often rape has been seen in explicitly sexual terms but it is clear that it is only secondarily sexual and is primarily an act of domination and degradation. [39]

The protection of the criminal law

The first of the remedies open to the battered wife is to invoke the processes of the criminal law. What protection is she afforded by this? Rape excepted, her husband can be prosecuted for any of the offences

179

against the person. It is unnecessary to list all these offences. They range from common assault to murder. Most marital violence thought serious enough even to consider criminal process is likely to amount to an assault occasioning actual bodily harm or one causing grievous bodily harm. [40] To constitute 'actual bodily harm' the harm need not be really serious. Lynskey J. said that it 'includes any hurt or injury calculated to interfere with the health or comfort of the prosecutor'. [41] This includes, so he held, a hysterical and nervous condition resulting from an assault. It seems to follow that many, if not most, acts of molestation will come within the concept. The more serious offence is committed when 'really serious' [42] bodily harm is caused.

If criminal proceedings are brought the wife is a competent but not a compellable witness against her own husband. [43] In fact, though, if she is an unwilling witness the police may well be hard put to prove the charge. Provocation is a defence only to a charge of murder (reducing it to manslaughter), [44] so a husband may not claim that he was driven to assault his wife. However, we know that juries do take account of such 'defences', [45] rather as they regard contributory negligence as a defence to a charge of rape. [46] Furthermore, the battered wife's view of her own role in the event may lead decide not to mobilise the criminal justice system. [47]

There have been several cases in England recently of wives who killed brutal husbands. Two of them, the *Bangert* [48] and *Pulling* [49] cases, got a lot of sympathetic press coverage. To Mabel Bangert, who killed her husband by stabbing him repeatedly in the back as he went to attack their crippled son, Milmo J. said: 'you have lived your life with a tyrannical, violent and cruel husband. Your provocation was as severe as any I have come across'. She was convicted of manslaughter and received a suspended sentence. Valerie Pulling shot her husband when she feared another beating from him. May J. told the jury that it was important to assess the case without emotion; he advised an acquittal if they felt it was not Mrs Pulling's intention to kill or seriously harm her husband. The jury did not, it seems, put emotion aside and, in a perverse [50] but arguably justifiable verdict, acquitted her. It is difficult to estimate how typical these cases are; my own suspicion is that both judges and juries take a more lenient attitude to such crimes than they would have done a decade ago.

In some legal systems, though not the English, wife beating is a distinct nominate crime. This is the case in California, Texas and Hawaii. [51] In California a statute dating from 1945 states: 'any husband who willfully inflicts upon his wife corporal injury resulting in a traumatic condition . . . is guilty of a felony' and this is punishable by a gaol sentence of between one and ten years. In *People* v. *Burns* [52] it was held that to satisfy this provision visible bruises and injuries had to be present. According to Del Martin police and district attorneys have been unwilling to charge an assailant with this offence, which is a felony, because of the higher bail and potentially longer prison sentence involved. [53] This statutory provision discriminates on the basis of sex and is therefore arguably unconstitutional. In 1975 its constitutionality was challenged successfully in the San Jose Superior Court. Judge Eugene Premo, dismissing a charge on this very basis, said, 'a wife inflicting the same injury and trauma can be subjected to no more than misdemeanour prosecution under assault and battery sections. [54] Del Martin has been forceful in her criticism of this decision which she accuses of taking advantage of the 'existing male bias within the criminal justice system' and 'denying the value of laws created to correct existing imbalances' [55] But, given that the criminal law is a blunt instrument in the war against domestic violence, it is dubious if the creation (or maintenance) of specific offences can be of much value.

Compensation for criminal injury

In Great Britain a scheme has existed since 1964 whereby victims of criminal assaults can claim compensation from the state. [56] The idea originated in New Zealand and has since spread. It has cost the British exchequer over £40 million. Applications each year are up on the previous year. In 1976-77 there was a 22.3 per cent increase over the applications of 1975-76. [57] Wives who suffer personal injury at their husbands' hands are, however, excluded from obtaining compensation under the scheme, as are cohabitees. The scheme is non-statutory. Paragraph 7 of it reads:

> Where the victim who suffered injuries and the offender who
> inflicted them were living together at the time as members
> of the same family no compensation will be payable. For
> the purpose of this paragraph where a man and a woman
> were living together as man and wife they will be treated as
> if they were married to one another. [58]

In the first 13 years of the operation of the scheme 433 applicants for compensation were ruled out of order on the basis of paragraph 7, that is, 3 per cent of all applications have failed because the injury was caused in a domestic setting. There were 76 such cases in 1975-76 (4 per cent of the total number of applications) [59] and 98 in

1976-77 (5 per cent of the applications). [60] Many of these applications are made on behalf of children. [61]

The battered wife's plight was aggravated by a decision of the Divisional Court in 1972. [62] Lord Widgery C.J. held that the words 'living together . . . as members of the same family' had their ordinary, natural meaning and were not to be read in the light of general matrimonial law. He concluded that a couple were 'living together' although the wife, terrified for her own safety, slept in a bedroom with her two daughters, leaving her husband to sleep on a sofa in the living room. There were no sexual relations between them and, although we do not know from the report about other domestic arrangements, we may assume that he would have been held to be in desertion and that they would be 'living apart' for the separation provisions of the divorce legislation. [63] In view of this the decision is to be deprecated.

A wife who is separated from her husband is eligible for compensation as are divorced women. Thus, where a former husband slashed his former wife's hands, lacerating tendons and ensuring that she was no longer able to work, the Criminal Injuries Compensation Board paid her compensation (his behaviour was subsequently held to be sufficiently 'obvious and gross' to be taken account of when the question of a transfer of property arose). [64]

The British system is not alone in excluding victims of family violence. [65] So far as is known the only system which does not so exclude them is that which operates in California. [66] How is one to explain the exclusion from the British scheme of victims of family violence? The Board itself pointed to the injustice involved as long ago as 1972 in its 8th report. [67] The exclusion was one of the main areas of concern of the Interdepartmental Working Party which began to look into the scheme in 1973 and finally reported in 1978. [68] Defences set up to justify the exclusion emphasise first, the difficulties of proof in a family situation and the dangers of fraudulent claims; second, the possibility of the state being flooded with a huge number of applications, many of them relatively trivial; and third, the danger that the offender will benefit from the compensation. [69] None of these defences is a satisfactory explanation. There are problems of proof in all cases, particularly where there are no witnesses. Fraudulent claims must be guarded against and subjected to criminal prosecution. There are unlikely to be many. The 'floodgates' argument is also disingenuous as, with the number of violent crimes known to the police approaching 100,000 a year (that is something like seven times the number of applicants for compensation), they are potentially open anyway, for it is only lack of knowledge and 'legal competence' [70] which cut access to the Board down to manageable proportions. Nor should it be difficult to ensure that the offender does not benefit from an award.

A better explanation is found, in another context entirely, in Marx's recent study of violence in an Israeli township. [71] He argues that in the case of interpersonal assaults in the privacy of the home that 'the public interest is not at stake', with the result that 'law organs tend to apply a more restricted definition of violence to them'. [72] Of course, it is arguable that male violence against women is in the public interest as this is defined at present in that it is functional to the maintenance of male domination. [73] This makes it even more likely that the state should exclude battered wives from the scope of the compensation scheme. So long as husbands can legally rape their wives and some judges are still prepared to concede to them a liberty to spank them, it is difficult to see how the state could compensate wives for injuries inflicted by their husbands.

The Interdepartmental Working Party has, however, recommended reform. [74] It suggests that applications for compensation should normally be considered in cases of family violence but only where the offender has been prosecuted in connection with the assault, that family cases should be included experimentally in the first place and, as an interim measure, that compensation should be payable only in cases where the injuries merit compensation of at least £500. Furthermore, to ensure that the assailant does not benefit from the award, the assailant and applicant should have stopped living together before the application and it should seem unlikely that they will live together again. The Working Party estimates that the maximum additional compensation required would be in the region of £1.6 million a year though the limitations they suggest might cut the number of eligible cases by 70 or 80 per cent, resulting in compensation of less than £1 million. [75]

The Report must be welcomed, albeit with reservations. There seems no reason why inclusion of family violence within the scheme should be experimental, nor why it should be limited to cases which merit compensation of £500. The Working Party, in other words, sees family violence as different from other crimes of violence. Marx's explanation [76] seems to ring true in its implicit reasoning. The limitation to cases where cohabitation has ceased may also cause problems. The Working Party does not refer to *Staten*'s case, [77] so presumably approves of the Divisional Court's interpretation. It does, however, appreciate the difficulties of wives leaving violent husbands. [78] Yet it would seem to wish to deny a wife compensation who does all she can to cease cohabitation yet who remains under the same roof as her husband. It may be added that an award of compensation may assist the wife to set up elsewhere. Finally, the anomaly remains that no compensation will be payable for rape, since, when perpetrated on a wife, it is not a crime. No change has yet been made in the scheme as a result of these recommendations. It is hoped that the scheme will now be made statutory so that parliamentary debate on its details will be possible. This should enable the current anomalies and inconsistencies to be aired, and, it is hoped, to be removed.

The non-enforcement of the criminal law

In June 1973 the Home Office, in answer to a question tabled in the House of Commons by Jack Ashley, stated: 'the law does not discriminate between assaults by a husband on his wife and other assaults. Any assault constitutes a criminal offence'. [79] That is the theory but what happens in practice?

The main way in which the police hear about crime is when the victim of a crime complains to them. [80] But wives are reluctant to report assaults by their husbands. There are a number of reasons for this. They may expect to be degraded and humiliated. They may know (or worse still half-know) about police attitudes towards what are euphemestically designated 'domestic disturbances'. If they are frequent victims they may tend to refrain from reporting because the burdens of such reporting and follow-up actions may be intolerable. They may believe that, without a husband to support them, they will be in a worse position. They may sense that initiating police action is likely to cause them even greater distress: greater poverty, worse beatings-up etc. The publicity involved may also act as a deterrent. They may not wish to be instrumental in the imprisonment of their husbands; they may believe he needs 'help, not punishment'. The decision to seek legal assistance then is the result of a change in the wife's behaviour, not the husband's. [81]

But, given that they alert the police, what happens then? This depends on the character of the assault or rather on how it is interpreted by the police. It is not generally realised that in cases of common assault the legal remedy is for the wife to initiate proceedings in the magistrates' court. Legal aid is not available for private prosecutions. Pizzey suggests that the probation service will sometimes assist a wife through her case. [82] A police officer is not entitled to act as informant on a charge of common assault, [83] unless the person assaulted is so feeble, old and infirm as to be incapable of instituting proceedings because he is not a free agent but is under the control of the person committing the assault. [84] It is arguable that some battered women come into this category but the number is probably not large. [85]   In cases of more serious assault the police have the power of arrest, as well as the duty to follow up and prosecute. [86]   The Metropolitan Police in its evidence to the Select Committee said that the police took 'positive action in every case of serious assault' [87] but the tendency of the police is to interpret most marital violence as minor.

The police attitude itself is fashioned by a number of factors. The Association of Chief Police Officers of England and Wales and Northern Ireland in its evidence to the House of Commons Select Committee on Violence in Marriage cited as a consideration a factor that may well be at the root of the problem:

> [w]hilst such problems take up considerable Police time . . .
> in the majority of cases the role of the Police is a negative
> one. We are, after all dealing with persons 'bound in
> marriage', and it is important, for a host of reasons, to
> maintain the unity of the spouses. Precipitated action by
> the Police could aggravate the position to such an extent
> as to create a worse situation than the one they were
> summoned to deal with. [88]

And, expressing its approval of the provision of refuges for battered wives, it adds: 'every effort *should be made to re-unite the family*' (the emphasis is the Association's). [89]   In like manner the Chief Superintendent in Canterbury is quoted by Jan Pahl as criticising the Canterbury refuge on the ground that 'it makes it easier for people who want to opt out of their family responsibilities to go somewhere at someone else's expense'. [90]   In a similar way Parnas says of intra-familial violence that it is different from normal crime in that 'preservation of family relationships may be deemed a very important social goal'. [91]   What is wanted is a restoration of the equilibrium with a minimum of change. It is taken for granted that 're-uniting' the family, preserving family relationships, is desirable. But is it? Should not this commonsense assumption be questioned? And, in a society with a rapidly rising divorce rate which has just made divorce procedurally simpler, [92] is it not a little surprising that so much effort should be put into preserving violent marriages when so little is devoted to marriages which fail for other reasons? To this I shall return later in the chapter.

The attitude of the police is formed also by their training and environment. In England the police recruit learns almost nothing about the dynamics of marital conflict during his 16-week crash induction. Courses tend to be legalistic and the social science content is sparse. In the USA, according to Parnas, [93] what police learn about most is the danger involved in intervening in cases of marital conflict. Certainly, this is what remains in the policeman's memory. Since over 20 per cent of police deaths in the USA and 40 per cent of injuries to police occur on domestic disturbance calls, this is hardly surprising. [94] Very few police officers are killed on duty in England, and, though it was reported to the Select Committee that a policeman was stabbed while intervening between husband and wife, [95] no policeman has been killed in this country whilst responding to a marital violence call. Nevertheless, a low profile policy is kept.

Parnas found that it is common for the wife to go to the aid of her husband so that 'the danger quotient is high for both disputing parties'. [96] Wives may attack the police, such a reaction being elicited by 'emotional ties and habituated loyalty'. [97] Furthermore, as the Metropolitan Police Memorandum to the House of Commons Select Committee points out:

> the wife herself [in any subsequent prosecution] is an
> essential witness. Experience has shown that prosecutions
> have failed or could not be pursued because of a withdrawal
> by the wife of her complaint or because of her nervous
> reaction to the prospect of giving evidence against her
> husband. A woman no matter how cruelly treated is often
> reluctant to see her husband imprisoned or fined. [98]

This can reach a point where the police can accept marital violence as violence between 'consenting adults' and hence a 'private affair'. [99] Even where the wife wants a prosecution they may actively discourage her initiative.

Parnas [100] has shown that in the USA the police in the marital violence situation act as support figures rather than as instruments of control, seeing their prime objective as adjustment rather than arrest. This is consistent both with the conclusions of sociologists who have examined policing generally [101] and with what has been found in England. [102] The police have a number of roles: [103] law enforcement, peace-keeping (that is, group-level order problems), order maintenance (that is, community order) and public service functions. In marital violence calls the police must decide whether to adopt a law enforcement or a peace-keeping posture. [104] The greatest range of potential police discretion is found in police-initiated actions. Research indicates that the complainant's wishes significantly affect police discretion. [105] The initial call to the police may not be a request for criminal action at all. The public in England hold the police in high regard [106] and to many they are the first of the social services, acting as gatekeepers and filters to the other specialised services. The operational police officer carries a vast amount of knowledge around in his head. No other agency is known to function for 24 hours in a day. The police are influenced also by the demeanour of the accused. [107] They are less likely to arrest someone who is co-operative and shows respect for their authority than someone who is unco-operative and antagonistic. There are other criteria for choosing between arrest and mediation or arrest and caution. [108]

There are undoubtedly local variations. Thus we know, for example, that cautioning rates are much higher in rural areas than large cities. [109] The variations tend to reflect differences in the communities. A policeman cannot be an effective peace officer, he cannot act in a social support capacity, unless he understands, or better still participates in, the society he polices. Subcultural differences also affect patrol practices. Thus, Skolnick in *Justice without Trial* can write of the way police interpret a stabbing in the white community as a 'potential homicide' which in the black ghetto is 'written off' as a 'North Westville battery'. [110] Lambert's comments on policing in Birmingham describe similar tendencies there. [111]

The Association of Chief Police Officers of England, Wales and Northern Ireland in its Memorandum to the House of Commons Select Committee lists a number of factors which, it says, militate for or against a decision to arrest and prosecute in cases of marital violence:

(i)   the seriousness of the assault;
(ii)   the availability of witnesses;
(iii)   the character of the alleged assailant;
(iv)   age, infirmity etc. of the complainant;
(v)   previous domestic history;
(vi)   the wishes of the complainant; and
(vii)   if prosecution ensued against the wishes of the complainant, would the domestic situation be adversely affected. [112]

Parnas divides the decision making into two levels in both of which discretion operates. [113]

There is, he says, an initial screening undertaken by a dispatcher. [114] Many cases get no further. Cumming et al. found that when a complainant reported a dispute she had only a one in two chance of getting more than advice. [115] The interpretational latitude in a communications centre is great. Surprisingly, it has not been commented on at all in an English context, though it obviously exists.

Amongst the factors which Parnas [116] detects in the decision making which takes place in field operations are:

1   the motivation for calling the police (does the victim want an arrest or does she rather wish to scare the offender or get him out of the house?);

2   the question whether the victim can afford to have the offender arrested;

3   the subculture, if any, to which the disputants belong (is the conduct 'not seriously objectionable to the victim'?);

4   the danger that the offender may cause more serious harm upon his return;

5   the danger that it may cause temporary or permanent termination of family relationships or harm innocent family members;

6   the knowledge that the victim may change her mind;

7   reticence in the issuance of warrants and in prosecutions by prosecuting authorities (this is not relevant in an English context where police prosecute in addition to investigating the offence);

8   the knowledge that the victim may choose not to prosecute;

9   the knowledge of the courts' leniency in sentencing; and

10   the policeman himself having had similar experiences and his feeling that a 'man's home is his castle'. [117]

Suggestions as to the ways in which police performance can be improved take two forms. One view is that if the traditional role of the police in this area is adjustment and mediation, then the effectiveness of these techniques should be increased. The work of Bard and the New York Family Crisis Intervention Unit [118] are the best known examples of this philosophy, though it has been copied in other American cities [119] and in London, Ontario. [120] In New York selected police officers were trained as specialists in family crisis intervention techniques. The police were 'psychological intervention agents' though at the same time left in no doubt that they were police officers ('They restore the peace and maintain order, but it is "how" they do it that is the measure of their success'). [121] Of the New York experiment Parnas wrote:

[d] omestic problems can be deemed to be significantly
diverted from the criminal process only when the result
of a police service call is not only restoration of order
but activation of a process which at least has the
potential to resolve the source of the conflict. [122]

It is difficult to assess the success or otherwise of the New York
scheme. [123] The number of arrests increased as did the number of
family homicides though none of these occurred in families seen by
members of the Family Crisis Intervention Unit. The recidivism rate
was high. But all these 'facts' may reflect a number of unknown
variables. Bard himself has written that it showed 'promise of
demonstrating that policemen provided with skills appropriate to the
complexities of today's social existence succeed in minimizing
violence which might otherwise be exacerbated by their well-meant
but inept performance'. [124] The programme in fact ceased when
its federal grant was terminated. Its influence has, however, lived on.
Parnas, one of its strongest supporters, has in a recent paper rejected
the ideology embraced by the programme. [125] The main problems
with such programmes are twofold: first, they assume that therapy
rather than arrest is the best approach, for their primary concern is
with keeping the family together; second, as Parnas himself has now
written, 'there is simply no evidence that we know how to diagnose
much less treat disputants' problems in a manner that will prevent
repetition'. [126]

A slightly different approach is to suggest that the police should be
encouraged to make referrals of marriages in trouble to relevant social
welfare agencies. Thus Parnas wrote (and one may assume he now
rejects this too) that '[p] olice contact could also be used to refer
agencies to disputants'. [127] This would not seem to involve any
violation of privacy or any breach of confidential relationship.
Surprisingly, the sort of liaison which exists in the area of child abuse
does not operate here at all and does not appear to be particularly
welcomed, by some policeman at least. It was one of Pizzey's
complaints against the police that they do not notify relevant agencies
such as social services departments and the NSPCC. [128] The
question is whether the police are convinced that such agencies can
make an effective contribution towards solving the problem. At the
moment they would appear not to be.

A second view as to methods of improving police performance is
put forward in the House of Commons Select Committee Report. It
recommended that chief constables 'review their policies about the
police approach to domestic violence'. [129] Recruits should be

given special instructions about 'this difficult and delicate subject' and regular guidance issued by the Chief Constable. It is clear that what the Committee wanted was a more rigorous prosecution policy. The first authority to take this line was Bedfordshire.

In February 1976 their Chief Constable, Mr Anthony Armstrong, announced a tough, new prosecution policy against husbands who battered their wives. [130] Under this violent husbands are arrested, charged and taken to court whether or not their wives are prepared to give evidence against them. If the wife withdraws her complaint by the time the case gets to court, the police invite the court to bind the husband over to keep the peace. If there are further incidents, the husband can be brought to court and dealt with for that, as well as for breaking the order binding him over. At the same time Bedfordshire police force set up a special advisory service to help battered wives under which senior officers based at police stations in Dunstable, Luton and Bedford, the three main centres of population, are on a 24-hour call to advise and assist them. This idea is close in conception to the 24-hour crisis centre envisaged in the Select Committee Report. [131]

A report has been published on the results of the new prosecution policy during its first six months. [132] During the period, 288 acts of violence in the home came to the attention of the police. In 184 of the cases (63.9 per cent), following the initial intervention of a police officer and a discussion with the parties to the assault, the complainants did not wish to pursue their complaints. No further action was taken as 'any injuries visible did not justify police intervention'. In 104 cases, complaints were substantiated, arrests were made and proceedings commenced. In 18 of those cases (17.3 per cent), between the date the charge was preferred and the date set for the court hearing, the complainants withdrew their complaints and no further action was taken. Seventy-nine out of the remaining 86 cases had been disposed of by the time of the Report. Only 3 men were given immediate custodial sentences (we are not told the length of these sentences). So 285 men (that is nearly 99 per cent) responsible for acts of violence against their wives remained at liberty after their wives had appraised the police. Is it any wonder that battered wives are reluctant to invoke the criminal justice process against their husbands? [133]

Since our knowledge about disposition is so scanty, it may be useful to document the decisions taken in the remaining 76 cases. In four cases no action was taken by the police. We are not told why. Two offenders were cautioned by a senior police officer. Five men received suspended sentences and one a deferred sentence. Seventeen (that is 21.5 per cent) were fined, thus hitting equally at their wives and children. Another three were bound over as well as being fined. Five were placed on probation. Fifteen were conditionally discharged; two more were given absolute discharges. Eleven were bound over to keep the peace. A further three were bound over after the case had been discussed and evidence heard, and three more were bound over although the complaint was withdrawn. In one case a warrant was issued for arrest because the accused failed to appear. Four cases were dismissed and the men were not bound over. In total, 20 of the 79 cases resulted in men being bound over to keep the peace, that is nearly 26 per cent.

The role of the courts in prosecutions

Erin Pizzey has asserted that 'the court is not the proper place to resolve problems of the battered wife'. [134] She is critical of the willingness to grant bail and the derisory sentences. [135] She alleges that going to court is an ordeal, and that judges and officials are uncaring and unfeeling. Field and Field, however, argue that 'the function of the criminal law is altered dramatically in the domestic-assault situation and the classical bases for the employment of the criminal process — deterrence, incapacitation, prevention, retribution or rehabilitation — do not apply in a substantial way to these cases'. [136] It is difficult to see why this should be so. True, deterrence does not work particularly effectively with any expressive offence [137] (which wife beating must, I think, be taken to be). But there is no reason why the other 'classical bases' should not operate in this context. The criminal process may not work effectively at this moment but that does not mean that it cannot be made to work.

In the USA attempts have been made to tailor the traditional criminal process to take account of the special needs of spouses at war. Domestic violence has become an arena for experimentation. [138] In England, on the other hand, the traditional criminal process has remained intact, and courts adjudicate upon domestic disputes and violence as upon other criminal behaviour. We are urged by some to imitate American experiments. Susan Maidment, for example, regrets that the House of Commons Select Committee was 'not more inventive and innovative in its recommendations regarding the law available to battered women'. [139] She is sympathetic to the American approaches, particularly that which operates in Washington, D.C. [140]

The Washington scheme is just one of a number of attempts in the

USA to decriminalise domestic violence. In the courts of a number of cities, notably Chicago, Detroit, Milwaukee, New York and Washington the judge has become 'practically director of a welfare agency engaged in diagnostic and therapeutic rather than strictly judicial pursuits'. [141] This has met with nearly universal approval. Thus, Parnas, before his recent conversion, wrote that 'persons and institutions best equipped to deal [with marital violence] are not those trained primarily in the law — but in the workings of the mind itself and the conflicts peculiar to marriage'. [142] The details of the schemes may be sought elsewhere. [143] Briefly, they put a premium on counselling, there are cooling-off periods and pre-trial conferences. There is pre-trial screening often with unenforceable peace bonds. The courts appear to be more accessible than they are in England. Proceedings take place within the context of a family court. In New York the purpose of family offences proceedings is found in the Family Court Act. This states:

> [i]n the past, wives and other members of the family who suffered from disorderly conduct or assaults by other members of the family or household were compelled to bring a 'criminal charge' to invoke the jurisdiction of the court. Their purpose, with few exceptions, was not to secure a criminal conviction and punishment, but practical help.
>
> The family court is better equipped to render such help, and the purpose of this article is to create a civil proceeding for dealing with such instances of disorderly conduct and assaults. It authorises the family court to enter orders of protection and support and contemplates conciliation proceedings. If the family court concludes that these processes are inappropriate in a particular case, it is authorised to transfer the proceeding to an appropriate criminal court. [144]

This purpose clause gives some indication of the ideology and methodology to be found in American jurisdictions. Whilst agreeing that they appear bolder and more adventurous than anything being tried in England, I would caution against transplanting American programmes to England. I am not concerned with the obvious cultural differences in the two countries, for a scheme could be engineered to overcome such natural barriers. My concern is that the counselling, social welfare approach to intra-familial violence conceives of the problem wrongly.

We must ask ourselves with what we are dealing when we confront marital violence. Where we are met with petty assault, a couple who give as much as they take, with basically an ongoing relationship which needs sorting out, the family court approach may be desirable. Where parties are in a continuous state of social propinquity, resolution by adjudication is inconsistent with a continuing viable social interaction. [145] Even so, nowadays we would probably not deny a spouse in these circumstances a divorce. But too often in cases of domestic violence we are confronted with cases of brutal violence. Can the family court achieve anything then? Can mediation work in such a case?

The success of mediation [146] depends upon a number of variables, notably a common interest in having the conflict resolved amicably. But what interest do a brutal husband and a terrorised wife have in common? The standard answer is couched in terms of the children they may have and the importance of stabilising the family. Mediation looks to the future whereas an adjudication measures the husband's behaviour against the norm of criminal legislation. Mediation looks towards a compromise solution, whereas an adjudicator, employing traditional techniques, imposes what he regards as a just solution. Once within the family court setting and a social welfare counselling orientation we may lose sight of the fact that wife beating may be a brutal criminal assault and not just the symptom of a troubled marriage.

The question that needs to be asked of those who see progress as lying with family courts and counselling services is what they conceive to be the causes of wife beating. Their goal is clear: they want reconciliation and stability; they want the family to 'function as it should'. They want to preserve the family. They rarely articulate a theory of family violence but implicit is one of two assumptions: the batterer has behaved 'irrationally' because there is something patho-logically wrong with him; or he has problems resulting from inadequate resources. On either hypothesis the solution is seen in terms of the need for more social work intervention, courts develop-ing welfare functions, as well as better housing and employment prospects. Either way he or his environment can be 'treated' and he can be sent back to his family 'cured' and safe. These solutions are misconceived because they do not speak to the right problem. That they are not in the woman's interest goes without saying; they are not intended to be. The ideology of family courts is, however, very much in the interests of the state.

My conclusion is that violence against a wife should be treated like violence against a stranger. Women should have the right to expect that men who assault them are treated as criminals whether those men are their husbands or not. And, furthermore, just as Fox has asserted the right of a juvenile to be punished rather than treated, [147] perhaps we ought to allow the violent husband to make such a claim as well.

Compensation under the law of tort

The act of battering constitutes the torts of assault and battery. In England until 1962 a spouse was not allowed to sue the other in tort. [148] Two reasons were given for this immunity. First, the fiction that they were one flesh was put forward. [149] Second, it was said that such litigation was 'unseemly, distressing and embittering'. [150] 'If a husband "beats up" his wife, she cannot sue him, because to sue him would be unwifely'. [151] The majority of American states have still to abrogate the doctrine of interspousal immunity. [152]

Each of the parties to a marriage now has the same right of action in tort against the other as if they were not married. But, in order to prevent them from using the court as a forum for trivial domestic disputes, the proceedings may be stayed if it appears that 'no substantial benefit' will accrue to either party from their continuation. The quantification of benefit is no easy task. [153]

There are no statistics on the number of spouses who sue each other in tort or of the number of cases which are stayed. Nearly all cases will arise out of motor accidents and the spouse will only be the nominal defendant. Whilst the immunity was impossible to defend, it would be folly to pretend that its removal has in any way helped the battered wife. But, though rarely if ever used for such purposes, it was potentially of use before the passing of the Domestic Violence and Matrimonial Proceedings Act 1976 as a way of obtaining an injunction against molestation or to exclude a brutal husband [154] from the matrimonial home.

The Magistrates' Courts and their remedies

In England there are two types of matrimonial proceedings. A spouse may seek the 'summary, local and inexpensive relief' [155] offered by magistrates' courts or turn to the superior courts for the more long-term remedy of divorce and the relief associated with it.

The jurisdiction of the magistrates' courts has been radically re-moulded by the Domestic Proceedings and Magistrates' Court Act 1978. Previously, the court could make an order containing a non-cohabitation clause provided the applicant (or complainant as she was called in the old law) could prove an offence and had not herself [156] committed adultery. This relieved the complainant of her obligation to cohabit with the defendant. It was, however, simply a declaration and was not enforceable. It also had the positive disadvantage that it prevented the complainant relying on the defendant's desertion subsequent to the order. [157] Further, magistrates had no power to evict a violent spouse.

The 1978 Act has abolished the old 'squalid' [158] list of matrimonial offences, and replaced them with four grounds of application for financial provision. Adultery is no longer a bar to an application for financial provision. [159] The non-cohabitation clause has disappeared and has been replaced by much wider powers in s.16. The court may now make an order that (i) the respondent shall not use or threaten to use violence against the person of the applicant and of a child of the family, and (ii) where satisfied that violence has been so used or threatened, or where it has been threatened by a respondent who has used violence against some other person it may make an order requiring the respondent to leave the matrimonial home or prohibiting him from entering it. An order may only be made under (ii) where the applicant or a child of the family is in danger of being physically injured by the respondent. There is provision also for orders to be expedited. [160] The court is also given the power to attach a power of arrest [161] to an order which provides that the respondent shall not use violence against the person of the applicant or a child of the family or shall not enter the matrimonial home.

The 1978 Act is not yet in operation. The protection provisions are to some extent modelled on the Domestic Violence and Matrimonial Proceedings Act 1976, so that certain predictions as to its likely impact may be judged from the first year's experience of that Act. Comments on that Act follow later in this chapter. A number of criticisms of the new Act may, however, be ventured at this stage.

First, it only applies to matrimonial violence so that cohabitees will continue to be excluded from magisterial domestic jurisdiction. It seems ironical that a jurisdiction which was designed for the problems of those not deemed 'respectable' enough for the superior courts (i.e. working-class women in the late 19th century) should not now encompass the problems of women outside the bonds of matrimony. [162] The limitation was justified by Dr Shirley Summerskill on two grounds: first, the problem of distinguishing a couple living in the same household as husband and wife and one merely living in the same household would be too difficult for magistrates to tackle; and second, the inability of magistrates to resolve the question of occupation of a household on a more permanent basis. Neither of these defences is really tenable. As far as the first is concerned this reservation has not prevented magistrates being saddled with concepts like 'desertion'. Magistrates anyway have or should have legally trained clerks. The second defence should have prevented the 1976 Act being extended to cohabitees but it did not. Parliament has not yet faced up to the problem of the ultimate disposition of property of cohabitees in a situation where violence has been used or threatened.

Second, protection, as has been noted, extends to 'children of the family'. This includes children 'treated' as such by a non-parent. But, whilst it may be reasonable to limit the provision of financial support to such children, it is difficult to see why a personal protection order should not extend to children who have not been so 'treated'.

Third, whilst the 1976 Act refers to 'molestation', [163] the 1978 Act is more circumscribed in that it refers to 'violence'. Superior court judges thus have jurisdiction to grant injunctions where there has been mental cruelty, even arguably just pestering. [164] Magistrates do not have comparable jurisdiction. The Law Commission defended its rejection of granting magistrates this jurisdiction by arguing that 'adjudication on an allegation of psychological damage is a very difficult matter which may involve the assessment of evidence by psychiatrists. This is a highly skilled task which we do not think can appropriately be placed on magistrates'. [165] It is difficult to accept this reasoning. There is nothing in a judge's training or background which equips him to tackle such evidence. Some magistrates, indeed, will be in a better position to assess it than most judges.

Other criticisms may be made more tersely. The Act does not define the 'matrimonial home'. The couple may be living with inlaws or in a caravan in someone's garden. What, if anything, is the 'matrimonial home' in these situations? It is not possible to restrict a spouse under the Act to a part of the matrimonial home. But, as Dr Summerskill commented, in a stately home 'one could partition off the west wing for the husband and the east wing for the wife. But in the average council house I do not think the wife would like the thought that she might be put in one room and the husband in the other'.[166] There is no provision in the Act for a limit to be put on the period of the order. Since the Act envisages a short-term solution one would have been advisable. The problem of evidence has also not been tackled satisfactorily. The concept of the affidavit does not exist in magistrates' courts. There is little scope for such evidence in most magisterial proceedings. It may, however, be thought to be elementary justice where a drastic order such as that to exclude a man from his home is sought to give him advance warning of the evidence against him. But as the law stands there is no way in which he can be appraised of such evidence in advance of the hearing.

Whilst the Act undoubtedly improves the law and its administration it is, therefore, not without major blemishes.

Divorce as a remedy

Another option open to the wife is to seek dissolution of her marriage. Once accomplished, this does not mean she will then necessarily live in peace. The Law Reports are replete with examples of post-dissolution batteries. Indeed, as will appear later, the divorced woman may well be at a disadvantage in seeking an injunction against her former husband. Divorce is, of course, only open to those who are married; there is no mechanism by which the courts can declare a cohabitation of long standing as terminated.

There is no doubt that a woman battered by her husband can divorce him. Like many other systems English law now bases divorce on the concept of irretrievable breakdown. Unlike some systems, however, it does not leave the question at large [167] but specifies facts, proof of any of which raises a strong presumption that the marriage has broken down irreparably. A battered wife should have no difficulty in proving that her husband 'has behaved in such a way that [she] cannot reasonably be expected to live with [him]'. [168] And, indeed, she may well be able to prove other of the facts as well, notably his adultery coupled with her finding it intolerable to live with him. [169] His 'unreasonable behaviour' is, however, the more obvious line of approach. The courts consider not only the behaviour of the respondent but 'the character, personality, disposition and behaviour of the petitioner'. The question asked is 'can this petitioner, with his or her personality, with his or her faults and other attributes, good and bad, and having regard to his or her behaviour during the marriage, reasonably be expected to live with this respondent?' [170] In *Ash* v. *Ash,* Bagnall J. gave as an example the following: 'a violent petitioner can reasonably be expected to live with a violent respondent'. [171] But this should not be taken too literally. The *Rusic* marriage was so violent on both sides that Heilbron J. said one could hardly call their house a 'home'. Sticks, bricks, iron bars, pokers, even an axe was used. The judge granted cross-decrees. [172]

There are reported cases where wives have obtained decrees against husbands who have treated them violently. [173] In one case the

Court of Appeal accepted that a wife could not reasonably be expected to live with her husband 'even though she [was] in the same house with him — and in fact living with him', as she had no alternative open to her, 'nowhere else to go'. It was 'not reasonable to expect her to live there, but albeit unreasonable, she [had] no option but to be there'. [174] This wife had seven children living with her, two non-cohabitation orders for persistent cruelty and the local authority had refused to rehouse her until she secured a divorce against her husband. Her Catch-22 situation makes this case particularly instructive, for it highlights a not uncommon predicament.

Divorce is not generally available during the first three years of marriage. [175] A judge may, however, allow the presentation of a petition within that period if he considers the case one of exceptional hardship suffered by the petitioner or one of exceptional depravity on the part of the respondent. [176] In determining the application the judge is enjoined to have regard to the interests of any child of the family and to whether there is a reasonable probability of reconciliation within the three years. This provision was first introduced in 1937 and has been consistently defended by official committees [177] though it finds little support in academic literature. [178] It has never existed in Scotland or in most of the rest of the world. Its main effect is to delay divorce which in England reaches its peak after four years. As women who are going to be battered often find that the violence begins shortly after marriage, the bar to divorce is potentially a serious inconvenience. In the past the courts have construed serious cruelty coupled with physical injury as exceptional depravity. [179] In considering exceptional hardship the courts have considered what effect the facts have had on the particular petitioner. So, if a nervous wife suffered a breakdown because of her husband's conduct she might well get leave to petition within the three-year period. [180] Because of such interpretations battered women should not suffer unduly from the bar. They did, however, suffer under the old law relating to injunctions, when it was held that, under a summons asking for leave to petition within three years, the courts could not exclude the husband from the matrimonial home where this was in his name, although they could grant an injunction against molestation. [181] This is no longer the case since the implementation of the Domestic Violence and Matrimonial Proceedings Act 1976.

A further problem for the battered wife, and one which may have far-reaching implications, is the recent withdrawal [182] of legal aid from undefended divorces. She can still seek legal advice and assistance under the £25 scheme introduced in 1973 [183] but she

198

will have to negotiate the mechanics of the divorce herself. Legal aid remains available for the purpose of seeking injunctions, as it does for the so-called ancillary matters which follow a divorce relating to custody of children, property adjustment and financial provision.

One of the greatest advantages in securing a divorce is that the court is then given the power to undertake a complete restructuring of the parties' property relationship. On divorce (and on the granting of a nullity or judicial separation) the court is given the widest possible powers to deal with the matrimonial home and to take into account every possible factor. [184] Though the courts are reluctant to take conduct into account [185] they do sometimes do so. [186]

Divorce is an obvious remedy and is usually efficacious. But it is final. Many women, distraught, bruised and battered, and doubtless endowed with beliefs about the necessity of trying to 'make a go of it', will lack the mental composure to consider the long-term decision of divorce. As Baroness Phillips said in the House of Lords in July 1976: 'at the time of probably having been beaten, assaulted and thrown out of the house, bruised and frightened, the last thing a woman wants to do is start the complications of a divorce or separation proceedings'. [187] Nor must one forget her 'romantic delusions', [188] the 'beauty and the beast syndrome', [189] as Pizzey called it, how she can reform him and preserve the marriage for the sake of the family. Perhaps she also considers the alternatives: accommodation problems, living on state assistance, employment prospects, day care facilities for children. These may be the real reasons why she stays and does not seek a divorce; the romanticism may be merely rationalisation. Divorce applications will increase as the alternatives to married life improve.

The injunction weapon

A woman who does not want a divorce or does not want a divorce just yet, who sees her husband's violence not as a 'complete breakdown of relationship' but rather a 'bewildering impediment to an otherwise loving relationship', [190] nevertheless requires a remedy, a court order which directs her husband to leave her alone. She may hope that a temporary enforced separation will give him time to cool off and her a breathing space. It may bring him to his senses so that in due course they may resume a more normal married life together. Why she should think like this does not matter here; the fact is, rightly or wrongly, many women do. And for these women the injunction is the obvious remedy.

Matrimonial injunctions are of two kinds. There is the non-molestation injunction, which is an order not to molest which includes [191] assault, pester or otherwise interfere with the spouse concerned. Situations short of violence are thus also covered. Second, there is the injunction to vacate the matrimonial home. Additionally, the court may, instead of granting an injunction, accept an undertaking by the offender not to molest his spouse. The effect is the same for breach of injunctions and undertakings. Both constitute contempt of court, for which imprisonment can be imposed. But the real purpose of bringing the matter back to court in most cases is not so much to punish the disobedience, as to secure compliance with the order in the future. A committal order should be 'the very last resort'. [192] The existence now of the provision to attach a power of arrest [193] to an injunction should anyway diminish the necessity for committals. Contempt is purged by a promise of good behaviour in the future. In one case a man was only released from prison on condition that he did not go within 50 miles of his ex-wife. [194] The courts can attach various subsidiary orders to an injunction, for example, an interim custody order. More unusually they may make an order, for example, requiring the husband to restore heating to the wife.

Normally applications for an injunction are heard in the presence of the offender who is thus given a chance to be heard in his own defence. For this reason two days' notice of the hearing to the offender is required and a full hearing held seven days after the complaint. Sir George Baker, in evidence to the House of Commons Select Committee, said that injunction applications were given 'absolute priority'. [195] In cases of emergency, an *ex parte* application can be made and an interim injunction granted in the absence of the offender. According to Margeritte Russell the judges have to be presented with a 'near corpse' [196] before they will take emergency action. Several times recently the Court of Appeal has criticised the readiness with which judges have granted *ex parte* applications. In *Ansah* v. *Ansah* (where an *ex parte* injunction had been granted against the wife) Ormrod L.J. said that:

> This power must be used with great caution and only in
> circumstances in which it is really necessary to act
> immediately . . . [T]he court should only act ex parte
> in an emergency when the interests of justice or the
> protection of the applicant or a child clearly demands
> immediate intervention by the court. Such cases should
> be extremely rare . . . circumstances, of course, may
> arise when prior notice cannot be given to the other side;

for example, cases where one parent has disappeared with the children, or a spouse, usually the wife, is so frightened of the other spouse that some protection must be provided against a violent response to service of proceedings, but the court must be fully satisfied that such protection is necessary. [197]

In *Masich* v. *Masich* [198] an order had been made excluding the husband from the matrimonial home from 6 p.m. the same day on a *ex parte* injunction by the wife served at 3.30 p.m. on the husband without prior warning. No allegation of violence had been made against the husband but it was alleged that he was domineering. Ormrod L.J. said that there was nothing to justify turning the husband out of his home without hearing his side. Such a course should only be taken in exceptional circumstances. Applications to exclude from the matrimonial home should never be *ex parte*. The judge described them as 'an abuse of the process of the court' and threatened solicitors with having to meet the costs themselves should such applications be made in the future. This condemnation may well prove to be the death knell of *ex parte* injunctions in matrimonial matters, certainly where it is sought to exclude the husband from the matrimonial home. Judges granting an injunction now have the power to attach a power of arrest to it. Many judges, it is thought, will be reluctant to do this in the absence at the hearing of the husband.

Injunctions are a popular legal remedy. There are no real statistics though the Lord Chancellor's Office did conduct a small survey of *ex parte* applications for injunctions. It was found that in November 1975 there were 252 applications, three-quarters of them in large cities. [199] According to the Lord Chancellor, speaking in the House of Lords in July 1976, 'practically all of them involved physical violence to the person, and the very large majority related to couples who were still married'. [200] Only one application was made outside normal working hours. It was found that the problems of getting a judge were most severe in the North East, the Lake District and the Isle of Wight. When Sir George Baker, the President of the Family Division, gave evidence to the House of Commons Select Committee he noted that applications for injunctions during the long vacation in London had increased. In 1972 there had been 339 applications, in 1973, 468 and in 1974, 502. But outside London there was no evidence of any increase. [201] With the introduction of the Domestic Violence and Matrimonial Proceedings Act 1976 the increase in demand has continued. [202]

The High Court's power to grant injunctions is contained in the

Supreme Court of Judicature (Consolidation) Act of 1925. Section 45 of this states that an injunction may be granted 'in all cases in which it appears to the court to be just or convenient to do so'. The jurisdiction of county courts to grant injunctions is derived from section 74 of the County Courts Act 1959. By a process of interpretation the courts cut down their jurisdiction. They decided that there had to be a sufficient nexus between the subject-matter of the main action and the relief sought by the injunction. [203] It followed that an application for an injunction had to be ancillary to other proceedings. In theory these needed to be nothing more than an action for assault claiming £2 damages. In practice it tended to mean that a battered wife could not get an injunction unless she filed [204] a petition for divorce (or nullity or judicial separation). The cohabitee could not, of course, so petition; her only practicable course was to start proceedings for assault or trespass to land, claim damages and attach an application for an injunction to these proceedings. The courts also decided, though they hardly needed to, that an injunction could only be granted to support a legal right. [205] They then set about repairing some of the damage by holding that the wife's personal right to remain in the matrimonial home is such a right, [206] though this right ceased on termination of the marriage. [207] What jurisdiction they had they exercised most sparingly. The general attitude adopted until very recently emphasised property rights over personal protection and insisted that to exclude a husband from the matrimonial home, of which he was likely to be the estate owner or tenant, was a drastic step to be taken only in extreme circumstances. Thus, in *Hall* v. *Hall*, [208] the Court of Appeal said it would not order a husband out unless it was proved to be impossible for the spouses to live together. And in *Mamane* v. *Mamane*, the Court of Appeal said it would only make an order where it was 'imperative and inescapable'. [209] An order was refused despite the fact the husband was given to unbalanced emotional outbursts and acts of violence, and there were two young children.

The question of jurisdiction has been radically remoulded by the Domestic Violence and Matrimonial Proceedings Act 1976. [210] There is also evidence from the landmark decision of *Bassett* v. *Bassett* [211] that the way the court exercises its discretion has been liberalised.

The Domestic Violence and Matrimonial Proceedings Act 1976 provides that a county court shall have jurisdiction to grant injunctions against molestation and to exclude a spouse from the matrimonial home, a part of it or a specified area in which the matrimonial home is included, or requiring a spouse to permit the applicant to enter and remain in the matrimonial home or a part of it, whether or not any other relief is sought in the proceedings. The jurisdiction extends to a man and a woman living with each other in the same household as husband and wife: this refers to the 'parties' relationship before the incidents which gave rise to the application'. [212] A more literal interpretation would deprive a cohabitee of the power to seek an injunction if she left, or was driven out, before so doing. An injunction may also be granted restraining the other party from molesting a child living with the applicant. This is narrow: an injunction cannot, it seems, be obtained to restrain molestation of a child who has his home with the applicant but is living elsewhere (for example, a children's home or hospital) nor to restrain molestation of a child living with the other party.

The jurisdiction of the High Court was not altered by the Act as this required only an amendment to Rules of Court, and this has been made. [213]

The Act refers to applications 'by a party to a marriage'. Cohabitees, provided their union is stable and heterosexual (violence between a homosexual or lesbian couple is not provided for) are covered. So are husbands. Whether former spouses are is more doubtful. Certainly, on a literal interpretation a divorced woman is not 'a party to a marriage'. [214] It is to be hoped that the courts will adopt a more purposive construction than this. Otherwise it may be found that the Act has actually cut down jurisdiction. Certainly, before the Act, county courts had jurisdiction to grant injunctions restraining molestation of former spouses. [215] Indeed, though such jurisdiction was dubious, county courts have in the past excluded former husbands from the former matrimonial home where they considered it necessary to protect children. [216] The High Court, in exercise of its inherent jurisdiction to protect children, will continue to be able to exclude husbands from their property where the marriage is already dissolved, where it is necessary to protect the welfare of children. [217]

Injunctions may only be sought against 'the other party to the marriage' (or cohabitation). A wife with no proprietary interest in the matrimonial home cannot, therefore, exclude her husband's mistress or his relatives, for she has no legal rights against them and the Act confers none on her. In the past courts have ordered mistresses out of the matrimonial home. In *Adams* v. *Adams*, [218] the absence of the wife's legal right was referred to, but the order justified on the basis of the court's primary duty and primary concern for the welfare of three young children. In *Jones* v. *Jones*, [219] there were no young children, nor was there any discussion of the

203

wife's absence of any legal right, but the court felt no compunction in ordering the husband's mistress out. In the plain language of the 1976 Act the courts will no longer be able to do this.

Another problem is that the Act is limited to, and does not define, the matrimonial home. English law is still founded upon the separation of property. [220] A vindictive husband could thus, on being excluded from the matrimonial home, remove *his* furniture and household equipment and leave the wife with bare floorboards. [221] Against this it may be said that a husband does have a duty to provide his wife with a roof over her head. Lord Denning has described this feature of family life as 'elemental in our society'. [222] It would not take much imagination to extend this duty to the provision of basic household necessities.

The failure to define the matrimonial home causes a further problem. There must be considerable doubt as to whether a wife can exclude her husband from a home where the two of them have not lived together. [223] He may have sold the matrimonial home over her head and be threatening violence if she enters the house in which he is now living. There is no doubt that she could obtain an injunction restraining him for molesting her but it is dubious if she could exclude him from the house. She certainly cannot do so under the Matrimonial Homes Act 1967, even as amended by s.3 of the 1976 Act. [224]

The most difficult problem so far to have exercised the courts concerns cohabitees. Can a woman who cohabits with a man exclude him from property of which he is the owner or tenant under s.1(1)(c) and 1(2) of the 1976 Act? There is no doubt that those who drafted the Act, those who promoted it, and those who discussed it in Parliament assumed that the Act gave the courts the power to do just this. Thus, Miss Jo Richardson, in introducing s.1(2) said:

[i]n many cases it would be impossible for the woman to leave her home and to escape from . . . violence. This is particularly so where children of the association are involved, though in some cases, even where there are no children, the association may have grown up over a period and there may be nowhere for the spouse who is assaulted or molested to go. Therefore she . . . deserves protection. In these cases, under existing law, an injunction can be obtained only by means of an action for assault . . . Even an injunction obtained in this way would not extend to the question of occupation of the home where the applicant is not the sole owner or the official tenant. The President of the Family

Division . . . stated in his evidence to the Select Committee that there was a need for women in such relationships to be protected, and he suggested that, if the law relating to injunctions were to be amended, it should be extended to cover these cases. This is what we are seeking to do here. [225]

It is worth noting that the original clause would not have achieved this. The clause which was enacted, however, had the drafting assistance of 'the Lord Chancellor and his staff and Parliamentary Counsel' and took account of the Law Commission's suggestions. [226]

Nevertheless, in *B.* v. *B.* [227] and *Cantliff* v. *Jenkins* [228] two differently constituted benches of the Court of Appeal held that the 1976 Act had not altered the existing substantive law so as to empower the court to override the common law property rights of the parties. Section 1 was a procedural provision only. In *B.* v. *B.* the man was the sole tenant: in *Cantliff* v. *Jenkins* the man and woman were joint tenants. To the criticism that this interpretation rendered s.1(1)(c) nugatory, as far as cohabitees were concerned, Stamp L.J. in *Cantliff* v. *Jenkins* said that it enabled one cohabitee to exclude the other from his or her house, though not from the other party's own home, nor from premises of which the two of them were joint owners. As very few homes will be in the sole name of the woman partner, whatever Stamp L.J.'s protestations, this interpretation does, indeed, render s.1(1)(c), as extended to cohabitees, nugatory.

The consternation caused by these decisions prompted the Court of Appeal in a third case to convene a five-member court to consider the scope of s.1(1)(c) in its application to cohabitees. In *Davis* v. *Johnson*, [229] Miss Davis shared a council flat with Mr Johnson and their two-year-old daughter. It had been granted to Miss Davis, but at his request it was put into their joint names. Nevertheless, she paid the rent. He treated her brutally and she fled to Chiswick women's aid refuge. An order allowing her back to the flat and excluding him was made but withdrawn after the two Court of Appeal decisions just referred to.

Lord Denning M.R. thought the Act was 'perfectly clear'. [230] The words of s.1(1)(c) and (2) covered Miss Davis's case. He believed that where justice required it 'personal rights in a proper case should be given priority over rights of property'. [231] Sir George Baker, the President of the Family Division, rejected the idea that 'this provision [was] only a tiny miserable mouse incapable of even a nibble at the evil of domestic hooliganism'. [232] The Act was

'plain as a pikestaff'. [233] Shaw and Goff L.J.J. also thought that
B. v. *B.* and *Cantliff* v. *Jenkins* were wrong. Goff L.J.   (and
Cumming-Bruce L.J., who anyway was unable to hold that the earlier
cases were wrong) dissented on the ground that the Court of Appeal
was bound to follow previous decisions of its own, unless the instant
case fitted, which they held it did not, within existing exceptions to
that general rule. [234] The majority were, however, disposed, for
various reasons, to overrule the earlier decisions. Sir George Baker
hoped that *B.* v. *B.* would sink into 'merciful oblivion . . . unloved and
unread'. [235]

The House of Lords upheld the Court of Appeal. [236]
Viscount Dilhorne insisted that s.1(1) was 'not concerned with
property rights . . . It was not intended to provide a means for the
enforcement of property rights but to give protection from domestic
violence and from eviction'. He saw clearly that such an injunction
would not affect 'the legal rights to the home. It will, or may', he
added, 'interfere with the enjoyment of those rights'. [237]
Lord Salmon saw 'the whole purpose of the Act' as being to afford
some protection to 'unmarried "battered wives" in particular'. [238]
Lord Scarman was far from surprised that Parliament should legislate
in such a way that property rights would not be allowed to undermine
or diminish the protection being afforded by the Act. He pointed out
that 'the restriction or suspension for a time of property rights is a
familiar aspect of much of our social legislation' and he cited the
Rent Acts which do just this. [239]

Critics of *Davis* v. *Johnson* point to the dangers of allowing property
rights to be overridden in the way in which the Court of Appeal and
House of Lords countenanced. This ignores the fact that for decades
the courts have done just this in cases concerning husbands and wives.
[240] More significantly it overlooks the unreality of the concept of
property rights in cases like *Davis* v. *Johnson*. Council tenants have
few rights as such against the local authority. [241] They are not
protected by the Rent Act. [242] They cannot assign and their
tenancy has no commercial value. To claim that Miss Davis who paid
the rent and was the local authority's choice as tenant should have
fewer rights against Mr Johnson than he had against the local
authority is preposterous. What an injunction purports to do is give
short-term protection [243] from homelessness while new permanent
accommodation is sought. Were it not for a refuge Miss Davis could
well have found herself on the streets with her baby in care. How
permanent injunctions become will very largely depend on how local
housing authorities interpret their powers under the Housing
(Homeless Persons) Act 1977. But they are intended to regulate

occupation [244] of property and not, on any long-term basis, to effect its transfer. [245]

The Domestic Violence and Matrimonial Proceedings Act 1976 is silent on the criteria for the exercise of its jurisdiction. Its sponsor, Miss Jo Richardson, thinks 'the court will exercise its discretion along the lines of the policy it has already developed'. [246] The courts were formerly most reluctant to order a man out of the matrimonial home. But in *Bassett* v. *Bassett* the Court of Appeal took a more practical approach to the problem. Ormrod L.J. accepted that ordering a spouse to leave was a drastic step but he was of the opinion that 'to refuse to make such an order may have no less drastic results, if the consequences of refusing to make an order is to inflict severe hardship on "the unsuccessful spouse"'. [247] He thought that, particularly in cases where the marriage has already broken down, the court 'should think essentially in terms of homes, especially for the children'. [248] It should balance the needs of the wife and children against the husband's. He believed that the husband would find it easier to secure accommodation for himself than the wife with a baby would. This is not necessarily so, as housing authorities have a greater duty towards mothers with young children than single homeless men. Ormrod L.J.'s reasoning could, therefore, rebound. [249]

It has not yet done so in any reported case. Decisions have, however, continued to use words like 'impossible' and 'intolerable'. Recently, the Court of Appeal in *Walker* v. *Walker* [250] has said that it was now time for these words to be dropped. Both were exceedingly vague and were being misused in argument far too frequently. Ormrod L.J. said that the court should solve the problem in terms of 'human beings and not legal quibbles' [251] and Geoffrey Lane L.J. said that the question was what in all the circumstances was 'fair, just and reasonable'. He continued:

> was it fair to exclude the husband from the matrimonial home taking into account the behaviour of the parties, the effect on the children if the husband stayed, the effect if he went, the personal circumstances of the wife and the husband, and the effect on their health, physical and mental. [252]

The husband was ordered to leave.

In *Rennick* v. *Rennick* [253] the emphasis was placed firmly on the welfare of the children. The wife had fled with the five children to her mother and was living there in cramped conditions whilst her husband, who had threatened to kill her, had remained in the four-bedroom matrimonial home. The Court of Appeal held that the children's interests were paramount and the matrimonial home was needed for their accommodation. As it would be wrong to oblige the wife to take her 'chance' again with her husband, it followed that he should be ordered to leave and not to return except with the wife's consent or for the purpose of access to the children until further order. Ormrod L.J. used the analogies of wardship jurisdiction and that of divorce: if these facts had surfaced in either jurisdiction, there was no doubt that the husband would be ordered to leave. So it was here.

The Domestic Violence Act, *Bassett, Walker, Rennick, Davis* v. *Johnson* have made the injunction a most useful weapon in the armoury of the battered wife. Unfortunately, there is evidence of a judge's backlash against injunctions. [254] Some county court judges are said to be 'antipathetic' to injunction applications regarding them as 'a kind of new industry invented by solicitors'. One judge is alleged to have said: '[w]e are inundated by these applications. We think they are just to increase costs'. [255] It may be a truism that in any area of decision making where discretion is involved justice is a very personal thing, but that certainly seems to be the case here. It is too early as yet to draw definitive conclusions but that there is inconsistency in the practice of different courts, and even in different judges in the same court, and disquiet in the legal profession and organisations concerned with battered women is incontestable.

Problems attendant upon the enforcement of injunctions have in the past meant that many were not worth the paper upon which they were written. They are frequently broken and up till the passing of the 1976 Act this has meant the woman returning to the court. If the court determined that the injunction had been breached it could order that the erring husband be fined or imprisoned. It rarely did either. Pizzey tells us of 'Joan' who took her husband before judges on 11 occasions before he was committed to prison. [256] The court must then issue a warrant for his arrest which is to be carried out by the tipstaff in the High Court, and the bailiffs in the county court. But 'they are scarce, they finish at 5.30 and they don't work weekends'. [257] Additionally, they only have jurisdiction within the court area and the judge must be asked to extend their power if necessary. It is the duty of the police to assist the bailiff, not to take the initiative in making the arrest. The Solicitor-General in his evidence to the Select Committee intimated that when asked the police did in fact co-operate by, for example, holding the husband until the bailiff arrived. [258] The police do, of course, have a power of arrest under the criminal law if a criminal offence, such as an assault occasioning actual bodily harm, takes place, as well as for conduct likely to cause breach of the peace. Margaret Gregory writes of one case where the man 'contrived to avoid being served with the warrant for breach of injunction for six months, continuing all the time to commit further breaches'. [259]

The reluctance of the police to get involved is as evident here as it is in the area of the criminal law. The Metropolitan Police, however, do not think that there is an enforcement problem. In its evidence to the House of Commons Select Committee it argued that 'the civil and criminal law have always been separated for good reasons, and it would be wrong both constitutionally and practically to extend the criminal law to enable police to exercise powers to enforce orders made within the civil jurisdiction of the courts'. [260] The police say they prefer to rely on the criminal law but this is hardly a fair strategy to adopt when their performance on domestic violence calls is so pusillanimous. The Select Committee recognised this problem and recommended that judges should have the power to back the injunction with a power of police arrest. [261] This recommendation formed the basis of s.2 of the Domestic Violence and Matrimonial Proceedings Act 1976.

This section does not extend the criminal law but brings the police into the enforcement of one aspect of the civil law. [262] It gives a judge power to attach a power of arrest to an injunction where (a) he grants an injunction containing a provision restraining the use of violence against the applicant or a child living with the applicant or makes an exclusion order and (b) he is satisfied that the party to whom the injunction is directed has caused actual bodily harm to the applicant or the child and (c) he considers he is likely to do so again. The police are given the power of arrest without warrant where the constable concerned has reasonable cause for suspecting breach of the injunction by reason of the use of violence or entry into the excluded premises or area. Persons so arrested must be brought before a judge within 24 hours. The police are not allowed to bail a person so arrested. [263]

In *Lewis* v. *Lewis* [264] the Court of Appeal made a number of general comments on s.2. First, it declared it to be general so that a power of arrest could be attached to an injunction sought outside the jurisdiction conferred by s.1, for example, in divorce proceedings. Second, the court emphasised that the person applying had to satisfy the court on both (a) and (b), as set out above. Third, 'the power of arrest is not to be regarded as a routine remedy'. [265] It was 'very useful for exceptional cases where a man or a woman persisted in disobeying an injunction'. Fourth, notice should be given in an application for an injunction that it was proposed to ask the court for a power of arrest. The court reasoned that a man might submit to an injunction but oppose the power of arrest.

This new provision is potentially of value. But one must not read too much into it. It does little, at least directly, to alter current police attitudes towards intervention in cases of domestic violence. It only applies where an injunction with a power of arrest has been issued and disobeyed. One must not lose perspective; most people, even violent husbands, obey the law. [266] Police operations at the pre-injunction stage, then, are not affected. Much depends on how the courts and the police interpret their powers. Both have a discretion. The courts, we have seen, regard the power of arrest as an exceptional remedy. Judges throughout the country are said to be reluctant to attach powers of arrest to injunctions. Some find it unsatisfactory because they have to be disturbed to deal with the offender. One solicitor in Birmingham told the Legal Action Group that not one of his firm's applications for powers of arrest to be attached had been granted. [267]

Even if a power of arrest is attached, there remains considerable uncertainty as to whether the police will use it in the event of a breach. Some of the practical difficulties were spelt out by Mr Alex Lyon for the Home Office in evidence to the Select Committee:

> if the husband denies that there is an injunction against him, or if there is some doubt in the situation, how does the constable on the beat first of all decide that an injunction has been ordered, how does he know what are the limits of the injunction . . . [W] e do not think it is feasible to do what is in fact the judge's job in a civil court. [268]

The Home Office antipathy to the concept is reflected in its circular [269] to chief constables. It emphasises the permissiveness of the power of arrest and stresses that the police may arrest for a criminal offence or for conduct likely to cause a breach of the peace rather than for breach of the injunction. If they do this, the offender is taken to the magistrates' court, rather than brought before a judge in a civil court. And, as there is no duty on the police to inform the civil court of what has happened, it may never discover the full truth. Indeed, the magistrates' court may well dispose of the offender in ignorance of his previous history in the county court.

One of the greatest fears of the police has always been that a policeman's misuse of his powers of arrest will result in an action for false imprisonment. The potential for unlawful arrests is great in this area of domestic violence. Because of their policy of non-intervention they will probably not have been involved in the spouses' domestic problems at all. Then, summoned to a disturbance, they are told there has been a breach of an injunction to which a power of arrest has been attached. How is the individual constable to know how accurate this is? Serving injunctions on police stations may help. But, suppose the woman has left the neighbourhood and breach takes place somewhere else? The effective operation of this provision requires a centralised data bank. [270] Bringing an offender before a judge within 24 hours can also cause problems. It means that every weekend a judge has to be available and in turn this means that a court official has to be on call. Sir George Baker, in his evidence to the House of Commons Select Committee, did not think there would be any difficulty about this in the main centres, but he conceded that in rural areas it could cause problems. [271] Is 24 hours a long enough period? If not, ought it to be extended to, say, 72 hours, which was the period the Select Committee seems to have had in mind? [272] But, if so, are we prepared to countenance police detention without even the possibility of bail for such a lengthy period? With these problems it is hardly surprising that courts are showing a reluctance to attach a power of arrest to an injunction and the police continue to prefer (in so far as they prefer anything) to arrest for a criminal offence rather than for breach of an injunction. There needs to be consider-able administrative operational and attitudinal change before the power of arrest provision can be made to work effectively and efficiently.

Other ways of excluding the husband

Other ways of excluding the husband from the matrimonial home may be briefly considered. In *Gurasz* v. *Gurasz*, Lord Denning M.R. said that 'in an extreme case, if [the husband's] conduct is so out-rageous as to make it impossible for them to live together, the court will order him to go out and leave her there'. [273] He grounded this dictum in the common law duty of a husband to provide his wife with a roof over her head. He qualified this by stipulating that this applied 'so long as the wife behaves herself'. This principle and its limitation are no longer of much importance since the Domestic Violence and Matrimonial Proceedings Act 1976.

In theory a wife should be able to use s.17 of the Married Women's Property Act 1882. This gives the court power to make such order as it 'thinks fit' upon an application to it by either party about title to or possession of property. But as the wife's right to occupation is not exclusive, the court does not appear to have the power in proceedings under this section to exclude the husband from the matrimonial home. This was held in *McDowell* v. *McDowell* [274] where a wife had

211

obtained a decree of judicial separation and the circumstances of life in the jointly owned home were such that the husband's continued presence was virtually forcing the wife to leave.

The Matrimonial Homes Act of 1967 in s.1(2) allows either spouse to apply to the court for an order (*inter alia*) 'regulating the exercise by either spouse of the right to occupy the dwelling house'. In *Tarr* v. *Tarr*, [275] the House of Lords held that this did not include a power to 'prohibit' the exercise by the entitled spouse of his (or her) proprietary right of occupation. An order to such an effect for a limited period was also excluded for it is, 'so long as it has effect, a complete prohibition of the exercise of the right'. [276] This decision has been overturned by s.3 of the Domestic Violence and Matrimonial Proceedings Act 1976. For the word in the 1967 Act 'regulating' are now substituted the words 'prohibiting, suspending or restricting'. There is thus now power under the Matrimonial Homes Act 1967, as amended, to exclude a spouse from the matrimonial home or to do so for a limited period or to restrict a spouse to part of the home.

These are wide powers, indeed. Hitherto, very little use has been made of the Matrimonial Homes Act. Indeed, according to the President of the Family Division, it has not been used in cases involving domestic violence. [277] Whether the new amendment will stimulate greater use of the 1967 Act remains to be seen. The liberalisation of the law relating to matrimonial injunctions renders this an unlikely development. The Matrimonial Homes Act is also limited, in that it covers only spouses, and not cohabitees, and only the matrimonial home.

The Domestic Violence and Matrimonial Proceedings Act has also extended (in s.4) the powers in the 1967 Act to joint legal tenants. Hitherto, short of a matrimonial injunction, they had to rely on the common law or use s.30 of the Law of Property Act 1925 under which the court in its discretion can order a sale but nothing else. Now one joint legal tenant will be able to exclude the other from the matrimonial home under s.1(2) of the 1967 Act.

Conclusion

In this chapter a number of legal remedies has been surveyed. The criminal law has been under-used. It is not as blunt an instrument as it is when dealing with child abuse. The powers of the magistrates' courts are too limited for much faith to be put in them. Divorce is usually, although not always, an effective remedy, should it be desired. But, so long as alternatives to married life remain so bleak for so many women, many battered wives will not be able to contemplate a clean break. All in all, injunctions remain the battered wife's best weapon: quick, cheap, flexible and relatively effective; for all their faults, they give the battered woman the protection she seeks. The law cannot solve her problem. Ultimately, only a restructuring of society can do that. It may not even be as useful to her as the sanctuary of a refuge. But it is there, to be used, and in conjunction with other remedies, notably the recent changes in social policy towards the homeless, should go a long way towards giving the women in question some peace of mind. We must, however, not expect the law to bear the burden of society. [278]

Notes

[1] Graphically described in vol.1 of Sir W. Blackstone's *Commentaries on the Law of England*, T. Tegg, 1765. A good account is K. De Crow, *Sexist Justice*, Random House, 1974. See also L. Kanowitz, *Women and the Law — the Unfinished Revolution*, University of New Mexico Press, 1969.

[2] By O. McGregor, *Divorce in England*, Heinemann, 1957, p.67.

[3] Blackstone's term (*Commentaries*, p.433).

[4] Good discussions of the disabilities are K. De Crow and L. Kanowitz, op.cit., note 1. See also B. Brown et al., *Women's Rights and the Law*, Praeger, 1977.

[5] On sex discrimination in social security see R. Lister and E. Wilson, *The Unequal Breadwinner*, NCCL, 1976 and R. Lister, *Patching up the Safety Net?*, CPAG, 1977, p.78ff.

[6] The expression is K. von Savigny's (*System of Modern Roman Law*, 1840).

[7] See Y. Dror, *Tulane L.R.*, vol.33, 1959, p.789; G. Massell, *Law and Society Review*, vol.2, 1967, p.179; V. Aubert, *Acta Sociologica*, vol.10, p.99. See generally, M.D.A. Freeman, *The Legal Structure,* Longman, 1974, ch.3.

[8] *Cf* J. Eekelaar, *Family Security and Family Breakdown*, Penguin, 1971, p.44.

[9] *Ante*, p.141.

[10] 1 Hawkins P.C.130.

[11] Quoted in Blackstone's *Commentaries*, op.cit., note 1.

[12] Op.cit., note 1, p.445.

[13] *Per* R. Graveson in R. Graveson and F.R. Crane, *A Century of Family Law*, Sweet and Maxwell, 1957, p.16.

[14] *R. v. Jackson* [1891] 1 Q.B.671, 682.

[15] *Cochrane*'s case (1840) 8 Dowl. 630.

[16] *Meacher v. Meacher* [1946] P.216.

[17] *McKenzie v. McKenzie, The Times*, 5 June 1959, commented on in J. Biggs, *The Concept of Matrimonial Cruelty*, Athlone Press, 1962, p.147.

[18] See 'No Comment' in *Ms.* August 1975.

[19] *Cf* E. Pizzey, *Scream Quietly or the Neighbours Will Hear*, Penguin 1974, p.33.

[20] R. Gelles, *The Violent Home*, Sage, 1972, p.59.

[21] R. Parnas in *Wisconsin L.R.*, 1967, pp 914, 952.

[22] *The Daily Mirror*, 20 March 1974.

[23] *The Daily Mirror*, 18 January 1974.

[24] J.S. Mill commented that a 'female slave has (in Christian countries) an admitted right . . . to refuse to her master the last familiarity. Not so the wife: . . . he can claim from her and enforce the lowest degradation of a human being, that of being made the instrument of an animal function contrary to her inclination' (*The Subjection of Women*).

[25] *R. v. Clarke* [1949] 2 All E.R.448. The non-cohabitation order no longer exists. See Domestic Proceedings and Magistrates' Courts Act 1978.

[26] *R. v. O'Brien* [1974] 3 All E.R.663.

[27] *R. v. Miller* [1954] 2 Q.B.282. In *R. v. Steele* (1977) *Criminal Law Review*, p.290, the Court of Appeal held that when a husband gave an undertaking to a court not to 'assault, molest or interfere with his wife' he also gave up his sexual rights so that he could be charged with raping his wife.

[28] *R. v. Reid* [1972] 2 All E.R.1350.

[29] *Holborn v. Holborn* [1947] 1 All E.R.32.

[30] *Foster v. Foster* [1921] P.438.

[31] See E. Livneh, 'On Rape and the Sanctity of Marriage', *Israel Law Review*, vol.2, 1967, p.415.

[32] Del. Code tit 11, para. 763 (Supp. 1976). The code distinguishes between rape in the first and second degree. Rape of a wife comes into the latter category. (See also Hawaii, Penal Code, paras 730-2, 1972.

[33] S.D. Compiled Laws Ann. para. 22-22-1 (Supp. 1976). See also J.A. Scutt, *Australian Law Journal*, vol.50, p.615 (1976).

[34] HC Standing Committee F, 24 March 1976; *cf* HC, vol.911, col. 1952ff. See also Lord Dunedin in *G. v. G.* [1924] A.C.349, 357.

[35] See V. Greenwood and J. Young, 'Notes on the Theory of Rape and its Policy Implications', Paper presented to London group on

Deviancy, 1975.

[36] S. Griffin, 'Rape: The All-American Crime', *Ramparts*, September 1971, p.28.

[37] A. Davis, 'Sexual Assaults in the Philadelphia Prison System' in J. Gagnon and W. Simon (eds), *The Sexual Scene*, Aldine, 1970.

[38] H. & J. Schwerdinger, 'Rape Myths', *Crime and Social Justice*, vol.1, 1974, p.18.

[39] See C.H. McCaghy, *Deviant Behavior*, Macmillan, 1976, pp 129-39. For the impact of the feminist movement see V. Rose, *Social Problems*, vol.25, 1977, p.75.

[40] See Offences Against the Persons Act 1861 ss 47, 20. See also s.18 (wounding).

[41] *R. v. Miller* [1954] 2 Q.B.282, 292.

[42] *D.P.P. v. Smith* [1961] A.C.290, 334 and J.C. Smith and B. Hogan, *Criminal Law* (4th ed.), Butterworths, 1978, pp 368-9.

[43] *Hoskyn v. Metropolitan Police Commissioner* [1978] 2 All E.R. 136, overruling *R. v. Verolla* [1963] 1 Q.B.285, *R. v. Lapworth* [1931] 1 K.B.117. G.D. Nokes's comment that decisions to the contrary would have constituted 'a charter for wife-beaters' in R. Graveson and F.R. Crane, op.cit., note 13, p.148 is interesting considering when it was written (1957). So is Lord Edmund-Davies's dissent in *Hoskyn*.

[44] Homicide Act 1957 s.3.

[45] A good example, though not involving an offence against a wife, is that of the Indian hot-dog salesman in S. McCabe and R. Purves, *The Jury at Work*, Oxford Penal Research Unit, 1972, p.33.

[46] See H. Kalven and H. Zeisel, *The American Jury*, Little Brown, 1966, p.249.

[47] A. Reiss, *The Police and the Public*, Yale University Press, 1971.

[48] *The Times*, 28 April 1977.

[49] *The Times*, 27 April 1977. Another case concerned Mrs Newsome (*The Times*, 15 September 1977) given a 2-year suspended sentence after being convicted of the manslaughter of her husband who was said to have ill-treated her for 10 years. The case got minimal press coverage compared to the earlier two cases.

[50] That is, according to 'professional' expectations. It may, however, be argued that decisions of this nature which are certainly in tune with community sentiment are part of the jury's function.

[51] Discussed in E. Truninger, *Hastings Law Journal*, vol.23, 1971, p.259 and D. Martin, *Battered Wives*, Glide 1976, pp 100-1.

[52] *People v. Burns* (1948), 88 Cal. App. 2d, 867.

[53] D. Martin, op.cit., note 51, p.100.

[54] Quoted from *San Jose Mercury*, 5 November 1975 by D. Martin, idem, pp 100-1.

[55] Idem, p.101.

[56] It is non-statutory. It is found in annual reports and as Appendix 4 of Home Office/Scottish Home and Health Dept, *Review of the Criminal Injuries Compensation Scheme*, HMSO, March 1978.

[57] See *Annual Report of CICB*, 1976-77, Cmnd 7022 (13th report).

[58] The origins of the exclusion are found in Cmnd 1406, para. 38.

[59] Cmnd 6656, Appendix D.

[60] Cmnd 7022, Appendix D.

[61] A striking illustration is in the 10th report, Cmnd 5791, pp 10-11.

[62] *R. v. CICB exparte Staten* [1972] 1 All E.R.1034.

[63] *Cf Hopes* v. *Hopes* [1949] P.227, *Mouncer* v. *Mouncer* [1972] 1 All E.R.289, *Fuller* v. *Fuller* [1973] 2 All E.R.650.

[64] *Jones* v. *Jones* [1976] Fam.8.

[65] See S. Schafer, *Victimology — the Victim and his Criminal*, Reston, 1977, ch.3.

[66] See J. Brooks, *Crime and Delinquency*, vol.21, 1975, p.50.

[67] Cmnd 5127, para. 9.

[68] Home Office/Scottish Home and Health Dept, *Review of the Criminal Injuries Compensation Scheme: Report of an Interdepartmental Working Party*, 1978.

[69] See, for example, idem, para. 7.1.

[70] J. Carlin and J. Howard, *UCLA Law Review*, vol.12, 1965, p.381.

[71] E. Marx, *The Social Context of Violent Behaviour*, RKP, 1976.

[72] Idem, p.18.

[73] See *ante,* p.141.

[74] Op.cit., note 68, ch.7.

[75] Op.cit., note 68, Appendix 2 (paras 7-11).

[76] Op.cit., note 71.

[77] Op.cit., note 62.

[78] Op.cit., note 68, para 7.10.

[79] HC, vol.858, *Written Answers*, cols 149-50 *per* Mr M. Carlisle.

[80] See R.O. Hawkins in *Law and Society Review*, vol.7, 1973, p.427.

[81] R. Gelles in *Journal of Marriage and the Family*, vol.38, 1976, pp 659, 660.

[82] Op.cit., note 19, p.109.

[83] *Nicholson* v. *Booth* (1888) 52 J.P. 662. It is also said (*sed dubitante*) that there is no power of arrest unless it is committed in the view of the police (*Minutes*, p.375).

[84] *Pickering* v. *Willoughby* [1907] 2 K.B. 296.

[85] *Cf* M. Dow, in M. Borland (ed.), *Violence in the Family*, Manchester University Press, 1976, p.132.

[86] On their reluctance to intervene see HC *Minutes*, pp 361-91 and M. Dow in M. Borland (ed.), *Violence in the Family*, Manchester

University Press, 1976, p.129.

[87] Metropolitan Police Evidence to Select Committee, *Minutes*, p.376 (para 13).

[88] Idem, p.366.

[89] Idem, p.369.

[90] J. Pahl, *The Canterbury Women's Centre 1975-76*, University of Kent, 1977, paras 6, 19. Pahl comments that the police see their role as to enforce the law, whereas the women want protection from the police so that they can stay in their own homes (6.26). The accommodation problem seen in these terms is really a problem of inadequate policing. See also *Family Service Unit Quarterly*, 1974, no.vi.

[91] R. Parnas in *Law and Contemporary Problems*, vol.36, 1971, pp 539, 542.

[92] On the new 'special procedure' see M.D.A. Freeman in *Family Law*, vol.6, 1976, p.255.

[93] R. Parnas in *Wisconsin L.R.* 1967, p.914 at p.920.

[94] Idem.

[95] *Minutes*, p.79 *per* M. Russell.

[96] R. Parnas, op.cit., note 91, p.543.

[97] Idem.

[98] *Minutes*, p.376.

[99] *Per* M. Field and H. Field, 'Marital Violence and the Criminal Process: Neither Justice nor Peace', *Social Services Review*, vol.47, 1973, pp 221, 227. See also C.A. Coleman and A.K. Bottomley, 'Police Conceptions of Crime and "No Crime" ', *Criminal Law Review*, 1976, p.344 at pp 352-3.

[100] R. Parnas, op.cit., note 93.

[101] See M. Banton, *The Policeman in the Community*, Tavistock, 1964.

[102] See M. Punch and T. Naylor in *New Society*, 17 May 1973, p.358.

[103] J.Q. Wilson, *Varieties of Police Behavior*, Harvard University Press, 1968.

[104] The police have a wide discretion to treat law-breaking incidents as peace keeping. See E. Bittner 'The Police on Skid-row', *American Sociological Review*, vol.32, 1967, p.699.

[105] See D. Black, 'Production of Crime Rates', *American Sociological Review*, vol.35, 1970, p.733. This gives crime rates 'a democratic flavour' (p.739). Black did, however, find that the police were less likely to comply with requests for legal action where family was involved.

[106] See W. Belson, *The Police and the Public*, Harper and Row, 1975.

[107]   See I. Piliavin and S. Briar, 'Police Encounters with Juveniles', *American Journal of Sociology*, vol.70, 1964, p.206; D. Black and A. Reiss, 'Police Control of Juveniles', *American Sociological Review*, vol.35, 1970, p.63.

[108]   See D. Steer, *Police Cautions — A Study in the Exercise of Police Discretion*, Oxford Penal Research Unit, 1970.

[109]   J.A. Ditchfield, *Police Cautioning in England and Wales*, HMSO, 1976.

[110]   J. Skolnick, *Justice Without Trial*, Wiley, 1967, pp 171-2.

[111]   J. Lambert, 'Race Relations: the Role of the Police' in S. Zubaida, *Race and Racialism*, Tavistock, 1970, p.73.

[112]   *Minutes*, p.367.

[113]   R. Parnas, op.cit., note 93; and in *Law and Contemporary Problems*, vol.36, 1971, p.539.

[114]   R. Parnas, op.cit., note 93, p.922 ff.

[115]   E. Cumming et al., 'Policeman as Philosopher, Guide and Friend', *Social Problems*, vol.12, 1965, p.276.

[116]   R. Parnas, *Wisconsin L.R.* 1967 at 922, 929.

[117]   *Cf* E. Pizzey, *Scream Quietly or the Neighbours will Hear*, Penguin, 1974, p.30.

[118]   See M. Bard and B. Berkowitz, 'Training Police as Specialists in Family Crisis Intervention', *Community Mental Health Journal*, vol.3, 1967, p.315 and M. Bard in S. Steinmetz and M. Straus, *Violence in the Family*, Dodd, Mead, 1974, p.152.

[119]   For example Louisville and Oakland.

[120]   See J. Eekelaar and S. Katz, *Family Violence*, Butterworths, 1978.

[121]   M. Bard in (eds) S. Steinmetz and M. Straus, *Violence in the Family*, Dodd, Mead, 1974, p.138.

[122]   R. Parnas in *Law and Contemporary Problems*, vol.36, 1971, pp 539, 551.

[123]   For comments upon it see R. Parnas, idem and M. Field and H. Field, op.cit., note 99, pp 237-8.

[124]   Op.cit., note 121, pp 134-5.

[125]   R. Parnas, 'The Relevance of Criminal Law to Interspousal Violence', Second World Conference of the International Society of Family Law, Montreal, 1977. (Also in op.cit., note 120).

[126]   Idem, p.6.

[127]   R. Parnas in *Indiana L.J.* vol.44, 1969, pp 159, 180.

[128]   Op.cit., note 117, p.99.

[129]   HC Select Committee Report, *On Violence in Marriage*, 1975, para. 44.

[130]   *The Daily Telegraph*, 28 February 1976.

[131] *Ante*, p.161.

[132] Bedfordshire Police, Reports on Acts of Domestic Violence committed in the County between 1 February 1976 and 31 July 1976.

[133] A similar point is made by M. Fields 'Representing Battered Wives', *Family Law Reporter*, vol.3, 1977, p.4025.

[134] Op.cit., note 117, p.129.

[135] Idem, p.120.

[136] Op.cit., note 99, p.227.

[137] See W. Chambliss, 'Types of Deviance and the Effectiveness of Legal Sanctions', *Wisconsin L.R.*, 1967, 703. *Cf* J. Andenaes, 'Deterrence and Specific Offenses', *University of Chicago Law Review*, vol.38, 1971, p.537.

[138] Discussed in R. Parnas, *Minnesota L.R.*, vol.54, 1970, p.584 and S. Maidment, *I.C.L.Q.*, vol.26, 1977, p.403.

[139] S. Maidment, idem, p.442.

[140] Discussed idem, pp 437-42.

[141] M. Rheinstein, 'The Law of Divorce and the Problem of Marriage Stability, *Vanderbilt Law Review*, vol.9, 1956, pp 633, 636.

[142] R. Parnas, op.cit., note 138, pp 585, 643.

[143] Good discussions are S. Maidment, op.cit., note 138 and R. Parnas in *Criminal Law Bulletin*, vol.9, 1973, p.733.

[144] Quoted in Maidment, op.cit., note 138, p.435.

[145] See further M.D.A. Freeman, *The Legal Structure*, Longman, 1974, p.38.

[146] On which see T. Eckhoff in *Acta Sociologica*, vol.10, 1966, p.158; in V. Aubert, *Sociology of Law*, Penguin, 1969, p.171.

[147] S.J. Fox, 'Reform of Juvenile Justice: The Child's Right to Punishment', *Juvenile Justice*, vol.25, 1974, p.2.

[148] The law was changed by the Law Reform (Husband and Wife) Act 1962.

[149] *Cf* W.E. McCurdy, *Villanova L.R.*, vol.4, 1959, p.303.

[150] *Per* J. McCardie in *Gottliffe* v. *Edelston*, [1930] 2 K.B. 378, 392.

[151] *Per* Glanville Williams in *Modern Law Review*, vol.24, p.101.

[152] See M. Ploscowe, H. Foster and D. Freed, *Family Law: Cases and Materials*, Little Brown, 1972, pp 852-4.

[153] *Cf* H. Street, *The Law of Torts*, Butterworths, 1976, pp 468-9.

[154] It was probably used more against a cohabitee, where matrimonial proceedings were not available.

[155] *Per* Law Commission, *Law Commission*, no.77, 1976, para. 3.15.

[156] Or himself. For convenience the assumption is that the

applicant is the wife.

[157]   See now Domestic Proceedings and Magistrates' Courts Act 1978 s.62.

[158]   *Per* Lord Harris of Greenwich, H.L. vol.388, col.581.

[159]   Conduct may be taken into account (see s.3(1)(g)).

[160]   S.16(5)-(8).

[161]   S.18. On the Act see M.D.A. Freeman, *Domestic Proceedings and Magistrates' Courts Act 1978*, Sweet and Maxwell, 1978.

[162]   The magistrates' courts today 'deal exclusively with what used to be called the lumpen proletariat . . . the poorest, the least literate, the worst informed section of the population' *per* O. McGregor in *Proceedings from Conference on Matrimonial Jurisdiction of Magistrates*, Institute of Judicial Administration, Birmingham, 1973.

[163]   See *post*, p.202.

[164]   It has been held that an injunction not to molest is broken by pestering (*Vaughan* v. *Vaughan* [1973] 3 All E.R.449). There is no reason why an order should thus not be made for pestering. See also, for agreement, J. Masson, in *Family Law*, vol.7, 1977, p.29.

[165]   Law Com. No.77, 1976, para. 3.12.

[166]   HC Standing Committee B, col.74.

[167]   The Law Commission (*Field of Choice* Cmnd 3123) thought the proposals of the church commission (*Putting Asunder*) which would have left the question at large impracticable. See, for a discussion of this, M.D.A. Freeman in *Current Legal Problems*, vol.24, 1971, pp 183-5.

[168]   One of these facts (see s.1(2)(b) of Matrimonial Causes Act 1973).

[169]   See s.1(2)(a) MCA 1973.

[170]   *Per* Bagnall J. in *Ash* v. *Ash* [1972] 1 All E.R.582, 585.

[171]   Idem, pp 585-6.

[172]   *The Times*, 20 December 1975.

[173]   *Ash* v. *Ash*, op.cit., note 170 and *Bradley* v. *Bradley* [1973] 3 All E.R.750 are but two reported examples.

[174]   *Bradley* v. *Bradley* [1973] 3 All E.R.750. Another example is in *Select Committee Minutes on Violence in Marriage*, q.1082-3 (*per* Mrs S.)

[175]   M.C.A. 1973 s.3(1).

[176]   M.C.A. 1973 s.3(2).

[177]   Morton Commission Cmnd 9678, 1956, ch.5; *Putting Asunder*, SPCK, 1966, para. 78; Law Commission, *Field of Choice*, Cmnd 3123, para. 19.

[178]   M. Hayes, *Family Law*, vol.4, 1974, p.103; J.G. Miller, *Anglo-American Law Review*, vol.4, 1975, p.163; B. Mortlock, *The Inside of Divorce*, Constable, 1972, pp 11-15.

[179] *Bowman* v. *Bowman* [1949] P.353, 356-7 *per* Denning L.J.
[180] *Hiller* v. *Hiller* [1958] P.186.
[181] *McGibbon* v. *McGibbon* [1973] Fam.170. *McLeod* v.
McLeod (1973) 117 Sol. Jo. 679 is sometimes cited as an authority to
the contrary but there the wife was the tenant.
[182] As from 1 April 1977. On the withdrawal see M.D.A. Freeman
in *Family Law*, vol.6, 1976, p.255, and G. Davis and M. Murch in
Family Law, vol.7, 1977, p.71.
[183] By the Legal Advice and Assistance Act 1972 (see now Legal
Aid Act 1974). The limit is £45 where the solicitor drafts the petition.
[184] See particularly s.24 of MCA 1973.
[185] *Wachtel* v. *Wachtel* [1973] Fam. 72. Registrars apparently do
not show the same reluctance. See W. Barrington Baker et al. *The
Matrimonial Jurisdiction of Registrars*, SSRC, 1977, paras 2.20-2.23.
[186] See *Jones* v. *Jones* [1976] Fam.8.
[187] HL, vol.373, col.1438. See also HC vol.905, col.858 *per*
Miss J. Richardson.
[188] *Per* E. Truninger, *Hastings L.J.* vol.23, 1971, pp 259, 260.
[189] Op.cit., note 117, p.41.
[190] D. Marsden and D. Owens, *New Society*, 8 May 1975, p.334.
[191] *Cf* note 164.
[192] *Ansah* v. *Ansah* [1977] 2 All E.R.638.
[193] s.2 of Domestic Violence and Matrimonial Proceedings Act
1976.
[194] *Vaughan* v. *Vaughan* (see *The Times*, 7 May 1974).
[195] *Minutes*, q.1803.
[196] Idem, q.389.
[197] *Ansah* v. *Ansah* [1977] 2 All E.R.638, 642.
[198] *Masich* v. *Masich* (1977) 7 Fam. Law. 245. The courts
continue to be worried by *ex parte* applications. A survey apparently
has shown that nearly half such cases were 'unmeritorious' (see *The
Times*, 25 July 1978, Practice Note [1978] 2 All E.R.919)
[199] *LAG Bulletin*, June 1976, p.125.
[200] HL, vol.373, col.1441.
[201] *Minutes*, q.1800.
[202] About 350 injunctions under the 1976 Act are being granted
monthly (figures for first 5 months of the Act). Nine per cent of
applications are being refused. See *LAG Bulletin*, February 1978, p.28.
In the first 10 months 4272 injunctions were granted under s.1 of the
1976 Act (1201 had a power of arrest attached). Injunctions with a
power of arrest attached are uncommon on the North-Eastern circuit
and in Wales and Chester. See HC vol.951, cols 1383-4 *per*
Miss J. Richardson.

[203] *Des Salles d'Epinoix* v. *Des Salles d'Epinoix* [1967] 2 All E.R.539.

[204] Or agreed to file, usually within 14 days.

[205] *Montgomery* v. *Montgomery* [1965] P.46.

[206] *Jones* v. *Jones* [1971] 2 All E.R.737.

[207] *Robinson* v. *Robinson* [1965] P.39, *Brent* v. *Brent* [1974] 2 All E.R. 1211.

[208] *Hall* v. *Hall* [1971] 1 All E.R.762.

[209] *Mamane* v. *Mamane* (1974) 4 *Family Law*, 87. A digest of recent cases is in *LAG Bulletin*, June 1976, p.137.

[210] On the Act see M.D.A. Freeman *New Law Journal*, vol.127, 1977, p.159, 'Man's Inhumanity to Wife' in MLR (forthcoming). There is a detailed legal commentary in *Current Law Statutes Annotated*, Sweet and Maxwell, 1976. See also J. Masson in *Family Law*, vol.7, p.29 and S. Maidment in *Family Law*, vol.7, p.50.

[211] *Bassett* v. *Bassett* [1975] Fam.76.

[212] *Per* Lord Denning M.R. in *Davis* v. *Johnson*, [1978] 1 All E.R.841, 850, *cf* Bridge, Megaw L.J.J. in *B.* v. *B.* [1978] 1 All E.R.821, 832, 834.

[213] S.I. no.532, 1977, para. 5.

[214] *Cf* R. Lane, *New Law Journal*, vol.127, 1977, p.298.

[215] *Ruddell* v. *Ruddell* (1967) 111 Sol. Jo. 497.

[216] *Phillips* v. *Phillips* [1973] 2 All E.R.423.

[217] *Stewart* v. *Stewart* [1973] 1 All E.R.31;

[218] *Adams* v. *Adams* (1965) 109 Sol. Jo. 899.

[219] *Jones* v. *Jones* [1971] 2 All E.R.737. See also *Bowens* v. *Bowens*, *The Guardian*, 10 August 1973.

[220] See Married Women's Property Act 1882 s.1. The Law Commission has rejected community of property. (See *Law Com.* no.52). It has recommended statutory co-ownership of the matrimonial home (see *Law Com.* no.86).

[221] *Cf W.* v. *W.* [1951] 2 TLR 1135 in the light of *Pettitt* v. *Pettitt* [1970] A.C.777. See *Law Com.* no.86 (Book 3).

[222] *Gurasz* v. *Gurasz* [1970] P.11, 16.

[223] *Cf* the facts of *Nanda* v. *Nanda* [1968] P.351.

[224] See s.1(8).

[225] Domestic Violence Bill Standing Committee F, col.9.

[226] Idem, cols 9-10 (*per* Miss J. Richardson).

[227] *B.* v. *B.* [1978] 1 All E.R.821.

[228] *Cantliff* v. *Jenkins* [1978] 1 All E.R.836.

[229] *Davis* v. *Johnson* [1978] 1 All E.R.841.

[230] Idem, p.847.

[231] Idem, p.849.

[232] Idem, p.860.
[233] Idem, p.860.
[234] Idem, p.879ff.
[235] Idem, p.860.
[236] *B. v. B.* [1978] 1 All E.R.1132.
[237] Idem, p.1145.
[238] Idem, p.1150.
[239] Idem, p.1156.
[240] At first under the so-called 'palm-tree' justice of s.17 of the Married Women's Property Act 1882 and then under S.24 of the MCA 1973.
[241] On these see D.C. Hoath, *Council Housing*, Sweet and Maxwell, 1978.
[242] Rent Act 1977 s.14. But see J. Davies (1976) *LAG Bulletin*, 158.
[243] This is recognised in a Practice Note of 21 July 1978 ([1978] 2 All E.R.1056). It states that consideration should be given to imposing a time limit on the operation of an injunction. Three months is the suggested limit. See also *Hopper v. Hopper* (1978) 122 S.J.610.
[244] See C.H. Sherrin, *Family Law*, vol.8, 1978, p.176.
[245] This can be done on a divorce, judicial separation or nullity under s.24 of MCA 1973.
[246] HC vol.905, col.859.
[247] *Bassett v. Bassett* [1975] Fam. 76, 82.
[248] Idem, p.84.
[249] The House of Commons *Report on Violence in Marriage*, 1975, HC 553-i, thought the approach in *Bassett* right, para. 50.
[250] *Walker v. Walker* [1978] 1 WLR 533.
[251] Idem, p.539.
[252] Idem, pp 536-7.
[253] *Rennick v. Rennick* [1978] 1 All E.R.817. See also *Spindlow v. Spindlow* (1978) 122 S.J.556 (couple not married).
[254] See *LAG Bulletin*, December 1977, p.274.
[255] Letter by D. Darwin, quoted idem.
[256] Op.cit., note 117, p.119.
[257] Idem, p.118.
[258] *Minutes*, pp 401-2.
[259] M. Gregory in M. Borland (ed.), *Violence in the Family*, Manchester University Press, 1976, p.117.
[260] *Minutes*, p.378.
[261] Select Committee Report, para. 45.
[262] The Lord Chancellor thinks this will make the job of the police 'easier than it is now' (HL, vol.373, col.1443).
[263] This is in striking contrast to the Bail Act 1976 which creates

a statutory presumption in favour of bail.

[264]   *Lewis* v. *Lewis* [1978] 1 All E.R.729.

[265]   Idem, p.731 *per* Ormrod L.J. See also *Crutcher* v. *Crutcher*, *The Times*, July 18, 1978. Payne J. there held that if it was desired to obtain in the High Court a power of arrest, proceedings for some substantive relief must have been started or there must be the usual undertaking to start proceedings forthwith.

[266]   HC, vol.905, col.879 *per* Mr I. Percival.

[267]   See *LAG Bulletin*, December 1977, p.274. Apparently about one-third of injunctions have powers of arrest attached to them. Not many, however, lead to an arrest (this may be because they are not broken or because the police either do not arrest for breach or arrest for some criminal offence instead). There were 18 arrests in June 1977, 47 in October 1977. Six men were committed to prison in June, and 16 in October. Statistics showing the rate of refusal of applications for powers of arrest have not been collected. (See *LAG Bulletin*, February 1978, p.28).

[268]   *Minutes*, q.1684.

[269]   Home Office Circular no.68/1977 (May 1977).

[270]   There are over 4,000 injunctions a year; nearly 1,500 will have powers of arrest attached, if early experience is representative. The rules provide for copies of injunctions to which a power of arrest has been attached to be delivered to the officer in charge of the police station for the applicant's address (S.I. 1977 no.532 and 615). But battered wives move about the country.

[271]   *Minutes*, q.1815-6. This problem is now partially tackled by the provision in the Domestic Proceedings and Magistrates'Courts Act 1978 that in reckoning any period of 24 hours no account is to be taken of Christmas Day, Good Friday or any Sunday. See Sch.2, para. 53.

[272]   Idem, q.1815. No period is mentioned in the Report.

[273]   *Gurasz* v. *Gurasz* [1970] P.11, 16.

[274]   *McDowell* v. *McDowell* (1957) 107 L.J.184. But *cf* Lord Denning in *Gurasz*, op.cit., note 273.

[275]   *Tarr* v. *Tarr* [1973] A.C.254.

[276]   Idem, p.265.

[277]   Quoted in *Law Com.*, no.77, para 3.27.

[278]   See C. Smart and B. Smart, *Women, Sexuality and Control* RKP, 1978, p.1.

PART III

OTHER FAMILY VIOLENCE

9 Battered husbands

The suggestion that husbands are battered by their wives is apt to
produce a wry grin. Yet, as has been indicated earlier in the book, [1]
the indications from the latest American research suggest it is as
prevalent as wife battering. We have become used to hearing of wife
battering as the most unreported crime. But it may be that it is in
fact husband battering which surpasses it as the most 'hidden crime'.
   Only rarely has the phenomenon of a husband brutally assaulted
by his wife surfaced to public attention. In 1974 a Mr Gadsby was
granted a divorce on account of the gross violence perpetrated upon
him by his wife. [2] Another husband, but only one it seems, wrote
a letter to the House of Commons Select Committee on violence in
marriage to inform it that marital violence was not one-way traffic.
[3] Divorce actions involving mutual violence are sometimes
reported. [4] In this country there is little evidence of battered
husbands. But then ten years ago few believed that wives were
beaten by their husbands. When evidence is produced, and there were
a few references to American research in the popular press and on the
radio early in 1978, [5] it is met with stunned amazement, incredulity
or just sheer laughter.
   As was indicated earlier, [6] even if the incidence of husband
battering is higher than that of wife battering, the latter remains the
more serious problem. Reasons for this have been given. But we must
not turn our back on the more newly discovered phenomenon.
   There is no need to consider legal responses to it, for the remedies
already considered are equally applicable. A husband or male
cohabitee may use the Domestic Violence and Matrimonial Proceedings Act 1976 in just the same way as his female counterpart. [7] A
married man was formerly able to seek a non-cohabitation order in the
magistrates' court [8] and a divorce citing his wife's behaviour in a
superior court. [9] The Matrimonial Homes Act 1967 is equally
applicable to him. [10] So is the criminal law, [11] though it is
thought that police reluctance to get involved in 'domestic
disturbances' is hardly likely to be altered by the fact that a man is
being beaten up. There are, as yet, no refuges for battered men.
Indeed, little or no attention is as yet given to the men who batter
their wives. [12] Their accommodation problems, once they are
excluded from the matrimonial home, are glossed over most scantily
by those who are concerned with marital violence. Neither they nor

battered men are singled out as priority cases for housing allocation policies. The recent Code of Guidance [13] issued under the Housing (Homeless Persons) Act 1977 mentions neither the male perpetrators nor the male victims of domestic violence.

Why do we hear so little about battered husbands? It is unlikely to be because the problem is so rare. There is, of course, no 'Men's Movement' as such; whereas we know the presence of an active Women's Movement is closely related to the identification of battered women as a problem. Few men complain to the police about their wives' violence. Why? Masculine ideals in our culture discourage husbands from reporting the abuse to which they have been subjected. Men are 'supposed' to be physically tough, rough, strong and dominant; women weak, delicate and submissive. An admission that one has been beaten up by one's wife is, therefore, an admission that one is not 'really' a man. [14] Whilst women may be afraid to reveal their husbands' violence, men may be ashamed to confess that they are the victims of their wives' assaults. They may find it necessary to give false explanations of their injuries to colleagues at work or to the family to obviate the expected sniggering that the truth will produce. Such rationalisation is not always successful and the battered husband may find himself the target of jokes, comment or innuendo. The cultural ideals are such that the man who alleges he has been beaten up by his wife is likely to be disbelieved, especially in those cases in which he responds to his wife's violence by behaviour in kind. His behaviour is more susceptible to the label 'wife abuse' than is her behaviour to that of 'husband battering'. Indeed, the tendency on dissolution or even before to award home and children to the wife inevitably means that the husband who retaliates stands the chance of losing everything. [15]

Whilst there is little evidence of violent assault on husbands (though the research indicates its prevalence, at least in the USA), the statistics demonstrate that murder of a husband is not uncommon. Some examples were given in chapter 8. [16] The Gibson and Klein study of murder in the period 1957-68 reports that eight men were murdered by their wives or by women with whom they were living. A much larger number of men (an exact figure is not given but it is likely to be about 100) were killed by wives or cohabitees in circumstances which led to verdicts of manslaughter, by reason of provocation or the woman suffering from diminished responsibility, or where the woman was found 'unfit to plead' or subsequent to the crime committed suicide. [17] These figures are almost certainly an underestimate: murder by poisoning, a form of homicide for which women have the greatest opportunity, is notoriously difficult to detect. In this country more wives are killed by husbands than vice versa. In the USA FBI statistics, which indicate that in 1975 15 per cent of homicides were between husband and wife, show that in 7.8 per cent of the cases the husbands were victims, while in 8 per cent of the cases the victims were wives. [18]

One possible explanation of 'husband homicide' is put by Eisenberg and Micklow in their Michigan study published in 1977. They attribute her violence to the 'lack of any meaningful protective measures available' to her, 'as well as a minimizing of the seriousness of her situation'. For, 'faced with a violent husband and no alternatives, she may equalize the situation herself by using a deadly weapon such as a gun or knife'. [19]

We do not know how many women assault their husbands or cohabitees. In the USA Curtis reported that violence by women against men accounted for only 9 per cent of the reported assaults (violence by men against women was responsible for 27 per cent). [20] But one must not draw the conclusion that women commit only one-third as many assaults as men for 'non-fatal violence committed by women against men is less likely to be reported to the police than is violence by men against women'. [21] Steinmetz's random sample of New Castle County (Delaware) families in 1975 revealed no husbands as victims of serious assault among the study population, but in two of the cases reported to the police the victim was the husband. From this she extrapolates that 540 incidents (or 574 per 100,000 families) occurred in New Castle County during 1975. [22] It is noteworthy that in both incidents of husband beating, a neighbour, not the husband, reported the abuse. In O'Brien's study of divorce applicants in a large mid-Western metropolitan area in the USA spontaneous mentions of overt violence were recorded in one-sixth of the 150 interviews. Sixteen per cent of the reports came from men. [23] Levinger noted that of 600 husbands in mandatory conciliation interviews in greater Cleveland 18 said that 'their partner hurt them physically'. [24] These figures show a low incidence of husband beating but are undoubtedly considerable underestimates of the true amount of violence perpetrated on husbands.

First, the male interviewees are unlikely to mention what amounts to their own physical weakness to an outsider. Second, in Levinger's study there were nearly twice as many complaints by women as by men. As Steinmetz comments, 'unless one is willing to assume that it is the husband's fault when a marriage fails, it appears that women might be more comfortable voicing their complaints'. [25] Further, husbands are expected to take the blame for marriage failures so that social etiquette demands that they allow their wives to initiate proceedings; it would seem to follow that husbands might be less ready to expose their wives' faults.

It is clear that there is gross under-reporting of husband battering. Nevertheless, the revelation in the latest American research, already referred to, [26] that almost as many wives battered husbands as vice versa and that violent women tended to engage in violent acts more frequently than husbands comes as something of a shock. This finding, revealed by Straus at conferences in 1977 [27] and to be published in 1978, [28] confirms the indications of earlier pilot studies. Thus, Gelles found that nearly one-third of wives in his sample hit their husbands and 11 per cent did so at least half a dozen times a year to as much as daily. [29] Straus's study of 385 couples showed little difference in the frequency with which husbands and wives committed physically violent acts against each other. [30] Steinmetz found in her sample of 57 New Castle County families that virtually identical percentages of husbands and wives resorted to throwing things, hitting the other spouse with their hand, and hitting the other spouse with some hard object. The only mode which husbands used more frequently than wives was pushing, shoving and grabbing, which require superior physical strength. Men, she found, also did more damage, and this she attributes, rightly I believe, to their greater physical strength. [31]

Why these findings should come as a shock is not entirely surprising. We expect women to be weak and submissive. Our stereotype of women pictures them as more verbal and better able to control impulses. Yet we have known for some time about child abuse and that child abusers are more likely to be women. Women have throughout history been primarily responsible for infanticide. [32] However these facts are explained, they do demonstrate women's potentiality for violence.

The causes of husband battering have not been the subject of any research as such. One may, however, hypothesise that it is the product of a complex of factors. First, women grow up in families and these, we have seen, are veritable cradles of violence, training grounds in the use of violence to solve problems. Women learn to use violence much as men do from the way their parents treat them and each other. Second, it may be a manifestation of the frustration caused by women's oppressed position in the social structure. If the purpose of male violence to women is to control them, [33] then female violence may be akin to the violence perpetrated in a slave rebellion. We know so little of husband battering that it is difficult to pass judgement, but it may turn out to be desirable and beneficial. What Bienen wrote in a completely different context, i.e. that 'to treat violence as a phenomenon outside of "normal" social process . . . hinders analysis' [34] may be an important consideration in our understanding of this phenomenon.

But, third, one must not ignore either the pathological considerations or the structural factors that will be present in some or even many of the cases we are considering. Some battering wives will be psychotic, alcoholic or addicted to drugs and many will live in poor economic circumstances, in bad, overcrowded and isolated housing etc. But, as has been stressed throughout this book, neither pathology nor structural conditions explain violence though they may be mediating factors. [35] Further, some of the men will not be physically strong. As Langley and Levy have written: '[a] wife need not be an Amazon to abuse her husband. Sometimes a woman is physically stronger than her husband because the man is sick, handicapped or much older than his wife'. [36] Finally, it should not be overlooked that some 'husbands' are beaten up by the men with whom they live in a homosexual relationship. Frank Marcus's well-known play *The Killing of Sister George* [37] showed that violence can also exist in lesbian liaisons.

Pleas for more research are common refrains in academic literature. In making one here I am drawing attention to the fact that our knowledge of a problem that is close to all of us is just non-existent. It may be predicted that as much attention, which, be it admitted, is not very much, will be given to the phenomenon of husband battering in the next few years, as has been devoted to wife battering in the last eight years or so. It may be hypothesised that intensive research into violence against men may further our understanding also of violence against wives.

Notes

[1] *Ante*, p.132.
[2] *The Daily Telegraph*, 12 March 1974.
[3] Select Committee on *Violence in Marriage*, HC 553, 1974-75, Appendix 5.
[4] The *Rusic* case is one such: *The Times*, 20 December 1975 and *ante*, p.197.
[5] *The London Evening Standard* reported it on 30 January 1978 and an interview with Roger Langley took place on the 'Today' programme on 31 January 1978.
[6] *Ante*, p.133.
[7] *Cf, ante*, p.203.

[8]   *Cf, ante,* pp 194-5.
[9]   *Cf, ante,* p.197.
[10] *Cf, ante,* p.212.
[11] *Cf, ante,* p.179.
[12] A point made in the *Annual Report* of the Lambeth Community Law Centre, 1977. Chiswick has now set up a 'Men's Aid'.
[13] Discussed *ante,* p.165.
[14] *Cf* J.O. Balswick and C. Peck, 'The Inexpressive Male: a Tragedy of American Society', *Family Coordinator,* vol.20, 1971, p.353.
[15] See, further, on this R. Langley and R. Levy, *Wife Beating: the Silent Crisis,* Dutton, 1977, pp 190-4.
[16] *Ante,* p.180.
[17] *Murder 1957-68,* HMSO, 1969. See also *Criminal Homicide in England and Wales,* 1957-68, Interim Report of Homicide Research Project, Bedford College, London.
[18] FBI, *Vital Statistics Reports, Annual Summary for USA,* vol.24, no.13, Nat. Center for Health Statistics, 1976.
[19] S. Eisenberg and P. Micklow in *Women's Rights Law Reporter,* vol.3, 1977.
[20] L. Curtis, *Criminal Violence: National Patterns and Behavior,* Lexington Books, 1974.
[21] *Per* G.M. Wilt and J.D. Bannon, *Violence and the Police: Homicides, Assaults and Disturbances,* Police Federation, Washington DC, 1976, p.20.
[22] S. Steinmetz, *The Cycle of Violence: Assertive, Aggressive and Abuse Family Interaction,* Praeger, 1977. See also in M. Roy (ed.) *Abused and Battered Wives,* Van Nostrand-Reinhold, 1978.
[23] J. O'Brien, 'Violence in Divorce-Prone Families', *Journal of Marriage and the Family,* vol.33, 1971, p.692.
[24] G. Levinger, 'Sources of Marital Dissatisfaction among Applicants for Divorce', *American Journal of Orthopsychiatry,* vol.36, 1966, p.803.
[25] In M. Roy (ed), op.cit., note 22.
[26] *Ante,* p.132.
[27] M. Straus, 'Wife-Beating: How Common and Why?', Stanford and Montreal.
[28] M. Straus, R. Gelles and S. Steinmetz, *Violence in the American Family* (forthcoming 1978).
[29] R. Gelles, *The Violent Home,* Sage, 1972, p.52.
[30] M. Straus, 'Leveling, Civility and Violence in the Family', *Journal of Marriage and the Family,* vol.36, 1974, p.13.
[31] Steinmetz, op.cit., note 22.
[32] See S.X. Radbill in R. Helfer and C.H. Kempe (eds), *The*

Battered Child (2nd ed. 1974), University of Chicago Press, p.3.

[33] *Cf ante,* p.142.

[34] H. Bienen, *Violence and Social Change*, University of Chicago Press, 1968.

[35] *Ante,* chs. 2 and 6.

[36] Op.cit., note 15, p.190.

[37] F. Marcus, *The Killing of Sister George*, Hamish Hamilton, 1965.

10 The rest is violence

The family is not the idealised haven of love that finds its way into romantic stories and on to cereal packets. It is, as this book will have made clear, a cradle of violence. Until relatively recently few believed that babies were battered by their parents or wives or cohabitees beaten up by the men with whom they live. The battered husband is still the subject of amusement rather than serious reflection. The web of violence has spread even further and none, not even the family cat, would appear to be immune.

In this final chapter two further areas of familial violence will be explored: violence by children against their siblings and parents and 'granny bashing'. Though the two phenomena are not always mutually exclusive, they are best kept separate. Neither of them has yet emerged as an identifiable 'problem' causing general concern. To the general public violence between siblings is trivial, and 'granny bashing' is macabre and unbelievable; the 'experts' have not devoted much attention to either problem. But it may be predicted that both will emerge in the near future as recognisable problems of considerable dimension, rather as child abuse did in the 1960s and battered wives a decade later.

Violence by children

Extreme violence by children occurs infrequently. But inter-sibling conflict which is nearly universal covers a multitude of sins. Behavioural psychologists have been interested in infant sibling rivalry and the ways in which this is expressed for some time. As a result there is considerable psychological literature on interaction patterns, discussions of jealousy and aggression and ways of modifying such behaviour patterns. [1] Unlike child abuse or wife battering, violence between infant siblings has been generally acknowledged to exist for 50 years or more. But because it has been deemed to be universal and therefore 'natural' it has been studiously ignored by researchers. Until Steinmetz's research, published in 1977, [2] there was, so far as is known, no empirical research into the problems of physical aggression between brothers and sisters.

First, she found in a small exploratory study that nearly all her respondents, students at a large urban university in the USA, reported the use of verbal aggression and some 70 per cent physical aggression to resolve sibling conflicts. [3] Her study of families in New Castle County, Delaware, first revealed in a paper to the Second World Congress on Family Law in Montreal in June 1977 [4] and now published in *The Cycle of Violence* found that 78 per cent of the sibling pairs aged 8 or younger used physical violence to resolve conflicts. Most of these conflicts centred round possessions, mainly toys. Sixty-eight per cent of the pairs between 9 and 14 engaged in physical violence. Among this group, conflicts tended to revolve around infringement of personal space boundaries, touching or making faces. Even among siblings of 15 or over, where fewer conflicts were recorded and those there were tended to centre on obligations, responsibilities and social graces, 63 per cent used high levels of physical violence. [5] This is consistent with Straus's earlier finding that 62 per cent of high school seniors used physical force on a brother or sister during the previous year. [6] Steinmetz found that, although male sib pairs used more throwing, pushing, and hitting than did female sib pairs, the highest use of physical violence occurred between boy-girl sib pairs. She noted that fighting between children is considered 'inconsequential' [7] and, therefore, normal or expected behaviour. As a result there are no strong social sanctions against it.

Straus's as yet unpublished research, [8] to which reference has already been made, confirms these conclusions. Seventy-five per cent of the families with children aged 3-17 in his sample of 1,224 families reported the use of physical violence between siblings, with an average of 21 acts of physical violence per year. Thirty-eight per cent engaged in kicking, beating and hitting; 36 per cent hit with an object; 14 per cent reported a 'beating up'. 0.8 per cent reported that a child had threatened to use a knife or a gun on a sibling and 0.3 per cent had actually done so (that would amount to 138,000 in the USA). When the analysis was based on 'ever happened' rather than limited to the survey year, 5 per cent (that would amount to 2,300,000 children in the USA) had threatened a sibling with a knife or gun. Wolfgang found that 3 per cent of the homicides which occurred in Philadelphia between 1948-52 were sibling homicides. [9] There are no later figures and no figures at all for this country.

A recent article by Adelson [10] has pointed out that pre-school children are capable of homicidal rage when provoked by what they consider to be a threat to their position in the family unit and in the immediate human environment. Sargent's case study of two children who killed siblings puts forward the view that they were the recipients of both overt and covert commands from their adult environment to commit murder. [11] Steinmetz's research does not deal with the question of the extent to which parents are implicated in repeated serious assaults by one child on another. To this extent sibling violence may be a surrogate form of child abuse with an older child acting out a parent's wish to be rid of a younger child. [12] Whether or not this is the motivation, and no matter how conscious such a desire is, there is no doubt that such violence is carefully screened off from public view. Weston's analysis of abused children revealed that in 14 per cent of the cases, the batterer was a sibling. [13] But, Tooley argues, 'to maintain a degree of intrafamilial solidarity' the parent rationalises violent sibling behaviour as 'accidental' or normal 'horseplay' gone wrong. 'The defence of denial' [14] is used to a startling degree. To the student of child abuse this is all very familiar.

Another strategy employed, so Tooley argues, is to smooth out life space around the problem child, to placate and make allowances to forestall temper outbursts and attack. Indeed, she suggests that a younger child may be employed as the family's 'sacrificial lamb bearing the brunt of considerable physical punishment from an older sibling and deflecting such abuse from other family members'. [15] How much of this takes place we do not know. Tooley's hypothesis is based on her own clinical case histories. There are no sociological data as such, and this constitutes a real gap in our knowledge.

That children learn to act violently towards their siblings from watching their parents is substantiated by Steinmetz's research. She found intergenerational patterns of conflict resolution. In her small exploratory study, already referred to, [3] she found a relationship between the method of conflict resolution used by spouses to resolve marital conflict and the methods children use to resolve disagreements between themselves and their brothers and sisters. These findings support the social learning perspective outlined in the opening chapter. So do findings by Steinmetz [16] and Bellak and Antell [17] that children emulate the child-rearing techniques they experience in conflicts between themselves and other children.

Children also act violently against parents. Indeed, when children kill they usually choose their parents as victims. [18] In a study of homicide by children under 15 in Finland, Hellsten and Katila reported that such children are encouraged by one parent to act aggressively towards the other. [19] Most studies of such child violence view it as a pathological response to very poor relationships between parent and child. In some cases there is a history of parental brutality to respond to or model behaviour upon. These interpretations once again individualise the problem and criticisms similar to those already made might be repeated here. This is, however, a very under-researched area.

Is there anything that the law can do to help tackle violence by children? There is, of course, the criminal law provided the child is 10. Between 10 and 14 it is necessary to prove that he is *doli capax*, capable of distinguishing right from wrong. The penal system has been much troubled by its inability to cope with child killers like Mary Bell. [20] The difficulty is not the sentence (which is detention during the Majesty's Pleasure) but where to detain and when to release. For other offences a child under 17 may be committed into the care of the local authority and, if over 15, sent for 'borstal training'. [21] Civil care proceedings may be brought at the parent's request by a local authority on the ground that the child is beyond control. [22] This procedure is not extensively used and can seldom, if ever, have been used to prevent further violence by a child against a sibling or parent. In one recent case [23] when a 19-year-old son continually assaulted and maltreated his mother she successfully sought injunctions restraining him from entering the house and committing further assaults. Though a somewhat unusual remedy there is no reason why it should not be used again in similarly grave circumstances.

'Granny bashing'

Numbers of old people in the population are rising constantly. More people are now living to 65 though the expectation of life of a 65-year-old has hardly altered in the last century. Eight million people are above retiring age. By the mid-1980s it will be nine million. The number of those people who survive in their 80s and 90s is increasing all the time. Many of the elderly need constant care and attention from relatives or health care workers. A particularly difficult problem concerns those aged persons (and as many as 20 per cent of those aged 80 or over come into this category) who suffer from dementia. But, as the number of the elderly increases, the numbers admitted to hospital have declined. Both general and mental hospitals have be-come increasingly reluctant to admit the senile in the wake of the abuses exposed by recent committees of inquiry into hospitals such as Ely and Whittingham. [24] With insufficient resources being given to the care of elderly patients, hospitals are cutting down on the number of admissions. [25] Already admissions since 1970 have dropped by between one-third and a half. Someone must look after those of the elderly who cannot live by or care for themselves, and who need constant attention. Today's houses, however, are not built for three generations. Often the mother or mother-in-law is out at work. The elderly parent becomes a nuisance.

The elderly bruise easily and accidents are common. [26] Indeed, three-quarters of home accidents affect those over 75. Falls, it is said, account for most of these accidents. Further, three-quarters of the fatal falls affect old people over 75 years of age. Hazell, in *Social and Medical Problems of the Elderly*, attributes falls in the elderly to seven causes: loss of consciousness, transient imbalance, 'drop' seizure, defective power of co-ordination, polyneuritis, muscular weakness, and poor eyesight. [27] A further cause is not listed by Hazell: assault by a relative. We do not know how many, but a significant number of old people do not fall: they are pushed, shoved or tripped. Nowhere in Hazell's otherwise comprehensive survey of the problems of the elderly is the possibility of their suffering abuse at the hands of relatives even mentioned. Similarly, Howells, the author of that passionate account of the Colwell affair (*Remember Maria* [28]) nowhere includes any reference to the problems of abuse and neglect of the elderly in his *Modern Perspectives in the Psychiatry of Old Age*, [29] a book of over 600 pages.

Equivalent books on the care of children 20 years ago made little reference to child abuse. Parents who took an injured child to a hospital casualty department or doctor's surgery and explained that he had 'fallen out of his cot' were by and large believed. Now the suspicions of the medical profession are aroused. Equal suspicion may be called for in dealing with accidents to old people. Unlike babies, they can contradict the explanation preferred by relatives, if they are not too confused or frightened to do so. Some elderly people are admitted to hospital with injuries explained as falls, returned home and re-admitted, sometimes on more than one further occasion. 'Granny bashing', as this is coming to be known, is a common reason for this. Grandfathers must be included in this term. There are fewer of them so that fewer may suffer abuse. The problem is the same. With children we know about the brutality of some of the assaults that occur. Fortunately, the problem with the elderly does not seem to have reached these proportions. They are pushed, grabbed, shaken and shoved but rarely, it seems, hit with hard instruments, strangled or burned. This does, of course, mean that the injuries inflicted are less easy to detect. And too few doctors, it would appear, are prepared to search for suspicious signs.

The causes of 'granny bashing' are relatively easy to comprehend. Situations are not all the same. In some cases her presence will exacerbate a family situation where there is already stress. In others, an elderly parent, once welcomed, will now be a thorough nuisance, interfering with the lives of the rest of the family, making demands which are no longer regarded as reasonable, querulous, never satisfied and needing constant attention. Some of the strain could be relieved by day centres but at present there are only some 14,000 day centre places. Some of the problems themselves could be eliminated by more research into the causes of debilitating conditions like dementia. Little is at present known about why the brain of some but not others should go into such rapid decline. More health care resources could be channelled into rectifying ailments of the elderly.

Those who have been abused must also be helped. It may be thought desirable to extend some of the management techniques currently being developed in the field of child abuse to 'granny bashing'. Incongruous as it may seem, there are elderly persons who would benefit by being removed or retained by something akin to a 'place of safety' order. But the question is — to where? It is because of known institutional abuse that the hospitals are admitting less of the elderly, and there are few enough places at old age homes where the victims of abuse might be happier. And would the panoply of registers of suspected cases and case conferences do much more than salve society's conscience? Unless it would be a stimulus to positive action there would be no point in setting up the machinery, and it is dubious if society cares enough to plough more resources into the care of those who no longer have anything economically valuable to offer. [30]

Some concluding comments

From the cradle to the grave we are the objects of violence from those nearest and dearest to us. And it is a never-ending cycle for there is considerable evidence of intergenerational transmission of family violence. We know that individuals exposed to a high degree of physical punishment as children are more likely to resort to family violence as adults. Children reared in an environment of violence batter their children and spouses and in turn may find themselves exposed to violence in their latter years from their own children, who in turn were brought up by violent parents. A book which opens by discussing child abuse should close with a consideration of 'granny battering'. The wheel has come full circle.

Notes

[1] S. Steinmetz, *The Cycle of Violence*, Praeger, 1977, pp 177-8 contains a full bibliography.
[2] Idem.
[3] S. Steinmetz, 'The Use of Force for Resolving Family Conflict', *Family Coordinator*, vol.26, 1977, p.19.
[4] S. Steinmetz, 'Violence between Siblings' paper presented to the Second World Conference on Family Law, Montreal, June 1977.
[5] Op.cit., note 1, ch.4.
[6] M. Straus, 'Leveling, Civility and Violence in the Family', *Journal of Marriage and the Family*, vol.36, 1974, p.13.
[7] Op.cit., note 1.
[8] M. Straus, R. Gelles, S. Steinmetz, *Violence in the American Family* (forthcoming 1978).
[9] M.E. Wolfgang, *Patterns in Criminal Homicide*, Wiley, 1958.
[10] L. Adelson, 'The Battering Child', *Journal of the American Medical Association*, no.222, 1972, p.159.
[11] D. Sargent, 'The Lethal Situation: Transmission of Urge to Kill from Parent to Child' in Fawcett (ed.) *Dynamics of Violence*, AMA, 1971.
[12] M. Tooley in *Social Casework*, vol.58, 1977, p.25.
[13] J.T. Weston, 'A Summary of Neglect and Traumatic Cases' in R. Helfer and C.H. Kempe, *The Battered Child*, University of Chicago Press, 1974, pp 193-201.
[14] Op.cit., note 12, p.28.
[15] Idem.
[16] S. Steinmetz, 'Intra-Familial Patterns of Conflict Resolution: United States and Canadian Comparisons', Paper to Society for Study of Social Problems, 1974.
[17] L. Bellak and M. Antell, 'Intercultural Study of Aggressive Behavior on Children's Playgrounds', *American Journal of Ortho-psychiatry*, vol.44, 1974, p.503.
[18] R.L. Sadoff in *Psychiat Q.* vol.45, 1971, p.65.
[19] Hellsten and Katila in *Psychiat Q. Suppl.* vol.39, 1965, p.54.
[20] On which see G. Sereny, *The Case of Mary Bell*, Eyre Methuen, 1972.
[21] Children and Young Persons Act 1969 s.1(2)(f).
[22] Idem, s.1(2)(d).
[23] *Egan* v. *Egan* [1975] Ch.218.
[24] Report of Committee of Inquiry into Allegations of Ill-treatment at Ely Hospital, Cardiff, (1969) Cmnd 3975 and Report of Committee of Inquiry into Whittingham Hospital, (1972) Cmnd 4861.

[25] See D.J. Jolley and T. Arie 'Psychiatric Service for the Elderly: How Many Beds?' in *British Journal of Psychiatry*, vol.129, 1976, p.418.
[26] Registrar-General's Quarterly Return.
[27] J. Hazell, *Social and Medical Problems of the Elderly*, Hutchinson (3rd ed), 1973, pp 240-1.
[28] J. Howells, *Remember Maria*, Butterworths, 1974.
[29] J. Howells, *Modern Perspectives in the Psychiatry of Old Age*, Churchill Livingstone, 1975.
[30] Now that adoption has become a method of providing care rather than a service for the infertile, it may be worth considering why an age limitation should be set upon it. Would adoption of the elderly, subsidised if necessary, be a feasible approach towards their protection?

Appendix

A socio-legal study

U.S. Department of Health, Education and Welfare, Social Security
Administration, Children's Bureau: Proposal for Reporting Law
Legislation

AN ACT FOR THE MANDATORY REPORTING BY
PHYSICIANS AND INSTITUTIONS OF CERTAIN
PHYSICAL ABUSE OF CHILDREN

1. *Purpose*

The purpose of this Act is to provide for the protection of children
who have had physical injury inflicted upon them and who are further
threatened by the conduct of those responsible for their care and
protection. Physicians who become aware of such cases should report
them to appropriate police authority thereby causing the protective
services of the State to be brought to bear in an effort to protect the
health and welfare of these children and to prevent further abuses.

2. *Reports by Physicians and Institutions*

Any physician, including any licensed doctor of medicine, licensed
osteopathic physician, intern and resident, having reasonable cause to
suspect that a child under the age of ——* brought to him or coming
before him for examination, care or treatment has had serious physical
injury or injuries inflicted upon him other than by accidental means
by a parent or other person responsible for his care, shall report or
cause reports to be made in accordance with the provisions of this Act;
provided that when the attendance of a physician with respect to a
child is pursuant to the performance of services as a member of the
staff of a hospital or similar institution he shall notify the person in
charge of the institution or his designated delegate who shall report or
cause reports to be made in accordance with the provisions of this Act.

3. *Nature and content of Report; to whom made*

An oral report shall be made immediately by telephone or otherwise,

---

*It is recommended that the maximum age of juvenile court jurisdiction in the State be used.

and followed as soon thereafter as possible by a report in writing, to an appropriate police authority. Such reports shall contain the names and addresses of the child and his parents or other persons responsible for his care, if known, the child's age, the nature and extent of the child's injuries (including any evidence of previous injuries), and any other information that the physician believes might be helpful in establishing the cause of the injuries and the identity of the perpetrator.

4.   *Immunity from liability*

Anyone participating in good faith in making of a report pursuant to this Act shall have immunity from any liability, civil, or criminal, that might otherwise be incurred or imposed. Any such participant shall have the same immunity with respect to participation in any judicial proceeding resulting from such report.

5.   *Evidence not privileged*

Neither the physician-patient privilege nor the husband-wife privilege shall be a ground for excluding evidence regarding a child's injuries or the cause thereof, in any judicial proceeding resulting from a report pursuant to this Act.

6.   *Penalty for violation*

Anyone knowingly and willfully violating the provisions of this Act shall be guilty of a misdemeanor.

Index

Biderman, A. 149
Bienen, H. 230-1, 233
Biggs, J. 214
Birrell, R. & J. 117, 123
Bishop, E. 7
Black, D. 186, 217, 218
Blackstone, Sir W. 177, 213
Block, R. 149
Bohannan, P. 5, 8
Booth, M. 74
Boriskin, J. 117, 123
Boudouris, J. 130, 149
Box, S. 152
Briar, S. 187, 218
British Association of Social
  Workers, 77, 95, 101, 106
  code of practice, 79, 102
  view of wife abuse, 139, 153
British Paediatric Association,
  14, 35
Brody, H.L. 110, 111, 121
Brooke, R. 160, 173
Bromley, P. 154
Brown, B. 213
Brownmiller, S. 155
Bullough, V. 142, 153
Burning children, 16

Caffey, J. 14, 34
Cain and Abel, 4, 7
Calvert, P. 7
Canada
  corporal punishment, 118,
  124
  mandatory reporting of
  child abuse, 95
  Robinson committee, 118,
  124
Canterbury Women's Centre,
  163, 174
Care proceedings, 53-60
Carlin, J. 162, 173
Carter, J. 85-6, 87, 104

Case conferences, 88-91
Casey, M. 6
Castle, R. 16, 23-4, 28, 35, 37,
  38, 39, 80, 88-91, 102, 104,
  107
Catharsis myth
  of wife battering, 135-6,
  151-2
Chambliss, W. 191, 219
Chappell, D. 151
Charity Organisation Society,
  43, 68
Chase, N. 40
Chastisement,
  husband's right to chastise
  wife, 177-8, 183, 213-4
Chester, R. 131, 150
Child abuse, pt I, passim
  meaning of, 11-12, 34
  as a label, 26-7, 38-9, 110,
  121
  bonding failure and, 116, 123
  causes of, 21-32, 37-40
  'discovery' of, 12-16, 34-5
  effects of, 32-33, 40-41
  social isolation and, 114, 122
Childhood,
  concept of, 42-5
Children Act 1948, 61, 73, 78,
  101, 114-5, 122
Children Act 1975, 42, 44-5, 54,
  58, 59, 65, 72, 73, 75, 115,
  122
Children and Young Persons
  Act 1933, 45, 49-52, 58, 60,
  61, 65, 69
Children and Young Persons
  Act 1963, 77, 78, 116, 122
Children and Young Persons
  Act 1969, 56-62, 71, 72, 73,
  74, 78, 123, 237, 240
Chiswick Women's Refuge, 167,
  169-70, 176

251

Index of Cases

DATE DUE

~~DEC 1 1 1980~~		
APR 9 1981		
OCT 2 1 1982		
NOV 1 8 1982		
FEB 3 1983		
FEB 2 4 1983		
APR 7 1983		
DEC 6 1984		
MAY 2 2 1992		
DEC 1 3 1996		
NOV 1 8 1997		
MAR 2 4 1999		